The Walking Wounded

The Walking Wounded

*the journal of a homeless
Vietnam veteran*

WINFRED "Wayne" ROY COMPTON II

Rocky
Shore
Books
Marquette MI

ISBN 978-0-9823319-7-2
Copyright © 2012 Jeanne Oleniczak
Printed in U.S.A.

PUBLISHED BY

Rocky
Shore
Books
Marquette MI

Design: Doug Hagley
Printing: McNaughton & Gunn, Saline, Michigan

~ ACKNOWLEDGMENTS ~

This book is in thanks to the glory of God for causing the spirit to move me in the right direction to get my brother Winfred Compton II's story out in the hope that others may be helped.

A thank you to Kelly Trudell for her Eternal Vigilance Concert on June 26, 2010. Cold Sweat awakened me, as though my brother Winfred was reaching out to me. I knew that his story could wait no longer.

Thanks to Jeannie Lewis who answered my phone call and helped me get started and for referring me to a mysterious stranger who read my brother's manuscript and believed it was a story worth telling.

Last but not least, thank you, Winfred, for filling in the blanks of those years you were missing. And to my family, who never gave up on me, I love you all: parents, brothers, sisters, husband, sons, daughters and grandchildren. And may these words be read and thought about by the generations to come.

— Jeanne Oleniczak
Winfred's little sister

Sgt Winfred R Compton
H.Q.S. J 85 Maint Bn.
San Francisco, California
9649,

Free

Mrs. David Wall
1562 Blud. Drive
Okemos, Michigan

4-886 SEP 15 1968

SOUTH EAST
OF BIEN HOA
ABOUT 7 MILES

THIS IS
WHERE I'M
STATIONED

This is the story of my brother's journey from a hard-working, academically gifted person to a homeless Vietnam veteran. A journey many have taken.

Winfred (Wayne) Compton II was born on January 6, 1946. His family lived in Haslett and later in Muir. While the parents were away one night, social services, who had been watching the family, came in and took the six children. The three oldest, including Winfred were placed with family members, the three youngest were placed in foster care. There was one child born after the family split up. The parents divorced in 1957 or 1958, and the three boys were placed in Haslett with their father. In 1959 Winfred was sent to live with his mother in Muir, where he remained until graduation from high school in 1964.

During his high school years, Winfred worked at a local store. He was the star guard on the high school basketball team. In 1961 he met a "carnie" whom he worked for every summer, traveling with the carnival wherever it went. He graduated fourth in his class behind a valedictorian and two salutatorians. Three days after graduation he began working at Oldsmobile in Lansing.

Winfred married his high school sweetheart and in April of 1965 they had a son, Winfred Compton III. The marriage failed in July of 1966 and in March of 1967 Winfred II enlisted in the Army. His basic training was at Ft. Knox in Kentucky, and his AIT training (communication center specialist) was at Ft. Gordon in Georgia.

September 28, 1967, Winfred left for Vietnam where he never used his special training. He operated a switchboard, a radio, a radio teletype. He was a lineman and a security guard and drove a ten-ton truck.

On security watch with a friend one night, they saw a Vietnamese boy approaching. They told him to stop, but he kept walking toward them. Both had their guns pointed at the boy and shouted for him to stop again. Winfred's friend could not shoot; however, Winfred knew if he did not shoot the boy, the two of them would die. He pulled the trigger and shot a boy around his son's age. He said it was as if his son was walking toward him with his arms outstretched. The image haunted him the remainder of his days.

Winfred kept a journal after he returned from Vietnam. Winfred's story is now in your hands—his ups and downs after his return from Vietnam until the time he died. He was in Louisiana when Hurricane Katrina hit. He was in a wheelchair by this time. After the hurricane, three older couples and Winfred had difficulty moving. They were told by rescuers that someone would come back for them. No one did. They made their way to the roof of the apartment building and eventually they were helicoptered out and taken to the coliseum. The conditions there were atrocious and Winfred watched the six people who'd been evacuated with him die within days of their arrival. Winfred was then transferred to Texas where his sister found him after talking to a friend who had family in Texas and they were able to search for him.

When he knew he the end was approaching, he sent the journal to me, his sister, Jeanne, for safekeeping. He included a letter giving me the right to do whatever I wanted with it.

I have chosen to do what I feel my brother would have wanted. I am publishing his story and would like the profits to somehow help homeless Vietnam veterans. It is not an easy story to share; however, it needs to be done.

— Jeanne Oleniczak

Your Loving Brother Always
Winfred H.

This book is dedicated to all those—the Homeless—who gave their lives so that their voices may be heard. The Homeless who are still out there, as well as those to come in the years ahead, and those who have been but are no longer among the "Walking Wounded." That through these pages one might better understand that we all were not bad people, just people down on our luck who were trying to do the best we could in a bad situation.

To my family who lived for years in anguish, not knowing where I was, and for the many prayers that sustained me through those years.

To Betty and her family for finally making me see that I could be somebody, and I could be loved and needed; for the three years of their lives that they so freely gave to me that at the time were the happiest of my life and that finally gave my life some meaning.

And to the many tireless workers who toil endlessly, trying to help the homeless in a system with sadly inadequate resources.

To the Salvation Army and the many other Missions around the country who love the homeless even when they can't love themselves; to The Bridge House in New Orleans, which never gave up on me even when I wanted to give up on myself; and to Alchoholics Anonymous, an organization that has helped so many return to productive lives when nothing else worked.

The list could go on and on, but the result is the same: some of us make it and some of us don't. The reasons why are as numerous as the number of people out there who face the dilemma of being homeless and the prejudices that go along with that label every day.

— Wayne Compton

~ CONTENTS ~

Through the Eyes of the Heart

Have you ever looked across a meadow and seen
The hour that a flower begins
To bring life and beauty to a world so hurt
That God renews again and again

The endless contentment of a child at play
The hours that they spend within
The innocence of eyes that know no hate
It's a place where we all begin

The majesty of a bird flying so high
Reaching for the endless skies
The beauty of a snow-capped mountain stream
Seasons that go by and by

Look around you, it begins with each new day
It's a way we'd all like to be
It's in nature that we see God's realy plan
It's through the eyes of the heart we see

— 1982

~ IN THE BEGINNING ~

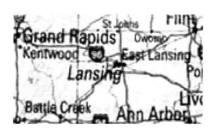

It seems like an eternity, so long, long ago, that my journey began, and yet at times it seems just like yesterday. The lives that touched mine, the people I met, the stories they told and the lessons I learned, so fresh in my mind it's as though I can just reach out and touch them. All of the old feelings come back to me

It is said that the things that touch a person's life serve to shape their being. Many factors figure in to make a person who they are today, and that affect the path that they travel. I guess I have to say this is true, because I believe my journey began long before I became homeless.

I begin my series of stories by telling you a little bit about mine. I grew up in what I believed to be a normal and healthy family, and for all intents and purposes it was. My parents loved me as they did all of us in the family. You see I grew up with nine brothers and sisters. I believe my parents did the best they could under the circumstances. I can never remember going without. There was always plenty of food on the table, a roof over our heads, and clothes on our backs, with plenty of love to go around. Oh believe me, we were punished when the occasion called for it, and I can honestly say when I was punished I deserved it — but even then I always knew I was loved. I went through the normal stages of growing up, although I may have been quite a handful: I started to get into a lot of trouble at a young age. Many other things happened that deeply affected me as I grew up. My parents separated and divorced when I was still very young. I bounced back and forth between them, as we all did, before settling down with my mother and stepfather when I was twelve years old.

I was considered what you might call an adventurer, even at the age of three and four. My parents had to keep a close eye on me because I often wandered off. I always had to see what was around the corner, on the next block, and even on the other side of town — a trait that I would carry through my adolescence and adult years. I was never happy where I was. I wanted to see the world, and believe me, before I was done I did just that.

I started working when I was very young — at twelve I was working on a farm to earn spending money. When we moved from the country into town, I got a job at the local grocery store bagging groceries, taking out the trash; anything they asked me to do, I done it — another trait I showed throughout my adult years.

I was a good student in school, an above-average student. Although I missed a lot of school skipping classes, and even whole days, I managed to keep my grades up, and my teachers thought I could do no wrong. I was quite the con man — still another quality that I would keep into adulthood.

My mother tells me that during this period we went through some hard times, but I don't recall things being any different. My mother must have hid it from us really well. I used to have run-ins with my stepfather from time to time, and it took me many years to realize that all he taught me and tried to teach me would be very useful in the hard times to come.

Little did I know at the time that events were already taking place that would shape my future. All the years of growing up as an adolescent, I remained somewhat of a loner. I had friends, but I was very selective of the people I allowed near me. Even then I kept them at a distance. In my high school years I wasn't what you'd call really popular, and yet I wasn't want you'd call unpopular either. I had a close-knit group of friends that I hung around with all the time, and they did not change much over the years. I had my share of girls, too. But now I look back and think it odd that I never dated anyone in my own class; that is to say, the grade I was in at the time. I always sought those who were apart from that which was near to me — someone in another grade, or better yet, another town.

Another event was about to take place that was to have one of the biggest impacts on my life, then and to this day. Between my sophomore and junior years in high school I met a man who traveled with the carnival and owned carnival shows. I worked for him at our local fair, and we became quick friends. His way of life intrigued me and I wanted to be like him. The next summer, between my junior and senior years, he invited me down to Florida, where he and his family lived, to help get his shows ready to go on the road again. I worked for him the rest of the summer traveling to different fairs around the country until school started in the fall. After that summer I was never quite the same. I was never satisfied with where I was or what I was doing. I knew from that time on that I had to see the world and who and what was around the next bend.

Then something happened that was to put those plans on hold for the time being. The girl I was dating at the time became pregnant right after I graduated. Me being a man, who I believed to be of high moral fiber, did the right thing and married her. My son was born soon after and for a while I tried to make the best of it, but something was missing and the marriage was doomed from the start. Two years later it ended in divorce, and she gained custody of my son.

I was now free to seek what I thought was missing in my life. I bounced around for a while, traveling with different carnival shows around the country, spending a winter in Florida and coming back to Michigan in the summer. This all took place in 1965 through early 1967. In March 1967, I made another decision, maybe the most important one of my life: I enlisted in the Army, right at the height of the Vietnam War. I knew this would be my vehicle to see the world, while at the same time fulfilling my obligation to my country.

I went to basic training at Ft. Knox, Kentucky, then A.I.T. at Ft. Gordon, Georgia. After a short leave home and a good-bye to my parents, I was on my way to Vietnam before the year was out. I won't get into what happened to me over there that changed my life so drastically and seriously affected my frame of mind at the time and the way I perceived things to be back then. That's another book. I can only tell you now that I came back a different person than I was when I left. My family and even my closest friends will attest to that — the person who went over to Vietnam was not the person who came back.

I hastily remarried, and upon reporting to my new duty station in Carlisle, Pennsylvania with my new wife, I soon realized something was wrong. My marriage, once again, was doomed from the start and lasted only a few months before my then-wife returned to her parents and filed for divorce. Alone again, I sought relief in the only way I knew and had learned in Vietnam, alcohol. I literally drowned myself in it. I couldn't adjust to stateside duty and I rebelled every chance I got until after many stints of being AWOL, the Army finally gave up on me and turned me loose.

For the next twenty-five years, I wandered the country, living in the streets most of the time. I never established roots anywhere because I never stayed in one place for more than a few months at a time. I moved around as the mood struck me. Here today and gone tomorrow, that was my motto. I won't go into much more of my own story, except at certain places in this book that seem appropriate, because that's not the story that I want to tell here. Instead I'll tell you about the people I met along the way who influenced my life a great deal. I will relate to you the facts as best I can remember them, and the way they were related to me. Although the chronology, names and exact locations may or may not be exact, the essence of the stories remains true. My many years of alcohol abuse have caused my memory to be less than exact, so please bear with me. I'll do the best I can to stay with the facts and give you a true account of the streets as I seen them from my perspective.

The Neon Jungle

Amidst the walls of concrete and cement
Lies a world that few really get to know
In the ambiance of the neon Jungle
Where the lonely and the broken go

Where most just visit by the day
The nights are left to chance
To those who call the Jungle home
Who are there through happenstance

The great walls become their skyline
And the pavement becomes their home
They lay their heads where few dare to tread
As they wrestle the pain of being alone

Alone in a world filled with others
Who walk the streets, yet do not see
The misery that lies around them
In a world that just cannot be

Driven by their own ambition
Blinded by the aspirations of life
They turn away and neglect to see
The anguish of another's strife

It's an education that we, the people
Of the neon Jungle, quickly learn
You have to learn to survive, as best you can
The others you must learn to discern

So you try not to concentrate on what could be
But rather focus on the way it is
To do anything else could be deadly
It's the way you have learned to live

Amidst the neon Jungle
Where your education begins in reality's light
When a new day brings new problems
And you must learn a new way of life

Where every moment is precious
And every day a new lesson in being
Along in the world filled with others
The truth of a life that's fleeing

— May 1978

20

~ CHAPTER 1 ~

The Vagabond Years OR *Getting an Education*

I began my quest, as I came to call it, in the early fall of 1970. The weather was still warm, but the nights were starting to turn cool. So, like all good migratory species, I headed south, though for no particular reason; I was just tired of the cold winters and wanted something different. This would be my pattern from that time on.

I decided to head down toward the Eastern seaboard, not knowing where I was going or what I would do when I got there. I only had about thirty dollars in my pocket at the time, so I chose hitchhiking as my mode of travel. I knew I didn't want to spend my last dollar on transportation. I realized early that when traveling you needed a little bit in your pocket for the trip, as well as a few dollars in your pocket when you arrived, although many times in the years ahead I learned to travel with much less and sometimes nothing at all. I headed south out of Michigan, catching highway 70 out of Columbus, Ohio, and heading east toward the coast, through Pennsylvania and into West Virginia. Just outside Baltimore, I caught 95 south. I was on my way.

My third night out I found myself just a few miles north of Fayetteville, North Carolina, and it was getting dark. Hitchhiking in the dark was no good, so I looked for a place to spend the night unnoticed. As I was walking along I came across some railroad tracks, and I decided to follow them for a spell, thinking maybe I'd find a spot not too far off the highway where I could rest for the night. I must have walked maybe half a mile when all of a sudden I heard voices off to the side of the tracks, down in a little hollow. I walked down the hollow for a ways, following the voices, when I came across a camp of sorts, with four men who had taken refuge there, all sitting around a campfire. I was hesitant to enter the camp for a while, but then decided, what the hell, they seemed to be in the same fix I was in. I figured they'd understand. As I walked down a path about a foot wide, running off the tracks, I noticed the camp was located in a small clump of trees with a clearing in the middle. Running parallel with the camp was a small stream.

As I came closer, I saw a campfire with several bedrolls around it. The camp was for the most part clean of debris. About fifty yards from the camp itself, I made my presence known. At first there was no reply, then came a call to identify myself. The only thing I could think of was to say *I'm a fellow traveler, with no place to rest.* This was followed by a reply: *enter*. It was awkward at first, but after a few introductions, they seemed quite responsive. They offered me some stew they had made earlier, and I accepted. It was either very good or I was very hungry; in any case it made me feel welcome. So I settled in for the night. After a little bit of talk and getting acquainted, they made me feel at home.

There wasn't much else said that night, as it was getting pretty late. Soon after eating we all went to bed. They made a spot for me around the fire, and even offered me a blanket. Being new at this type of travel, I hadn't yet learned to carry a bedroll, a mistake I made only that one time. My survival training had begun, and I had a lot to learn.

I slept well that night, and the next morning I awoke with the smell of coffee. Only one of the other men was up at that hour, about five a.m., and his name was — you guessed it — Cookie. He was the designated cook of the group. Everybody seemed to have a certain task to perform every day for the benefit of all. The coffee was crude, but good. They had a small pot that they threw coffee grounds in the bottom of, added some water from the stream and put it over the campfire to boil. And presto, you had coffee. You learned right away to drink it black, because there were no luxuries like sugar or cream. You were lucky to have coffee, and that was the extent of breakfast. As the morning went along and the sun began to rise the others got up, one by one. I then learned that most of the day for them was planned around the campfire while drinking coffee. And one by one, I got to know them better. I wasn't too surprised to learn that they all went by nicknames; no one seemed to want to share his actual name.

As I said, Cookie was the first one I got to know by name, and he was a short, portly man, in his mid-forties, though exact age was another thing everybody seemed elusive about. He was dressed in an old pair of well-weathered blue jeans, as most of them were: jeans seemed to wear better and to last longer. He had on a well-worn plaid shirt with a hole in one of the elbows. His voice was very deep, almost like he had a frog in his throat, and well spoken. I knew he had some formal education, as did most of them, I later found out.

It was from Cookie that I learned about the jobs offshore on the oil rigs. He had spent many years working on them before becoming homeless, a choice he made after three of his closest friends were killed in a helicopter crash during a crew change. He couldn't force himself to return to that line of work afterwards, out of fear or choice, I don't know, but it had had a profound effect on him and he never wanted to discuss it in much detail. He had no family to speak of, at least that's the impression he gave you, and other than being briefly married once, he had no other such relations, and no children. I never knew where Cookie was from, although from his accent, I guessed somewhere in the Midwest

The next one to get up was Popcorn. I never did find out how he got that name — it wasn't discussed — that's just what everyone called him. Popcorn was an elderly black man in his late fifties. He wore a pair of denim coveralls with a dirty T-shirt underneath. Popcorn was the oldest in camp, and seemed to be the spokesman for the group. He was the one everyone looked to for advice. He had been homeless, from what I could tell, for the greater part of his adult life — a choice he made very early. I did learn from later conversations that he was once married and had two children. Popcorn was from New York City, and grew up in Harlem. He worked on the docks in his early years, unloading ships. It was a laborious job, you could tell. He looked a lot older than he actually was.

Divorce was the catalyst that seemed to have driven Popcorn to the streets; he couldn't face the fact that his family didn't want him anymore, and that he had to go on alone. He struck me as having been a devout family man, and it showed in his concern for the rest of the group. He was well organized, and always seemed to have a plan of action to get everyone through the day and the tasks at hand done, and Popcorn assigned those tasks. There was a degree of organization in what appeared to be simple anarchy. Last one in: low man on the totem pole, and I was that person for a while. I had to earn their respect, and be useful to the group.

The next one to rise was Bulldog, a name he came by in prison when he was very young. He was a stout man in his mid-thirties, very muscular, with huge hands and a rugged face with a nose that was bent to one side, a feature he came by while boxing in prison. He was a man who at first glance you knew you didn't want to mess with, though I learned later that Bulldog was a gentle and kind person. He made a mistake when he was young, and never had a serious run in with the law after getting out of prison. In fact he had a deep respect for the law after that time. As best as I could tell, Bulldog had a difficult time adjusting to society, as most of us define it; he needed direction, and got it from the group. He always functioned better with a plan, but was not educated enough to come up with one himself and stay out of trouble, otherwise he needed help to make a decision.

Bulldog grew up in the hill country of Texas. He was an only child, whose parents died when he was very young. Besides a few distant relatives he wasn't close to, he had no family to speak of. Bulldog liked to wear western shirts and cowboy boots, I guess from his up bringing. He also had an old beat-up looking cowboy hat — it looked like he'd been wearing it all his life without ever cleaning it. He'd often say it took years to get it broke in just right.

For the best that I could tell, he never held down a regular job, other than working out of the labor pools around the country whenever the need arose. Labor pools were a means of working if you had no regular job — your were assigned a job each day and paid the same way, by the day.

Many times throughout this book you'll hear these places discussed. They were known by us not only as *labor pools*, but also as slave markets, day labor, and work pools; not the best places to work for, but handy to have around when you needed a few quick dollars.

The next person to get up that morning was Professor. Out of everyone in the camp, he seemed the most out of place. He was extremely well educated. He grew up in a place called Rutland, Vermont in a fairly well-to-do family. He was educated at Princeton University, and had a degree in engineering. Although the clothes that he wore seemed pretty much the same as the others, they were always well kept. He'd go through the ritual of folding them just so every night and putting them under his bedroll, giving them as pressed a look as possible under the circumstances.

Professor was in his early forties, as far as I could guess, since he never mentioned his actual age. At one time he had been married, and had one son. His reason for being where he was, as he told it, was that he lost his position at the University due to a drinking problem, and for the same reason he lost his family, home and everything else he had worked for over the years. Other than that he didn't speak much of his past; he gave the impression that he had accepted his fate and was living with it as best he could. Quiet most of the time, he could be very opinionated when he felt strongly about something.

That morning Popcorn asked me if I wanted to stay for a while, but before being accepted to the group, they had to take a vote. I expressed my desire to stay, not having anything else to do, and not being in too much of a hurry to do it. Secret ballot: three accepted me and one voted against me. I never learned who was against my staying, although I felt it must have been Bulldog. We always seemed to have a personality conflict, although we did get along pretty well just by not stepping on each other's toes. It was during this time that I learned a great deal of my street knowledge of how to survive in a hobo camp, and how to survive being homeless.

For the first few days, Popcorn kept me pretty close to camp, not sending me out as he did the others. I always felt this was a trial period, to see if I was going to stay or go, and to check me out, seeing what I was all about. So I kept the site clean; Popcorn was a stickler for cleanliness. I gathered wood for the fire and carried water from the stream. From time to time I helped Cookie with the meals. During the first few days, I only left the camp one time, and that was just to go down the tracks a ways, to a farmer's field to pick some field corn for a soup that Cookie was preparing.

After the fourth day at the camp, I guess Popcorn decided I was going to stay for a while, and he sent me to town to try and get in the labor pool for a day and earn some money for cigarettes, alcohol, and any other items we needed for that day. Popcorn always sent two of us out to work for cash, thus insuring one of us would get work, because sometimes jobs were scarce. The others would either go to the blood bank (another way of making a few dollars quickly), or out to panhandle or search for food wherever we could find it, e.g., gardens, farmers' fields, handouts, and my personal favorite, the farmers' market.

I always, from the first day, had no trouble getting out to work. I was young and strong, and didn't turn any job down as some would. I always figured I could do anything for a day, and besides that I wanted to impress the others. So no matter what Popcorn asked of me, I made sure that the task was completed, and most of the time I exceeded the demands. Approval was then — and I guess still — very important to me.

One time Popcorn sent me out to get whatever food I could find for supper that night. I went into town and searched around for quite a while with no luck, and then I ran across a small farmers' market. With a little bit of savvy, and a little work, I managed to come up with two large burlap bags filled with potatoes, turnips, cabbage, onions, and carrots. I remember thinking, boy will Popcorn and the others be surprised; needless to say we ended up throwing away more than we used, since refrigeration was not a luxury we had in hobo camp. I learned quickly to only get what we could use in the immediate future; Popcorn didn't like to waste good food.

We all from time to time liked a little libation, so to speak. At that time in my life I was drinking almost every day, but was still able to function fairly normal. With the exception of Bulldog, we all pretty much maintained the same state of inebriation. Bulldog on the other hand could get quite rowdy, so Popcorn kept a close eye on him to see that he didn't get out of line.

It was during this time that I learned how to drink on little or nothing. Popcorn always had some homemade hooch (homemade wine) brewing, and when that wasn't ready or available I learned how to strain Sterno (canned heat) through bread and get a nice buzz going. Bay Rum (a skin conditioner) and mouthwash were other alternatives. We would drink anything to take the edge off and not have to think about our lives at the time, or the families we had left behind, not to speak of the stark loneliness you felt sometimes. But we usually could afford the good stuff; it was only on Sundays that we had a difficult time getting the over-the-counter brands, either because we drank too much the night before or we just forgot which day it was and didn't stock up for the weekend. It was near impossible to buy alcohol on Sunday back then.

I remember many times though when Popcorn got drunk, after going to sleep he would have terrible nightmares. He'd literally wake up screaming. I never found out what that was all about. He never discussed it, but it was clearly something bad from his past.

We all had many different duties in camp, and we all shared fairly equally. The only job I really hated was digging the latrine.

This consisted of a hole about four feet deep. We had constructed a makeshift bench out of logs to sit on when necessary, and we simply moved it from one hole to another. We usually dug the hole about a hundred yards from the camp and kept it downwind as much as we could. A new hole had to be dug every week, and the old one covered up so the smell wouldn't get too bad.

At that time, and I guess even now, Fayetteville wasn't that big of a town and every once in a while a couple of us would go on R&R (rest and recuperation), jump a slow freight heading west to Charlotte, and spend a few days there working out of the labor pools every day so we could drink every night. Sometimes we'd be gone for a week or so before returning the same way we came. I got pretty adept at hopping freight trains at that time. I learned to take water, a bedroll, and cigarettes. No stopping at the local grocery on the way.

Back in the seventies, hopping a freight wasn't so bad; sometimes the bull (yard master) would even let you know what train to catch to get to where you were going. As time passed, though, it got a lot tougher. Certain bad apples spoiled the barrel, leaving bad feelings between the bulls and the hobos. It got so we had to be pretty sneaky about boarding, and just hope like hell we had chose the right train and would get to where we were going, and wouldn't run into a bull in the process. I've known some to get some pretty bad beatings having a run-in with the bulls.

Living in the camp was a lot like living in a regular community. There were rules we had to live by, and each person contributed his, or sometimes her, own expertise. Popcorn was without a doubt the leader, the mayor if you will. Professor was the idea man, and Bulldog and I were more or less the enforcers and the workers. It was as democratic as possible, with everyone having an equal voice. Cookie on the other hand was more or less sanitation control, keeping the site clean, though we all helped with that particular task. As cook, he was also the dietitian. Duties changed from time to time as people came and went, as was often the case in this type of setting. We never knew when someone new would wander in, or someone else would leave. These things were random.

The first time this happened was about three months after I arrived. One morning we woke up and Professor was gone, not a word to anyone. As was often the case, he had just moved on.

Then about a week later, Sandy walked into camp. Sandy was unknown to me, but she was an old friend to Popcorn; she'd been in camp before. I learned that a lot of the hobos that wandered around regularly knew where all the different camps were all over the country, especially if they'd been around for a while.

Sandy (not her real name), I remember thinking, seemed a bit out of place, not because she was a woman, but because of her age and the way she looked. She was in her late twenties, but I learned she'd been living this way since she was a teenager. She'd run away from an abusive family when she was fourteen. How she got involved with the hobo lifestyle, I don't exactly know. I suppose it was pretty much the same way we all did. We just stumbled into it while looking for who knows what. Sandy was about five feet tall with sandy-brown hair and brown eyes. She only weighed maybe a hundred pounds soaking wet. I never seen Sandy wear anything but jeans, and usually a man's shirt. She was what I call a bubbly person, always joking around and laughing. I believed this to be a mask: she would laugh on the outside to hide the pain on the inside. You only had to look into her eyes to see that pain. She had obviously had an unpleasant childhood so she chose to block it out, as most of us did with painful memories. None of us ever discussed the circumstances of those memories, but every once in a while certain details would come out, depending on the trust factor.

Sandy was a natural worker; she could work with the best of them, and for her size, pound for pound could out-work us all, maybe because she felt she had more to prove than the rest of us because she was a woman. Sandy did not stay for very long, only about a month. To say there was no hanky-panky while she was there would insult your intelligence. After all we were all human, and had the normal urges everyone else did. But she would choose just one, and barring any ill feelings, stick with him until she left, which she always did alone when she finally did leave. She wanted no ties. I remember she once told me she had a sister who lived in Utah somewhere and from time to time she would visit her. But she never stayed long. The vagabond life was in her blood, and believe me, once there it is hard to change. I know. For some reason or other—who knows?—she felt safer with no ties. Like most of us, I believe she was afraid of being hurt again. In case you want to know,

I was not her choice at that time. She took a liking to Bulldog, and stayed with him for the whole month. Guess you could say I lost out, if you wish to think of it that way. I never did. I accepted it as normal selection—she just wasn't attracted to me.

About a month after Sandy left, Swampy wandered into camp. Swampy was a newcomer to everyone. He was a natural-born Cajun from Louisiana. He grew up somewhere back in the swamp, where there were no cars; you needed a boat to get around. He grew up a fisherman like his dad, but sometime after reaching legal age, he decided he wanted to see what the the world was like outside of the swamps. I never heard of any major tragedy in his life that made him choose this way of living. It seemed to come natural to him.

Swampy was a rugged-looking man in his early thirties. He had a full beard, and wore dungarees and a pullover shirt most of the time. He did carry with him at all times though, what I call "Cajun Reeboks": rubber boots for everyday footwear if you happened to be a fisherman raised in the swamps. While he was in camp, we ate a lot of fish. He could catch fish in a toilet, he was so good at it. He enjoyed the challenge. He was also an excellent cook, as most Cajuns were, although his food was pretty spicy. I learned most of my Cajun cooking from him—dishes like jambalaya, gumbo, and so on—a talent that would come in handy in the not-so-distant future, when I started working offshore myself, as a cook.

One time Swampy and I went into town together to have a few drinks and shoot some pool at a local bar we often patronized. We were beginning to feel pretty good when Swampy got into a controversy with one of the "locals" as we called them. It was over who had dibs on the pool table next. Anyways a horrendous altercation then took place that immediately made me realize never to mess with Swampy when he fought. He fought to win, in any way he could, with any instrument at hand. He simply went blind in a fight, and didn't come to until the dispute was over. I learned at that time the rules to street fighting: win by any means possible. There is only one loser, and you don't want to be him.

For the rest of the time I was in the camp, the personnel didn't change much. Oh, every once in a while someone would wander into camp, stay for a day or two and then move on, but for the most part, they were what we called loners. They didn't take well to rules and were more comfortable by themselves, a trait I would come into in later years, though at the time I felt better with others around. During this time I heard from Popcorn about other hobo camps around the country, and their approximate locations. One in particular interested me—it was just south of Jacksonville, Florida. By December of 1971, I wanted a place that was warmer. Although it didn't—by northern standards—get all that cold in North Carolina, it was better, I knew, in Florida.

One thing I learned while in that camp was that no two reasons are the same as to why people choose to live the way they do. I could only ascertain through experience that it had something to do with our upbringing. Who really knows why one man chooses go take off when faced with certain situations, and another can stay put and cope with the same situation? The ability to adjust to setbacks in one's life depends on his or her moral fiber and the way they were raised. I make no excuses; that's just life, the way things are in the real world. We all have different personalities that dictate the life choices we make. And that my friend, is a fact.

Anyways, I lived like this for almost a year and a half, learning everything I could, getting my education (or so I called it). Then one day without a word to anyone, I packed up and left, as was the way with most of us when we got ready to move on. Seems we all hated long good-byes, and we all knew and understood.

The night I left, I caught a slow-moving freight heading south. The next stop in my journey: Jacksonville, Florida.

It took me almost two full days to get to Florida. The train kept stopping to drop off railroad cars. I even had to change cars once because they dropped the one I was in off at Waycross, Georgia. On top of that, I ended up having to get off the train in Lake City, Florida because I had missed my mark by about forty miles west of Jacksonville. This often happens when riding the rails. There have been times when I missed my mark by a whole state, and sometimes even more. You had to take your chances and hope you hit your mark or at least got close. When I got off the train in Lake City, I must have walked for about seven miles before I ran across a truck stop, another place to get a quick ride when you needed it back then. In later years even this method became precarious: a hit or miss kind of thing, because as the years went by people got less and less trusting, and who can blame them with everything that was going on in society at that time? You got so you couldn't trust anyone. With an offer to a truck driver to help him unload his cargo when he got to Jacksonville, I quickly picked up a ride; not only that, he gave me twenty dollars for the help, which they often did back then.

We unloaded the cargo in a place called Orange Park, a suburb of Jacksonville.

The hobo camp I was looking for was between Jacksonville and St. Augustine, so I still had thirty or so miles to make up for, and believe me, I walked most of that distance. It took me most of a whole day before I found the camp, off the main highway (95), just north of St. Augustine. As I approached the site, I gave the usual salutations, and was invited in. This camp was quite different from the one I had just left. It didn't seem to be as organized or as supervised as the last one. People were more helter-skelter in their activities, with a more or less everyone-for-themselves attitude. Everyone did their own thing to suit themselves and the camp got by as best it could. The people in the camp seemed to change daily, with nobody staying for very long. The one outstanding person I do remember from the time I spent there was Blackjack.

Blackjack was from—you guessed it—Las Vegas, hence the name. He told me that when he was a productive member of society he worked in the casinos in there. I did find out that the reason for his life change was the death of his wife. She had been his whole world when she was alive, the support that kept him on track. When she died he not only lost his wife, he lost his best friend and his reason for going on. He couldn't deal with the loss; in his mind he had no more reason for trying to achieve anything. He had no children, but I understand that he left behind a house, boat and other various holdings. They didn't have any value anymore, he felt. Without his wife nothing had a purpose. Blackjack wasn't very old, maybe in his late twenties, but he seemed much older.

He'd been on the road for six years, but had picked up a lot along the way. He was very outgoing, and would give you the shirt off his back if he thought you needed it more than him. But if you crossed him, he could be your worst enemy. I made it a point to stay on his good side. He knew Popcorn. They had crossed paths about four years earlier, and had become good friends. I found out that a lot of people I ran into during these years knew Popcorn and considered him a friend. He was very well known.

The one thing I liked about this camp was that it was only a few miles from the ocean, and I loved the ocean. Many times in the years to follow, where I was would be determined by its proximity to the sea. When I did go inland, I didn't stay very long. I liked being near the water. Another thing I liked in Florida was the climate. Although it did have a tendency to get cool from time to time, still it was better than North Carolina, and much superior by far to the extreme north. They had a name for the camp — they called it Koogan's Bluff — why I don't know, except to distinguish it from the others. At any rate, I didn't rank the camp that highly; it seemed too random to me.

Many people came and went while I was there, some were regulars, and some weren't. No one stayed for very long. The camp seemed to be a rest stop on the way further south. I can recall with certainty only one person who was a regular. This was a gentleman in his late sixties called Big John. I don't know how long he'd been on the road. I do know he received a check every month, which made him very popular with the sponges—those who used others for their own ends without reciprocation—and there were a lot of them in such a setting. But you didn't have to *take* from Big John. He freely gave and shared all he had; that's just the way he was. He was a lonely man, and seemed to like the company as well as the attention. Big John was by all standards a full-blown alcoholic, and he liked to drink the cheap stuff—wine, that is. Before he ran out of money for the month he would buy wines like Mad Dog 20/20, and Wild Irish Rose. Not one grape went into making these wines; they were chemically created. But Big John would always say: "Better living through chemicals."

I did learn that John was from Wilmington, Delaware and at one time he had been the manager of a large department store there. He had been married for over twenty-one years, and had three children, before his wife left him for his best friend and associate, although that in itself didn't cause him to adopt the homeless lifestyle.

What did, I learned later, was his children's desire to put him in a convalescent home after he had a heart attack and couldn't work anymore. At first his illness caused him some physical disabilities, and his children didn't want to deal with them, opting rather to store him away somewhere, where someone else would have to take care of him. He would have nothing to do with that. He had been a proud and independent man all his life, and wasn't going to let a small setback keep him down. The only reason he left Delaware was because his children were trying to get the court to commit him and give them control over his life. He ran and never looked back. Eventually his physical condition improved, and I have to say I never met a man who seemed happier. He was free to lead his own life as he saw fit, with no interference from anyone, and that's just the way he wanted it. Who is to say if that's right or wrong? I know it seemed right to me.

I didn't stay at that camp very long, only a few months, but while I was there I kept pretty much to myself. I spent a lot of time working out of a labor pool in St. Augustine. I became a regular and got out almost every day, but during this time I spent almost every night drinking in the local bars. I had several opportunities to settle down to a regular job and a more stable life, but I wasn't ready yet. There was too much left to do, too many more places to go and to see. I hadn't found what I was looking for in St. Augustine.

I did meet a girl while I was there that I liked pretty well, and seen a lot of, but I wasn't looking for anything permanent. Besides, she was a lot like me in that she liked to drink, and was a pretty wild character. She could shoot pool with the best of them, and I often laid side bets on her while she was playing. Many a drink was paid for by her pool game. I wish I could remember her name, but to tell you the truth I cannot. I can't even remember what she looked like. I only remember her demeanor, and believe me, she was not the settling down type either. She was what I often refer to as a party girl—fun to be around but with no emotional attachments, just the way I liked women back then.

Anyways after about three months in St. Augustine, I was ready to move on, and move on I did. I was still headed in a southerly direction, and my next stop was Daytona Beach. I wasn't aware of a hobo camp there, but I had heard stories from others that in Daytona Beach at that time of year a lot was going on and you could find plenty of places to spread out a bedroll, including on the beach. You see this was in late February, the Daytona 500 was going on and shortly after that, Spring Break. I timed it just right. Daytona was a hub of activity at this time of year. The town was full of strangers and I could move about without even being noticed, just the way I liked it. I didn't like to draw attention to myself. As it turned out I was coming into town just as the Daytona 500 crowd was leaving. I never saw so many motorcycles heading in one direction in all my life.

It took me less than a day to go from St. Augustine to Daytona Beach. I followed highway A1A all the way down; it was only about forty miles. It was pretty late when I arrived—about one o'clock in the morning—so I found a secluded spot on the beach, spread out my bedroll and slept till morning. It was a beautiful experience: this was the first time I had slept so close to the ocean, and the sound of the surf, and the chanting of the birds was like being surrounded by a symphony. I cannot remember ever having slept better. The next morning I was up early and scoping the territory out for possibilities. It usually took a couple of days to get the lay of the land and locate the opportunities available to someone in the state of limbo, that is to say, just passing through. Back then there was only one labor pool in town, and to tell you the truth, there wasn't much work going out of it. I did manage to get a couple days' work a week though. The rest of the time I was able to parlay my panhandling skills. With all the tourists in town, I really didn't do all that bad, although in the future I was to become much more skillful at the art.

Then in mid-March all hell broke loose, the college kids hit town, and I do mean hit. It was like a horde, one moment no one, the next you couldn't move to spite yourself, there were so many people. Overnight, tents sprang up, with every exhibit from beach towels to beer. Seemed like every beer distributor in the country was there. I was astounded by the opportunities that presented themselves. It was hobo heaven. With parties around the clock, free food and free beer everywhere you looked, you could always find someone who'd offer you a beer or something to eat. I had more jobs offered to me that first week of Spring Break than I'd ever had offered me before in my life. At first I wasn't interested, but after the first week, I had to go to work to get some rest, if you know what I mean.

I accepted a job in a small food tent right on the beach. This for two reasons: one was because I knew a little about cooking, and secondly, free food. I can go on and on about the parties that I went to during that time, mostly uninvited. But that's the way it was, a party started and it continued to grow as the night went on; it was an open invitation to all. But I will not bore you with all the details—you can fill in the blanks yourself—after all one party was pretty much the same as the other. All I can tell you is that there was plenty of girls, plenty of sex, and plenty of alcohol, of all kinds. It flowed like water. There was one party, though, that stood out from all the others.

I was working late one night at the food tent when three girls in their early twenties came in. They were already not feeling much pain, and were on the verge of being rowdy to the extent that they were very outspoken and were kidding around with everyone. I remember they had Penn State T-shirts on, so I assumed they went to Penn State University, although that was not necessarily the case. Everyone traded T-shirts freely during spring break. It was sort of a tradition, so you couldn't tell with any certainty exactly where anyone went to school. Anyways they got to kidding around with me, and next thing I knew, I was invited to a party at their motel. Needless to say I figured I hit it really lucky. When I got off work I went to the office trailer and took a shower and changed clothes. (My boss often let me use the trailer to clean up. It was either there or the ocean and the beach showers.) The motel they were staying at was only a few blocks from where I was working. As I neared the motel, I could hear a hell of a ruckus coming from just about every room there, so I figured everyone in the motel was having a good time. Well they were, but they were doing it all together, the whole motel was an open party. No one's doors were closed and everyone just roamed from room to room, checking out the different fares.

Anyways the party went on for three days. I missed work, we drank, and had nonstop sex for the whole time—it was unbelievable, even to me. I never before or since have seen such permissiveness. The music back then was the best, a cross between the old rock of the 50s and 60s and the New Age rock of the 70s, with the British influence. It just roared from every room nonstop. I have never again been to anything like that to this very day.

Well everything must come to an end, and spring break was no exception. The town changed overnight, from a young crowd party town to a laid back typical tourist town like so many others along the east coast of Florida. Anyways after the party ended, so did my stay at Daytona Beach. I stayed just a few more days, then moved on to my next conquest, Ft. Lauderdale. It was a much larger town and the work proved to be more plentiful. I knew of only one hobo camp there, and even that wasn't near a railroad tracks—it was in a small wooded area just off AlA, almost right in town. It wasn't hard to locate, and I was quickly taken in and accepted. By now I had become adept to the ways of the land, and was pretty sure of myself and of being accepted with no problems.

I really ended up liking this camp: not only was it close to the ocean, but it only had a few regulars and the face of it didn't change much over time. It was fairly laid back, with not a whole lot of rules other than to get along, no fighting, even arguing was not allowed. All and all we got along well—we were all about the same age and of the same demeanor. I stayed in this camp for over a year. During that time I met some pretty interesting folks, many of whom were not of the same circle—that is to say, they were street people but they didn't live in hobo camps. Sometimes they slept in local flophouses, just a bunk for two or three dollars a night, or they camped out under the bridge. This was nothing like the hobo camp. When you were out alone and in the streets, it was every man for himself, and you stayed pretty much to yourself, with the exception of maybe one or two near acquaintances. Some of these people's stories were very interesting.

One of the first individuals I met in the hobo camp where I was staying at the time was Gunny, a nickname gave him in Vietnam because he was a real gung-ho Gunnery Sergeant in the Marines. Because he, too, was a Vietnam Vet, I felt a special kinship with him, although his problems were much different than those I experienced when I returned from 'Nam. Gunny was medium height and very thin; in fact he looked sick most of the time. I cannot recall how many times I saw him actually eat anything, although I'm sure he must have. He just didn't do it often. Gunny was one of those who never really left Vietnam. Oh, he did leave physically but mentally he was still in 'Nam, a characteristic I ran across many times in the streets when dealing with 'Nam veterans. Many of us had a hard time adjusting to life in general when we came home, but some, like Gunny, had lost all touch with reality and couldn't forget or leave the experience behind them.

Gunny always wore his camouflage fatigues and jungle boots. He had no other clothes except for those he wore while in 'Nam. He purchased any new clothes he got from the local Army Surplus store in town. He was always reliving his experiences in 'Nam—it seemed to be his whole life, his only reason for being. Many times I had to just walk away from him, I got so tired of hearing about it. I was one of those who wanted to forget the experience and move on with my life, while Gunny wanted to relive it every day. Even though he had been out of Vietnam for over four years, he still had nightmares. Sometimes his nightmares flowed over into reality to the extent that when he awoke, in his mind he was still in Vietnam fighting the war.

That made him very dangerous to be around during these times—you never knew exactly how he was going to react. The times Gunny did have somewhat of a hold on reality, he drank constantly. He had been wounded three times in 'Nam, and came home hooked on morphine. Well he kicked the morphine habit, but replaced it with alcohol. It was his way of blocking some of the memories as best he could, although the way he talked about the experiences from time to time left you with a feeling that he actually carried a kind of pride around with him about them. Most of us had none concerning what had happened to us during the war. But then just as quickly as his pride would show itself, he'd do an about face and break into tears when relating some of his experiences. You never knew how he'd react. For the most part Gunny was a great person to know. He'd do anything for you, it's just that he was so unpredictable you'd never know exactly how he might react in different situations.

One time when we were in town together he went absolutely mad. He practically scared me to death. We were walking by the courthouse downtown and there were some young kids (hippies, we called them back then) demonstrating against the war in Vietnam and our continued involvement there. Although I didn't like what they were doing either, I let the incident go. But Gunny was another matter; he went completely insane. He charged the crowd of about six of them, jumped right into the middle and started swinging. It was as though he went completely blind. I'm sure if he'd had a gun he'd have shot them right there on the spot.

After a melee that lasted for only about five minutes the police stepped in and broke it up, arresting Gunny and taking him to jail. It was about a month before I saw Gunny again, and it was as though nothing had happened. It was not even a memory to him, as though the incident never took place. This was typical of most of Gunny's confrontations—his mind would go blank about any occurrence of them at all.

I remember another time when Gunny's family came to visit him. He was from a small town in Texas, just southwest of Houston. His family always knew where he was, and that's where they wanted him to stay. I believed they loved him, but didn't know how to deal with his attitude. Anyways the one time I was there when they came, their visit seemed less than cordial. They asked if he needed anything, brought him some regular clothes that he just gave away when they left, and left him with a few extra dollars. Then they disappeared as quickly as they came. Gunny really never needed extra money. He received a disability check from the government every month from wounds that left one of his legs about an inch shorter than the other, causing him to walk with a noticeable limp. I guess the money was a way for the family to cope with the situation themselves, not knowing what else to do to help him. Other than that, Gunny never discussed his relationship with his family; when they were gone it was as though they didn't even exist.

Gunny and I would hang around with each other from time to time because I was one person he felt understood him to a certain point. Other than me, he didn't have any close friends; most of the others were scared of him. I really wasn't scared of him, just cautious around him in certain situations so that to a point I did have some control of him. Sometimes I could bring him back to reality before he got too far gone. But in retrospect, most of the time I just got out of his way because when he lost complete sight of reality, there was no reasoning with him.

I worked out of a place in Ft. Lauderdale called Handy Men, one of the many labor pools you'd find all across the country. That's when I ran across Chief, another person that I took an immediate liking to. Chief was a full-blooded American Indian from the Choctaw tribe in Oklahoma. He was raised on the reservation and he, too, was a Vietnam veteran. His demeanor was pretty much the same as mine; he wanted to forget the whole matter and put it behind him. He too had difficulty adjusting to life and family upon returning, and having never seen any part of the world other than the reservation and Vietnam, went searching for himself. Neither of us knew exactly what we were looking for; we just knew whatever it was, it was not at home. Chief stood about five-ten, and at 220 pounds was a formidable-looking individual though in fact, he was a teddy bear. He wouldn't hurt a fly if you paid him to but he could be intimidating when necessary. He always wore a big old western hat, with a large eagle feather sticking out of the brim. He was proud of his heritage, and this was his way of expressing it. We had many good times together drinking or just hanging out. We liked each other's company. When I finally did leave Ft. Lauderdale, I really missed him, although we were to cross paths a couple more times in the years to come.

Another person I met while staying in this area I met quite by accident. On the way to work every morning, I passed an old abandoned house just off the road about a hundred yards. At first I never noticed anyone, just a dim light that came from inside from time to time.

It was on a sunny Sunday morning that I was walking up to the store to get some cigarettes and beer for the weekend when I spotted a child playing outside the abandoned house. I figured it was just one of the neighborhood children playing around the place. Then I noticed a young lady coming out of the house, and at the time thought it was odd, but didn't think it meant anything. I went on to the store not giving it another thought, but on the way back, I saw the girl again. She was sitting outside the house on one of those old spools you see linemen leave along the side of the road when they have been putting up new telephone cable. As I neared the road that led back to the house, she called out to me to come near. I was hesitant at first, but then thought what the hell, I'll go see what she wants. As it turned out all she wanted was a cigarette, but that one cigarette was to lead to a beautiful relationship that almost took me off the streets right then and there.

Her name was Sara, and while I'd like to say she was the most beautiful woman I had ever seen, such was not the case. Although she wasn't bad looking, I'd seen much better as far as looks go, but none better as far as heart and personality go, then or since. She was only about five feet tall, and at 130 pounds not fat, but what I'd call full-figured. She had bright red hair and the prettiest blue eyes I had ever seen. She was freckled from head to toe and had a smile that could melt your heart. She also had this funny laugh that you couldn't help laughing with; it was totally intoxicating. Sara was from a small town in West Virginia, best known for coal mining. Everyone who lived within fifty miles worked in the mine. I learned that Sara had been married for four years to her high school sweetheart, although neither of them had actually completed high school. She was twenty-six at the time I met her, but like most who lived in the streets, she looked much older than her years.

Sara shared a lot with me about her past and I learned that for the first couple of years of her marriage, everything was pretty good. Then sometime after the second year her husband became very abusive towards not only her but also to her son. He had a drinking problem that escalated as time went along. Being from a kind of backwoods background as both her and her husband were, they were very family-oriented, and no matter how much she complained to her family or the authorities, they were encouraged to work things out. Several times she called the police on her husband because of physical abuse, only to have them do nothing. She tried getting help from every resource available, but being such a small town there wasn't that much there.

She even tried the church, and other than offer her and her husband some counseling—which her husband would never agree to—they couldn't do anything. Even her family seemed to be oblivious to the matter. Her own dad had been abusive to his family while she was growing up, and all her mother did was put up with it as best she could by ignoring the problem, the same as she advised Sara to do. This went on for quite a while, to hear Sara tell it, until she just couldn't take anymore. One night she packed her things, took her son and left with only eighteen dollars in her pocket and not knowing where she was going or how she would get there. She walked out to the highway, stuck out her thumb, and almost immediately got a ride. The end of the line came for her when she reached Ft. Lauderdale. She felt like she couldn't go on anymore and figured this would be as good a place for a new start as any. It was only after she'd been there a few weeks that she met me, or I met her, whatever way it was; anyways I was more than pleased to make her acquaintance.

From that time on we became somewhat of an item, although it didn't happen over night.

Sara was an independent woman. She didn't want to ask anyone for help, partly because of her upbringing, I would say, but also because she was afraid her family would find out where she was and take her son away, or worse yet, make them come home. She was adamant about not going back to that "hell hole," as she called it. But this attitude left her at a disadvantage. You see, with her son, she had to find a way to support herself and him without leaving him alone. At first she depended on picking up cans along the roadway and around dumpsters in the alleys behind bars, and for a while this went pretty good for her. She could take her son with her, and earned enough money to feed them and buy whatever other items they needed for cleanliness. As long as no police bothered her at the abandoned house she lived in, she was OK. Sara was a stickler for keeping herself and her son clean. They took baths regularly at the beach showers after dusk. Sometimes she washed their clothes out by hand, but when she had the extra money she'd go to the local laundry mat.

I used to stop by the house every night to check up on them, see if they needed anything, and just to talk. We had some marvelous conversations. Other times we just kept each other company. But for the first two months, when it got late I returned to my camp and she remained at her place. She was distrustful of men for quite a while, and I can't honestly blame her, from what she told me. Then all of a sudden there was a change in our relationship.

Sara got a part-time night job as a waitress at a local restaurant, but this required her to find someone to take care of her son, Brad. I was the only person she knew very well, and seeing as I essentially worked days, and her job was in the early evening hours, I guess she felt comfortable asking me for help. Needless to say, I was more than willing to help in any way I could. Brad and I got along quite well, and I loved children anyways, so to me this was no big deal, though to Sara it was. For a while everything worked out very well, her coming home from work early enough for me to return to my camp and still get enough sleep for me to go to work in the morning. The weekends were no problem, because I never worked weekends except in extreme circumstances, and that is when she put in the most hours. Then after a while her boss started taking advantage of her and asking her to work longer hours, holding over her the fact that if she couldn't, he would find someone else who could.

Sara was saving every cent she could so she could find herself and Brad a decent place to stay, and didn't want to start all over again after coming so far. So I began staying later and later, until one night she wouldn't let me leave to walk back to my camp, and only get a couple hours sleep myself before going to work. She asked me to stay, and I did. At first I had my place to sleep and she and Brad had theirs. But after about two weeks we somehow, I'm not sure exactly how it happened, ended up sleeping together. From that time on it was our plan to get out of the streets together, and put our lives back on track.

After about five months, between the two of us we had saved enough money to rent us a small efficiency apartment, not too far from where she and I worked. I wish I could say this was the end of the story and we both got our lives back together, but if I did, that would be the end of this book, and besides, other events took place that led to our demise. When Sara got off the streets and into her own place, she really straightened up—no more drinking, and everything revolved around the home. We never went out. It wasn't that I didn't care for Sara or her son, it was just that I wasn't ready to settle down yet, at least not to that extent. I still had too much to do, and too many more places to go and see. I was not ready to be responsible. I still wanted my fun as well as my freedom, and with Sara I couldn't have both. Our parting of the ways came as a mutual agreement and understanding. As far as I know Sara and her son never ended up in the streets again. Last I heard just before I left town was that she had found a man that was a cook where she worked and they were getting along famously.

I returned to the hobo camp and stayed for another three months. It was during this time that I met Ike, a transient of sorts, even for the streets. He'd had, in recent times, some stability in his life. He was from Arizona, somewhere around Tucson, but had lived on and off in New Orleans since leaving home. There he worked for the catering companies as galley hand or BR person (cleaning the rig, making beds, etc.), on the oil rigs out in the Gulf of Mexico. It was through him that I was convinced to make my next move, but other events were about to take place that would delay my departure for about two years.

Ike and I were drinking in a local bar one night when a guy came in selling some merchandise that was too good to pass up. I must tell you at this point that I wasn't so naive that I didn't suspect something. I figured that the merchandise could have been stolen, but after the initial thought, I let it slide. I bought a CB radio for ten dollars, a steal would be the right word for it. Anyways, during a routine check that the police did from time to time of the camp, and a check of simple serial numbers, I was nailed and taken to jail. They charged me with buying and receiving stolen property. With that charge and that charge only, the State of Florida, in their unlimited wisdom, made me a ward of the Florida Prison System in Raiford, Florida for a period of three years. During that time I learned a lot about another type of survival, the do-or-die kind that you can only learn in a place like that.

I managed to survive for a year and a half before being released on a work program that required me to stay in the system for another six months. By keeping my nose clean and staying out of trouble, I was released on parole. It was a non-reporting parole, so as soon as I was released from the system I headed for New Orleans in the hope that I could get a job offshore like Ike had described to me, the way we had planned before this unfortunate incident happened. At that time my only real concern was to get out of the state of Florida as soon as possible—with no intention of ever returning—although over the years I would return to Florida several times.

I bought a bus ticket to New Orleans, not knowing where to start when I got there to find a job offshore, except for a couple of names and places that Ike had told me about. That was the only recourse I had when I got there, but that proved to be enough.

Thus was to begin what I call my "maintenance" years. I no longer lived in the hobo camps, but still led the high life while managing to keep a roof over my head, such as it was, usually just a flophouse, as we called them: a bed in a large dormitory shared with several others, for just a few dollars a night. I'll go into greater detail in the next chapter, which is the next chapter of my life.

Persevering

It's hard to know from day to day
Just how things ought to be
When deep inside your soul is lost
And your mind don't have the key

From where to go or what to do
The next item on the list
When surviving is just a way of life
And you can barely see through the mist

You learn right from the beginning
That to maintain is the best you can do
In a world that doesn't see the problem
And each day brings something new

So you work each day just to survive
Trying to maintain your sanity
When all around are losing theirs
And you search for your sanctity

'Cause sacredness is being safe
When all around you danger lies
And to maintain means reaching another day
In a world that's often disguised

As other than you had imagined it
More than you were taught from birth
It's become a matter of persevering
Rather than to know one's worth

—May 12, 1997

~ CHAPTER 2 ~

The Big Easy OR *Persevering*

So it was that the latter part of 1974 found me in New Orleans. When I left Florida, I had saved a few hundred dollars from the work release program I was on after leaving prison. This was not one of my best ideas. New Orleans was a real party town, and for an alcoholic with a few hundred dollars in his pocket, having been in prison for over two years now, it was party central when I arrived, and the bars were open twenty-four hours a day.

It didn't take me long at all to find one of the places Ike had told me about that was to be instrumental for getting me offshore. The name of the place was the Dixie Bar and Hotel on Crondolet Street, right in the heart of skid row (a place where transients hung and drank and lived). I was in the hopes that I would somehow find Ike right away, but that was not to be so. After all it had been over two years, and I wasn't even sure if he was back in New Orleans. At any rate I wasn't to find him until I'd been there almost a year.

The Dixie Bar and Hotel was a small three-story building with a bar downstairs and living quarters on the top two floors. These quarters consisted of a series of beds in several rooms, shared by four or five others, depending on the size of the room. The accommodations were cheap. I paid only thirty-five dollars for the first week. From the second floor, I had easy access to the bar, just at the bottom of the stairs leading from my room. The next two weeks I spent all my time in the bar downstairs and exploring the other bars in the neighborhood, and there were plenty. Within a six-block area were a dozen bars, all pretty seedy joints if you know what I mean, but these were my kind of places. I always figured if I could walk into the front door of a bar and smell the men's room, I was drinking with the good ole boys, and these were all like that, with maybe a couple of exceptions.

I mostly hung around Irene's Zoo Review, right across the street from the Dixie; the Mansion, around the corner from the Dixie; White's Circle View at 81 Charles, the next block up from the Dixie; the Hummingbird, just down the street from the Circle View; the Camp Inn, right across the street from the Hummingbird; Rebetos, just down the street from the Camp Inn; and Dale's, across the street from Rebetos. There were others that I frequented, but it's been so long I can't even recall the names of all of them. For the next year and a half, these would be my main hangouts.

By far The Dixie was where I spent most of my time though, because I'd usually get so drunk there I didn't wander much further unless I had company, and that was something that I seldom wanted. Even back then the streets weren't too friendly—not as bad as they are today—but even then you had to watch your step, especially if you looked like you had money.

The Dixie was mostly full of men who worked offshore. The owner of the place, Harry Van Camp, ran somewhat of an employment agency to supply different catering companies with offshore workers, for a fee of course, which usually consisted of your first week's pay. Seeing that most of the jobs lasted two weeks, this supposedly left you with a week's pay when you came back in. Wrong. By the time he got you out, you'd be so in debt to him from the bar tabs he ran on you and the advance in rent, that when you did get back in you had to start back out on the tab right away. Thus he kept you more or less under his control, unless you were one of those guys that could go without drinking for long periods of time and not spend much money, which was not the case for most of us. We lived for today and let tomorrow fend for itself. In this way a pattern started in my life that almost killed me. I was at the Dixie over a month before Harry got me out to work. By then I'd been broke for over two weeks, and was indebted to him for quite a bit.

When I did finally get out to work, it took me another two months or more to get out of his debt to some extent, although I always had a bill with him. Sometimes my bar tab alone would run over four hundred dollars for the two weeks I was in from offshore, not to speak of my rent. But through it all, I worked pretty steady, going out for two weeks, giving me a breather from drinking, only to come in and do nothing but drink and party for the two weeks I was in. I met many interesting people during my stay there and will spend most of this chapter talking about them, rather than myself. After all we were mirror reflections of each other; we all had our reasons for being where we were, and the lifestyle was pretty much the same for us all, with few exceptions.

The first person I met at the Dixie was of course the bartender, Clarence. He helped me get my foot in the door; that with the fact that they knew Ike from previous encounters. I was at the Dixie three days before I met Harry. He was not one of those people who tended close to business. The place was really run down, and besides buying supplies for the bar to keep it stocked, he done little of anything else but see that when you owed him he'd get you out to work for a while so you could pay your bill. He always made sure you had to rely on him. He even required that you let him pick up your checks when you were offshore so he'd be sure to get his money first. That was a requirement for staying at the Dixie and being able to charge the room and drinks.

Anyways, Clarence the bartender was in his late thirties, and was Harry's right-hand man. The bar was even licensed under his name because Harry had something in his background that didn't allow him to hold a liquor license. Clarence pretty much ran the whole show, except for the books, which were maintained daily by him, but overall by Harry. Believe me he kept close tabs on you and knew exactly when to get you out to work to get his money, while keeping you indebted to him. Clarence, like most of the others I've described, looked much older than his years—the kind of life we led tended to do that to you. He was always neatly dressed. He was one of the few living at the Hotel that had his own room. There was a laundry room on the second floor, so you could keep your clothes clean while you were there and before going back offshore.

Except for an occasional barmaid that the Dixie seemed to change like toilet rolls because Harry wasn't known for timely payment—if he paid them at all after they paid their own bar tabs. Clarence was the main man, and the one you had to get along with in order to obtain regular jobs. He had the option to either let you stay or throw you out. Needless to say, I got on his good side right from the start. I had some money when I got there so that wasn't much of a problem. I was a free spender when I had the money; everybody drank when I got drunk, as was the case for most of us in that situation. We maintained each other. When one was broke, someone else had money and vice versa.

Anyways, as I said, Clarence and I became quick friends, and remained that way whenever I was in town. From what I learned through countless conversations with Clarence, he was a native New Orleanais, born and raised on the Mississippi River in the part of the city we called the Irish Channel, another skid row that I would frequent in the months to come. He came from a poor background; his family never had much. His dad was a longshoreman who drank quite a bit when he wasn't working, and died when Clarence was young, leaving him to provide for his mother. He was an only child. His mother was a housewife all her life, though in her latter years she worked as a bar maid in one of the many bars in the Irish Channel district. That proved to be her demise, because just a few years before I met Clarence she had been shot in a bar brawl where she was working.

How Clarence and Harry first got hooked up I'm not sure, except that in the beginning Clarence worked offshore like all the rest of us, then graduated to being Harry's right-hand man and running everyday affairs at his business. He didn't have much of a formal education, but was very good with figures, and very street-wise. I learned a lot from him about when and where to go, and what and what not to do in the streets. He taught me how to be aware of my surroundings and what was going on at all times, especially when out on the town and drinking. For the first two weeks I was there and had some money, he'd take me around to the different places and introduce me, so everyone would get to know who I was. We spent a lot of time together during his off hours, when he had someone else that could run the bar. It's like I said, they changed waitresses often, but mostly it was a circle of the same ones that he hired over and over again. They'd work a while, then quit. Someone else would take her place for a while, then the same scenario. It just kept going around in a big circle all the time between maybe three or four different girls.

The first girl I met was Barbara. She was from Boston, and worked once in a while as a barmaid at the Dixie. Barbara was a chubby five-foot-three and cursed like a sailor. She was more like one of the guys—she drank like a fish, and that's where all the money that she earned went, except for what she paid in rent. She lived around the corner from the Dixie at the Mansion, which had private accommodations for women. Barbara was a regular barmaid at several of the bars; she always worked at one or the other, making the rounds so to speak. But the Dixie and the Mansion were where she hung around most of the time, bumming drinks when she was broke, and working when she had to.

Her background was very dark from what I was able to ascertain from her conversations from time to time. Being sexually abused by her father from the age of four until she left home at thirteen was all she ever talked about her past, with the exception of a succession of men in her life that abused her terribly, both physically and mentally. She'd been living on the streets and fending for herself for most of her adult life, which at that time put her in her early thirties. She, for all the time I knew her, never settled down with one man. Seems she had a different one every week, depending on who was in from offshore at the time and who she'd take to. She didn't mess around with anyone except offshore workers, because she knew that's where the money was, until they went out again, and also that way she could have a variety of men, a situation she seemed to prefer. She didn't trust men in general, and never let any of them get too close. If they got serious, she got gone. I felt sorry for Barbara in many ways, and even though she chose to live the way she did, I could see a lot of pain in her eyes. I was never one of her circle of men, but we were good friends, and drank and run together a lot. I found her to be of above average intelligence, and a lot of fun to be around, except when she got terribly drunk, at which time she became a total bitch. She'd get you into a fight in a minute if you hung around long enough, she herself being a fighter: I seen her in some horrendous fights that left even a man to believe he didn't want to be on her bad side. Barbara never changed all the time I knew her, and as far as I know still lives the same way—if she's still alive. She had a lot of physical problems caused by her excessive drinking and lifestyle, and I haven't seen her for over seven years.

New Orleans was one of those places that I would leave and return to from several times over the years. I got good enough at what I done offshore (cooking), that whenever I was in town I could find a job with no trouble at all, even without help from anyone. I made the rounds pretty well the first time I was there, and was well known in the industry.

The next girl I met was also an occasional barmaid at the Dixie and her name was Sue. She was the complete opposite of Barbara, even though she had a similar background. Sue was from a town in northern Washington called Bellingham, only about twenty miles from the Canadian border. Sue's dad worked for the same lumber company all his life. She had three brothers, all younger than her, and one sister, the youngest of all. She was in her mid-thirties, and came to New Orleans looking for a better life. When she was only fourteen, her mother deserted the family, leaving Sue to take care of her brothers and sister, and having to quit school. Her dad worked from dawn to dusk, often seven days a week. Sue had to do everything—clean, cook, wash, and any other household chores she couldn't get her siblings to do. In effect, Sue had no childhood herself; she became a mother at fourteen. Her dad was a very strict disciplinarian and didn't allow Sue any time of her own. She had never been out with a boy until after she left home, and that wasn't until she was twenty-two years old and her brothers and sister were grown enough to take care of themselves. Even then she had to sneak away, because her dad threatened if she ever left he'd come after her, no matter what. I guess that's one reason she traveled so far before deciding to settle down somewhere.

She told me that in the beginning she had a pretty rough time of it; because of her lack of experience with the opposite sex, she got involved with some pretty seedy characters. They used her and abused her to their own ends, and she done a lot of things she'll say she's not proud of. She says it took her only a couple of years to wise up, then she struck out on her own.

At first she worked in the French Quarter dancing in the topless clubs. She quickly tired of that life, and opted for a waitress job at the restaurant beneath the Hummingbird Hotel, right next to the bar. From there she got to know the locals, so to speak, and became a well-liked regular around skid row. She had become hardened over the years, but still possessed a gentle quality about herself. She had the mother instinct, and it was very strong and made her feel as though she wanted to take care of all us so-called strays. Sue was a pretty good-sized woman, tall and husky, a very formidable-looking woman, but with a heart of gold. Unusual I'd say, being what she'd already been through, that she still somehow managed to keep her soul, something most of us could not do. We had lost something in the transition. She had dark black hair, and eyes so dark that they mirrored her very soul, and like so many others I had seen in the past, the pain was ever-present. We all carried it, just some different than others. All the time I knew Sue I only knew her to be with one man, and he treated her well. He worked offshore, but worked on the boats, so he was gone more than the rest of us. When he was in town though, he treated her like a queen, and I never knew her to cheat on him. He was to become another acquaintance of mine, in a long succession of acquaintances. I never figured I had any friends, only acquaintances.

His name was Binder. Why they called him that I never found out, maybe it was even his real name. Binder was an older man, in his early fifties—too old, I thought, for Sue—but then what did I know? He treated her well and that's all that really counted. He stood about six-feet, weighed about 220 pounds, had sandy blond hair and walked with a shuffle. Binder was from St. Louis, Missouri, and grew up on the Mississippi River, just a bit more to the north. He was raised around boats, his father being a captain on a tugboat. I guess Binder followed in his footsteps. Binder was a drinking man, but not like the rest of us. He took care of business first and drank second. I never knew him to cause any trouble. He and Sue always lived in one of the many hotels close by, never opting for an apartment because Binder said they were too restricting, and didn't allow for spontaneity. Just what he meant by that is anyone's guess. The whole time I was in New Orleans this time around I knew Binder to be off work only three times. Each time he'd stay in for about a month and then go right back out again, for who knows how long. It never seemed to be the same. Binder was one of those people who seemed to find it convenient to live the way he did, from one paycheck to the next. I believe he was afraid of anything that seemed permanent.

During this time in New Orleans I met many who in some ways, according to one's definition, did not seem to be homeless in the literal sense of the word. But all of these people were a part of the life I led for so many years. Due to their lack of permanenc or direction in life, they seemed just like the rest of us who had no other place to go and nothing to do when we got there except to survive. After all, survival was the name of the game. Even when I had a roof over my head and a job, I was still in a transient state, because from one minute to the next I had no other plan in life but to survive for just that day.

One of the other people I met early on at the bar was not even a person who worked offshore. He was a young man named Jerry. For all intents and purposes, he was totally out of place; it was obvious he belonged somewhere else. He was far from street-wise, even though he'd been in the streets for a few years now and was fairly well known by most of the locals. Jerry was in his mid-twenties. He was a big kid and his manner of dress was not one you'd say was dictated by style. He always looked like his mother had dressed him. Another thing that set Jerry apart from the rest of us was his mental state. You see, Jerry was not what I would call retarded, but he was what I call slow. He was like a kid in a man's body, if you know what I mean. Whatever schooling he had was less than adequate. He could barely write his name and could not read at all. He was from Scranton, Pennsylvania, where he lived with his parents until he ran away from home at sixteen. Since that time, Jerry lived in the streets, opting for abandoned buildings or wherever else he could find to keep himself out of the weather.

Jerry use to work from time to time out of the labor pools, but that proved to be difficult. There were some things he couldn't do. If it required any skill or mental ability, he was lost. Jerry was all brawn and no brain when it came to work. Occasionally, he rented a room for a night at the Dixie, just to have a place to clean up and relax for a while. I believe it was because he knew many of us at the Dixie, especially Clarence and Sue, and trusted them. They didn't take advantage of him like many of the others did, and he felt safe there. Mostly, though, he lived in the streets and nobody ever really knew where. Jerry would come and go, and there would be days, even sometimes weeks, when no one would see him at all or even know where he was. Jerry distrusted most people, especially the older ones, those who I guess reminded him of his parents, and this is where the sad part begins.

Jerry's parents were very disappointed in him, because of the way he was and because he didn't live up to their expectations. He was less than perfect, and anything that wasn't in the norm, so to speak, must be some type of punishment they had to endure. They were very strict, to hear Jerry tell the story, and they not only physically abused him, but he endured a state of mental abuse unlike any I'd ever heard of before. They constantly called him names like "stupid" and "retarded," and told him he'd never amount to anything, or be anybody, because he was a retard. He told me they used to lock him in a dark closet, sometimes for days on end, with no food or water, lying in his own waste, punishing him for something he done that they didn't approve of. His father use to beat him with a thick leather strap that left welts all over his body and sometimes even drew blood.

How Jerry, with the way he was, ever got the presence of mind or the knowledge to finally decide to leave home, is a complete mystery to me, but at sixteen he done just that. Even more mysterious to me is how he got to New Orleans, or even how he decided to come here in the first place. Where all these ideas came from, I can't imagine. It's just one of those things in life that will always be a mystery, because left to his own devices, Jerry didn't have that kind of presence of mind. But leave home he did, finally, and New Orleans is where he ended up. I do know he got here by hitchhiking. I guess God was looking out for him, and put the right people in his life at that time to help him make the adjustment. Jerry was happy living in the streets, and being independent. That was very important to him. It was like he was trying to prove to himself that he could do it, and that he wasn't the kind of person his parents said he was. He could make it on his own.

But in the end the streets proved to be Jerry's demise. He often told me he'd rather be dead than go back home again. The life he had now, he used to say, was better than anything he'd ever had before, regardless of how harsh it was at times. About nine months after I'd gotten to know Jerry, they found him dead under the Mississippi River bridge on a cold rainy morning, beaten to death and robbed. We would have never found out about it, except the police found an address in his pocket with Sue's name on it. She had to go down and identify the body, which was very painful for her. She had been close to Jerry, and it hit her, as it did the rest of us who knew him, pretty hard. Jerry never asked for the kind of life he led, he was only looking for something better than what he'd had. He didn't deserve his fate, and maybe if things had been different, his parents more understanding and loving, he would still be alive today. But that's the harshness of the streets. It was a fact of life that many of us knew about and had accepted. No matter how distasteful it seemed for many of us, it was something we had learned to live with.

I spent a lot of my time while in New Orleans working. As I said, I'd spent all my savings before getting out to work for the first time. When I did finally get out, I went to work for a catering company out of Houma, Louisiana. They assigned me to what we called a work-over rig. It was owned by the Penrod Company, and I was the night cook. My usual tour of duty was two weeks out and one week in. Sometimes I did work more, staying out for a month at a time, though this was not very often.

I liked my time off, and drinking, and when my two weeks were up, barring any major development, I was ready to hit the bank. Sometimes my time off extended longer than one week, depending on when I ran out of money, and the need arose for me to return to work to pay my bills. I lived from paycheck to paycheck with no other idea in mind except to maintain my current lifestyle. I worked for the same rig and crew for so long, and became so well liked, that there were times when I didn't show up for crew change that the crew would come looking for me, usually only to find me so drunk they had to carry me to the boat to make the crew change. Sometimes it took me the first couple of days to sober up to where I really felt like cooking. But back then that's the way it was, the crew was like family, and when someone was absent, it didn't feel right. It was in my times off that I met all the people I talk about in this book, and I met many whose stories deserve to be told, the so-called throwaways of our society.

I had been back in New Orleans for almost a year when I accidentally ran into Ike again. I hadn't been looking for him. I was in the Circle View one night drinking during one of my times off when in he walked. He'd been in town himself for only a couple of months, but hadn't been around because when he came back from Florida he'd brought a woman with him, and rather than work offshore he opted to work out of the labor pools. You see, he didn't want to be away from his lady for weeks at a time. Ike was more of a homebody—or had became one—and enjoyed, or so it seemed, his newly acquired family life. He'd only been working at the labor pools for a month when one of the places where he had been working offered him a steady job, which he gladly accepted.

57

Ike never liked the streets. He wanted a normal life and a family and was working to that end. His lady friend's name was Ellen, and she helped him out by working at a local hotel as a maid. They had gotten an apartment soon after saving enough money to do so, and were on their way to what I would call normalcy. Ike was one of the few people I came to know that wanted off the streets and worked to achieve that end. So you see, it was not impossible to do, I just believe that first and foremost a person needed not only a strong desire to do so, but also a catalyst to give them that extra drive. This is the way I see Ellen. She was that catalyst for Ike. To this very day, as far as I know, they are still together, and the last I heard, had two children. My hat is off to him. There were many that never found the catalyst that was the secret ingredient that gave them the extra push they needed.

I often hung out and partied in the French Quarter when I first came in and had extra money. I never resorted to hanging around where I lived until I was so broke that I had no other choice. Thus I came to know Rosie, one of the local street people who were ever present in the French Quarter. She was considered a regular at many of the small bars in the area.

Rosie had a unique story, in that all her life she had been a housewife, married to a wonderful man who took good care of her until his death, and children who tried to do the very best they could by her, under the circumstances. Rosie's story began after her husband's death, and the misfortunes she had experienced afterwards. Rosie was from Dayton, Ohio, where she had lived all her life and raised her family. Her husband worked for a local service company all his life as a bookkeeper, and was a well-educated man. Together, they raised three children and lived a normal family life, not one you'd expect to end up with Rosie as a local bag lady, which was completely out of sync with her character and upbringing.

Rosie had had a beautiful home, bought and paid for by her husband long before he died.

Her children were all grown, and had wonderful families of their own, who Rosie talked about often and proudly. Her problems arose through events that were beyond her control, and left her no other final recourse but the streets, or so she felt. Rosie's husband died of a massive heart attack eight years after his retirement. Even though Rosie was devastated by his death, she managed to move on with her life. She still had her home and her loving children. One of Rosie's main problems was that she never wanted to be a burden on her children; to her this was totally unacceptable regardless of how they felt. She was an independent woman and had a lot of pride. This was one of the resolutions that led to her ultimate decision to live the way she came to live. A chain events beyond her control was about to take place in her life that would lead her to make the ultimate sacrifice, to give up her home and family rather than being a burden on anyone.

It all started five years after her husband's death, when her own health started going bad. She had a series of setbacks. She developed breast cancer, and had one of her breasts removed. The doctors thought they had gotten all the cancer and at first this seemed to be the case. But two years later, it flared up again, and they found cancer in her uterus. Through a series of tests, they determined the cancer had spread to other parts of her body and her prognosis was not good. She never really said how long the doctors gave her, only that she should start making plans. For the next couple of years, Rosie was in and out of the hospital many times. It quickly ate up the money she and her husband had managed to save over the years, and before it was over would also take away her home. Rosie's last hospital stay left her almost helpless to fend for herself, to the point that she needed constant care.

Her children were unable to give her the type of care that she required at home, and she had already lost her own home and was living in subsidized housing. She lost that when she had to enter a permanent care facility to tend to her needs. Although her kids didn't particularly care for the arrangements, they, too, really had no choice in the matter. Their mother could no longer take care of herself. A social worker had found a place for her to stay that could meet her needs, but it was anything but ideal surroundings. It was a large convalescent home that catered to individuals that were semi-ambulatory, and some could get around pretty good on their own.

During Rosie's stay at this place she fought to make herself independent again. Her only thought was to get well enough to leave and take care of herself, and that is exactly what she done. After seven months, she was doing better, but during this time she was also badly abused by some of the staff. She told me that one attendant often got mad at her and not only cursed her, but at one time had even struck her with a hairbrush. She said there were times when she needed attention and no one would come. Time and time again they failed to give her the physical therapy she needed to get better. She endured this treatment for quite some time, and never complained to anyone about it because she didn't want to worry her children, but I believe it was also out of fear of reprisals. The people she had to go through to complain were the same ones who were neglecting her. The home also ate up all the income from her husband's retirement, not leaving her much, if anything, for her own personal needs. The time came when she had a choice of leaving and going to live with one of her daughters, but to Rosie this was unacceptable. She would rather live under the conditions she endured than be a burden on her children.

It was just not in Rosie to subject her children to that under any circumstances. So finally when Rosie was well enough to move about on her own she left like a thief in the night. She packed what little things she had, and took what few dollars she'd managed to hide from the others, bought her a ticket out of town, and came to New Orleans. Rosie was a survivor. She quickly found her niche in the streets, never asking for help from no one, not even the local programs that could provide her with the bare necessaries like food stamps. She preferred to make it on her own. She soon learned the places where she could get a free meal, how to pick up a few dollars collecting cans, and how to go through dumpsters and find little trinkets she could trade on the streets to get by.

Rosie was a frail-looking woman, but it was a mistake to misjudge her. She was more than capable of taking care of herself. She was almost born, it seemed, with the knowledge that was required to make it in the streets. She always wore several layers of clothing, even during the summer. Sometimes I don't know how she could bear the heat, but when it was cold she surely had no problem. She always pushed a grocery cart around, and always had a couple of animal strays she'd pick up along the way to keep her company and to take care of. Early every morning, even before daylight, you could find her somewhere in the French Quarter, going through the trash from the night before, taking what she wanted. I never knew

Rosie to drink, and although she frequented the local bars, it was only to collect cans or just for some company.

No one knew where Rosie spent her nights. My guess is that she had found someplace inconspicuous, where no one would bother her, but she was always around during the day. You could often find her resting on a bench somewhere around Jackson Square in the French Quarter during the day when she didn't have other things she felt she needed to do. She was well liked around the Quarter, and well known. For her circumstances, I never knew anyone to be better adjusted to their surroundings. She was even happy with what she was doing. She was independent and not a burden to anyone, and that's just the way Rosie liked it. Rosie loved her children, and from time to time would get hold of them to let them know she was OK. Just why, or even if, her children never made an attempt to take her away from all this is unknown to me. Maybe they understood better than anyone the way she felt, and just accepted it. As far as I knew, they left her alone.

Call it apathy or whatever, all I know is that Rosie, during the time I knew her, was a happy and well-adjusted woman, and she lived well beyond the time the doctors had given her years earlier. This I'm sure was due to her attitude. As far as I know she is still there in the Quarter somewhere today. Or come to think of it probably not: that would make her a medical miracle today, more so than she already was; she would be well into her eighties by now. But I like to think she is still there, making the world a better place because she's in it. She was a real sweetheart and I'm a better person for having known her.

I met many such people in the Quarter. It teemed with street people at any time of day. They ranged from street performers to vendors, and their stories are as elaborate as any I know. Some of them lived literally in the streets, others managed to keep some kind of roof over their heads. Many were without substance; they had neither purpose nor direction, except to make it through the day. Most of the street performers I knew were transient, in that they traveled the seasons and events. Some were permanent fixtures, and never left New Orleans, some never even left the French Quarter. That was their world, and beyond that no other world existed.

One such individual was Clappy. Now Clappy was a shoeshine man; he shined shoes for tourists in the Quarter. He got his name from his unusual music ability with a shoeshine rag; that's right, I said a shoeshine rag. He could literally make the rag sing when he shined shoes, or so it seemed. He was very popular among the tourists. He was not only a service vendor, he was also an entertainer. You could find Clappy in the same spot in the Quarter every day. Nobody messed with his spot. If somebody was in his place when he came, they quickly relinquished it to him. Everyone knew that was his spot. He was a regular icon in the Quarter.

Clappy was in his early fifties back in the mid- to late-seventies. He was a frail-looking black gentleman, five feet-two with salt-and-pepper hair and gray eyes. He wore glasses and without them was as blind as a bat. He always wore blue jeans and a brightly colored shirt. You'd swear he just came off a cruise. When he worked, he wore a long red apron over his normal attire, and his shoebox was his constant companion. Even it was elaborately decorated—it looked like a carnival poster.

Clappy grew up in New Orleans in one of the many projects in and around the city. His dad worked all his life in the service industry in the Quarter. Thus, as Clappy was growing up, he spent much of his time there. His mother worked baby-sitting, doing laundry, and whatever else she could do at home so she could take care of the family. He had one brother and one sister, both of whom were still alive, but for some reason or another had no contact with Clappy. Sometimes Clappy would take a room somewhere, just for sleeping, and other times he lived wherever he could find a place to crash, depending on how much he had earned that week, the time of year it was, and what was going on in the Quarter. Obviously, during Mardi Gras and the Jazz Fest he made more money than he would at normal times. These and many other events that took place in the French Quarter drew tourists, as well as your transient street performers.

Clappy liked to drink wine, although he never let it interfere with his making a buck. I would often buy a bottle, go to Jackson Square in front of the Cathedral, sit on the bench behind Clappy's spot, and share a drink or two with him while listening to marvelous stories of his years in the Quarter and the many people he had met. He had shined the shoes of many a celebrity who happened to pass his way, and was a walking history of the Quarter. He had a marvelous memory, and could not only tell you about specific events, but could also tell you what kind of day it was twenty years before. He was one of the more colorful characters among the many I met in the French Quarter.

I went through many a Mardi Gras celebration over the years, and they were all the same in my view. If you'd seen one, you'd seen them all. It didn't change from one year to the next; it was pure pandemonium, unadulterated confusion and hullabaloo. It was my second visit to New Orleans though, before I actually saw the parades and other events that took place during Mardi Gras. My first year was spent sitting on a bar stool in a bar on St. Charles Ave., looking out the door at it. I never drew a sober breath that first year.

One of my other hangouts when in from offshore was the Irish Channel. This area was in what they called Uptown, or the Garden District. It was one of the oldest sections of town, and at one time in New Orleans history, the place to be from. That's where all the money lived back in the twenties and thirties. There were many stately mansions in this part of town, although over the years many had been let go and were pretty decrepit. But there were still sections where the old homes were kept up well over the years. For now though, the area I frequented was on Magazine St., commonly referred to as skid row and pretty rundown. One of my other hangouts was Mom's Place, a bar among the many antique shops and thrift stores that monopolized that area. Most of the patrons of Mom's Place were offshore workers, transients, and blue-collar workers, a few of them longshoremen who worked on the docks.

One of the people I came to know in this area was a wonderful old lady who I always called Grandma. She was in her late seventies, a retired schoolteacher who sometimes had a place to live and sometimes didn't. Her manner of dress was such that you could see her coming from blocks away. She always wore the most colorful clothes she could find, and wore more makeup than the law should allow. Sometimes she lived in our world, and sometimes she'd live in a world of her own, completely oblivious to what was going on around her, and not caring. Her memory wasn't what it used to be, and she oftentimes forgot where she was or why she was there. Mentally she was in and out. She took medication to keep her stable, but there were times when you knew she hadn't taken it for a while. But a more loving and kinder lady, you'd never likely meet; she was a veritable sweetheart and wouldn't hurt a fly. She was a heavy drinker, which didn't help, especially when she was on her medication, which the alcohol enhanced the effect of. But everyone knew her and even when she was intolerable, which she often was, we watched out for her and made sure nothing happened to her.

She bought many a drink for many a street person, often sitting in the park across from Mom's Place, sharing a bottle with one of the many winos who frequented the park. But even they didn't take advantage of her. She was one of those people who demanded respect, no matter what her condition. She was also one of those people who made you a better person for just having known her. She treated people the way she wanted to be treated, and never judged anyone. She was a friend and confident to all who knew her. She was also one of those many street people who died the way they lived, in the streets. Her death was attributed to old age; at least, she didn't meet a violent death, like so many others before her. She was greatly missed by me and many others after her passing. I often think of her today. She will always be one of a kind in my book.

When you frequent the types of places I did, you run across all kinds of people, from the die-hards who live on the streets and off the land, to those who struggle every day to scratch out a living as best they can, and to those who never seem to have a problem in the world and everything seems to be going right for. Then there are also those few who seem normal in every sense, that have it all together and are living their dream. But every once in a while you meet someone who seems out of place, who don't seem to belong, and you wonder, where did this person come from, why are they here?

Shannon was one of the latter type. I met her in the Irish Channel at a bar I used to frequent called the Green Door. Of all the skid row bars in the area, this was one of the worst as far as clientele and location are concerned. It was on the corner of Magazine and Jackson streets, and was a regular hangout for the local winos. One of the reasons I use to go there was because I was infatuated with one of the barmaids.

Shannon was a petite, delicate-looking woman in her early thirties. She had blonde hair and blue eyes, and dressed like at one time she must have been a woman of means. Where she stayed or what she did to survive, no one knew. She always had money, but never carried a lot at one time. She came and went so quietly you hardly knew she was there. She was very quiet and reserved, and except for a chosen few of us, never spoke to anyone. She didn't talk about her past but in it you knew, just by looking in her eyes, lay a lot of pain. She was definitely running from something, and I don't mean the law. She was vague about where she was from, but from her accent, I'd say the upper East Coast—maybe the Connecticut, Massachusetts, or Rhode Island area—she had that type of accent. It was obvious to me that she came from money; that is to say, she was well bred, and well educated. She drank incessantly, but in my opinion was not an alcoholic. She was drinking to forget. She often sat in a corner of the bar and drank alone, never saying a word to anyone. Often she would sit there and cry uncontrollably for hours at a time. Mostly they left her alone when she was like that, because she made it obvious to everyone she didn't want to be approached when she was in that state.

No one ever knew her circumstances, and then one rainy fall day she walked out of the bar right in front of an oncoming bus. She was killed instantly. Some say she didn't see the bus coming, that she was too drunk, but I know different. I had been talking to her just an hour earlier, and she was as sober as a judge. She had too much sense to just walk into traffic without looking. She had been very despondent that day, something was bothering her more than usual. But she hadn't been crying. By this time I believe she had cried herself out. She just seemed to be cogitating on an event that had already taken place or was about to. I pride myself in being able to perceive certain aspects of a person's being just by sensing it. Many times my feelings have been right, and this was no exception.

Through a police investigation, they found out her name and located her family who had, months earlier, filled out a missing person's report on her. As it turned out she was from Providence, Rhode Island. Her family came from a wealthy background. She was married, but had no children. As it was discovered, her husband loved her very much and didn't mistreat her one bit. He was the one who came down to claim the body. Through the police he found out where she had hung out. I remember the day he walked into the Green Door he looked totally out of it, completely exhausted, like he'd been up for days. He came down to the bar, partly to make some sense out of what happened and to see where she had spent her last days.

Her husband's name was Glen. He was, like her, a well-educated and well-dressed gentleman. He was very soft-spoken, and showed a deep concern about his wife's last days. It was from him that I learned the source of Shannon's pain. In the past four years, she had had three miscarriages. She and her husband had been trying to have a baby for over six years with no luck. Shannon and her husband both loved children very much, and wanted a family more than anything. After the last miscarriage, Shannon's doctor informed her that she would never be able to bear children of her own, that their only recourse was adoption. Shannon's husband had resigned himself to this fact, and was already looking into methods of adoption. But for Shannon, it was too much, she snapped; she couldn't accept the fact that she would never have any children of her own, blaming herself that she couldn't give her husband a child. One morning he woke up to an empty bed and Shannon was gone. With no word to anyone, she just disappeared.

I also found out in my conversations with her husband that the day she died was one year to the day after her last miscarriage. Coincidence? I think not. Shannon was another innocent victim. She didn't ask to be barren, nor did she ask to be where she was. She couldn't bear the thought of never having her own family and being able to give one to her husband. She blamed herself for everything.

Truly she was one of the Walking Wounded. One of many I met along the way, and one of many who spurred me to write this book. The stories go on and on, endlessly, and even though I'm not a part of that life today, I often think about those people because they are still out there, looking for answers to questions that should never need to be asked.

Along with many tragedies, every once in a while you'd run across someone who beat the odds, someone who persevered, fought the fight, and dug themselves out of the muck to triumph in the end. Andy was one of them. Andy had come to New Orleans, like many before him, looking for work. He was from a small town in southeastern Michigan, and had just the year before been laid-off from one of the main automobile assembly plants. He drove fifty miles each way to and from work every day, and worked at the plant for over eight years when he was laid off. He had a wonderful wife and two children, and had, just before losing his job, purchased a home for his family. He had financed the home through the bank, and with his job had no trouble making the payments. Andy had had a good life, one that I'd often thought about for myself—a family and a home to go to, a loving wife and children. Nothing fancy, just being able to get by and pay the bills, with a little left over in the end. I figured that would have been better than what I had. Many of us thought about that kind of life, but we were so entangled in our present lifestyle, and so doomed to repetition, we couldn't see the forest for the trees.

Anyways, Andy had a goal when he arrived in New Orleans, and he never lost sight of it. He had stayed up in Michigan, looking for work until his unemployment checks ran out. But with no work available at that time, he quickly became desperate. The bank was threatening to foreclose on his home, his money was running out, and he had no place to turn. He read in the local paper about all the jobs available in Louisiana and finally out of desperation he felt it his only recourse to see for himself. He left Michigan without a dime in his pocket, leaving what little his family had left with them on the premise that he'd go to Louisiana, find work, save some money, and then when he was settled, send for his family. He hitchhiked out of Michigan, hanging out at the truck stops along the way, catching rides from the truckers.

It only took him two days to get to New Orleans. Without a dime in his pocket and no place to stay, he opted for one of the many missions in the area that put souls up for the night. After the first night, that was enough for him. He didn't like the crowds and the way the missions were set up, and figured he'd find another form of shelter. That next day he got a job at one of the many labor pools in town cleaning river barges, a nasty and dirty job. But Andy didn't mind; he was working, and that's all that mattered. The first few nights were really rough on him though, making only minimum wage—a little over three dollars an hour back then. If he rented a motel room and got something to eat, he'd have nothing left to send home. So he chose to live in the streets and save every dime he made to send to his family back up in Michigan, always putting back just a couple of dollars towards getting him and his family a place to stay so they could come join him.

Andy worked seven days a week when he could, and often came in from one job just to go back out immediately on another. It seemed he was constantly working. Andy's only vice was that he enjoyed smoking, but he even gave that up because it took too much away from what he had to send to his family. I had never, up to this time, seen a person so focused on one goal and one goal only. Andy lived mostly in old abandoned buildings, of which there were many around the area at that time. A few times he had to leave abruptly when someone reported a suspicious person in the area. For a while he lived under the Crescent City Connection (Mississippi River Bridge, leading over to the west bank), but quickly decided this was too dangerous. There was too much traffic and too many people wandering around that area looking for trouble. Andy only ate once a day if he ate at all, at one of the local missions.

When Andy arrived in New Orleans, he was a strapping young man of only thirty years. He lost a lot of weight during that first year, but he never once lost sight of his goal. Living like he was, it was difficult to find a steady job because he had no address, and working so much just to survive he never had time to look for anything else. That's the way it was when you were in that situation; it was difficult to just get by for the day let alone save for a better one. But that's just what Andy did. It took a lot of sacrifice on his part, and he endured many a sleepless night to achieve his goal, but never once did his focus leave his family. They were what was important, nothing else. About six months after Andy left home, the bank foreclosed on his house and his wife and children had to move in with her folks. This was almost unbearable for Andy.

He was proud, and in the end it almost killed him. Then after nine months of living that life and almost working himself to death, already in poor health, his luck broke. He was offered a steady job by one of the companies he worked for out of the labor pools. It was a simple warehouse job, but it paid more than minimum wage. This meant he could reach his goal much faster.

Still Andy would get off his regular job, then go to the labor pool to try to get more work for the evening hours. The first two weeks were the hardest, because he had to wait before receiving a full paycheck. But he made it, and in only two months had enough money saved to look for his own place. He finally found a place not too far from where he worked. It wasn't much, but it was a two-bedroom apartment big enough for his family, until they could find something better.

It was a little over a year from the time that Andy had left his family until he finally sent for them and they could be together again. I never knew anyone who had such dedication. Andy had, and this told me that a person could beat the streets if he tried hard enough, and was willing to give up the basic necessities.

Not all the street people you see are the hopeless type. Many are there through no fault of their own, that through circumstances beyond their control, found themselves homeless through a quirk of fate. Put there out of necessity, and having nowhere else to turn, Andy was one such individual. You'll begin to see that all homeless people are not winos, drunks, thieves, or drug addicts. Many are just like you. They could have been your next-door neighbor at one time, but were one paycheck away from losing everything they had and becoming homeless. Most do not want to be in the street—although some small number do. Many want a better life for themselves and their families, but circumstances led them down this path, and it was all they could do to survive.

Even those of us who chose to be where we were would not have passed up the opportunity for something better, if that's what we'd made our minds up to do. But first, you need the desire. For some of us that desire didn't come until it was too late, for others of us it came much later in life—after we had been beaten down time and time again and had finally became sick and tired of living the way we were—before waking up and trying to do better. But even then, when you reached that stage, the road was rough and usually required a catalyst to give you that extra incentive. It wouldn't be fair to you as a reader or consistent with the honesty of this book if I didn't tell the stories of the alcoholics, drug addicts, and others who do make up a part of the homeless population, though even some of these stories don't ring true to the stereotypes that most have of the homeless.

One such story is that of a man that I met soon after arriving in New Orleans. He was, for all intents and purposes, your typical alcoholic, but he had reached the stage in his drinking where he was becoming tired of it all and really wanted some help. Now most alcoholics know that Alcoholic's Anonymous is a program that can and does help millions of men and women. But even they will tell you that for some, AA is not enough. For many you have to treat the whole person, and for most you first have to get them into an environment that is conducive to recovery. For the homeless person, this can be difficult, if not impossible.

If you are homeless, there are not enough programs around that are willing or even able to help someone who has no means of support or the monetary resources needed to keep their programs running and helping people who can't help themselves. The few around are filled to capacity, with long waiting lists to get in. For the street alcoholic, time is not a luxury they can afford to waste; they must provide for their everyday needs, and this leaves little time for seeking and obtaining help. Each day in the streets for an alcoholic can be the last, especially when they've become despondent and truly want help but can't find it, when there is no room at the inn. Rodney was one such person.

Rodney was in his late forties, of average build with gray hair and brown eyes. His clothes were often tattered, dirty, and worn, and he spent all his waking hours drinking. Even when he worked, you could find a bottle close by. When he wasn't working, he was scheming to get his next drink. He could think of nothing else. Even when he decided to seek help, it was impossible for him to stop. As long as he was in the streets he needed that something to take the edge off. He had reached the point where he had to drink just to feel normal. He could not function without a drink. He drank even though he didn't want to drink anymore, a condition that only another alcoholic who had reached or gone through that stage already would understand.

It is a dilemma that all alcoholics reach if they drink hard and long enough. Rodney freely shared the story of his life with me, which wasn't unlike that of many others. He began drinking at a young age, around seventeen. For many years, he functioned well. He got married, had a family, a home, and a steady job. For years he was able to keep it all together, but as his drinking progressed, so his situation deteriorated. Bit by bit, without going into elaborate details, he lost it all—family, friends, home and children. Still in denial, he was yet unwilling to admit that his drinking was a problem. He blamed his problems on others: they just didn't understand, they were all out to get him. Sound familiar to anyone? If you are a practicing alcoholic, or even recovering, I'm sure you'll recognize the symptoms. Soon even his job was gone, and still unwilling to admit he had a problem, he had nowhere else to turn so he turned to what many of us turned to, the streets. There no one criticized you for the way you lived, and many were just like you, so they didn't care. In the streets were the answers to all your problems. People would leave you alone, so long as you didn't step on their toes and minded your own business.

Rodney had worked as a mechanic, and was a good one. Before his drinking got really bad, he often thought that one day he would have his own business. He was self-taught, but high school educated. He was far from dumb. His trade even afforded him extra money from time to time while in the streets, if he could stay sober long enough to work on and fix somebody's car, not an easy task but he occasionally did muster the courage to do it out of necessity. Otherwise, he was broke and needed money for his next drink. Rodney was one of those literal street people, meaning that even when he did have money, he opted to stay in a weed patch or under the bridge rather than spend any of his money for a room. After all that would mean he'd have less for alcohol, and at this stage in his life, alcohol was the most important thing—even more important than eating or having a roof over his head. Rodney would drink until he passed out, and when he woke up would start all over again.

You can see how one would tire of this, but for many it took years to get there. Usually, we had to hit bottom several times over to reach this stage. It is, by all standards, a slow and painful disease. It has to beat you down many times to get your attention.

The first few months I knew Rodney, he never talked about getting or even wanting help, but gradually I saw him change. He began talking about doing something to get out of his predicament. He wasn't sure then just what he would do, but he had reached a point that he knew he wanted to do something. He just knew if he could get help and straighten his life out, that he could get everything back that he had lost, including his family.

Now as any recovering alcoholic will tell you, these are all the wrong reasons. You have to want to do it for yourself, no one else. But a person has to start somewhere, and for many that's the way it was: we were going to do it for someone else, to get our old life back. I have to give Rodney credit though, he really tried. But time after time, he was told he had to wait. There was a waiting list to get into the free programs, and there were only a couple of them in the whole city. Then there was the time factor. Often when the openings did come up, if you were unable to check every hour on the hour, they went quickly, and if they couldn't get hold of you, you lost out. After all, our cell phones didn't work most of the time and the mailman seldom came to our house! Many times Rodney broke down and cried. He didn't know what else he could do. He wanted help so badly and really wanted to change, but it seemed to him and even to those of us who looked on, that the deck was stacked against him.

As time went by I saw him become more and more despondent. I could see that he was coming to a point where he felt, what's the use, no one really cares, so why should he? Then one day as we walked along the First Street Pier, down by the Jackson Street Ferry crossing, sharing a bottle and talking about what could have been, he just turned with no warning and jumped into the Mississippi River. Now anyone who knows the Mississippi knows what the current is like, not to speak of the numerous undertows. Anyone with any sense knew that jumping into the river meant certain death. Few have ever survived such an action, and it was impossible to overcome if that's what you wanted. And that's the point Rodney had reached. He got tired of being sick and tired, and not being able to get the help he needed, when he wanted and needed it. He gave up.

I have seen this story in the streets over and over again. Some were not as dramatic as Rodney's solution, some just drank themselves to a slow death. I seen a lot of death in the streets, and a lot of it could have been prevented if things had been different. If more people had reached out to those who seemed unreachable, or had taken the time to look at the homeless alcoholic as a person, just like us all, with a mother, a father, a wife and family just like they have—we are all part of God's kingdom. It's just that most people's lives are not completely turned upside-down.

I include Rodney among the Walking Wounded, another lost soul, an entity that passed unseen, and in the end paid the ultimate price. His family would see him no more, or know how he felt that last minute before he jumped. When Rodney died, so did his hopes and dreams of ever obtaining something better, of getting his life back, of getting to know his family again, or ever knowing happiness again. Another nameless face to so many who might have been affected by his gentleness and the quality of his character.

My days in New Orleans this time around were coming to a close. My drinking was getting worse and worse. When I came in from offshore, it was taking me a couple of days just to get out of the bars, and sometimes much longer. I was quickly tiring of the repetition of it all. Even as big a drunk as I was then, I still figured there should come a time in every man's drinking days when he should be asked to leave.

In New Orleans, where the bars are open around the clock, this is not so, especially if they knew you well. They'd just prop you up in a corner booth somewhere, and let you sleep it off for a while. When you woke up, you could start all over again. Besides, I was getting restless. I had been in one place too long, especially for me. There was a lot more I wanted to do and see. The whole world was at my doorstep, and I was wasting too much time in one place. But somehow I always knew in the back of my mind that I would be back someday. New Orleans was that kind of town, it got in your blood, and would call to you from time to time when you were away.

I wasn't sure where I wanted to go, except I knew I had to head west, and west is exactly where I headed. I didn't go far. I ended up in Houston, Texas, where my life would change drastically from what it had been in New Orleans. Although I worked most every day, I turned to living in abandoned buildings, weed patches, under bridges, anywhere I could find to lay my head without going into my pocket and my liquor money. Thus begins the next chapter of my life, and a new batch of acquaintances. Come with me now, as I enter my "Itinerant Years," when my wandering knew no bounds.

Seeking to Find

As I wandered the highways and byways
Of this country, seeking to find
A purpose for my dismal existence
In the endless multitude of mankind

I envisioned the pain and the suffering
Of the lowly and déclassé of this day
I walked in their shoes to master
The feelings that lie in the way

In the way of doing much better
In a life filled with so much pain
Pain that comes with the lost and lonely
In a world that is so inhumane

So you wander the neon jungles
Seeking to find what you lost
Or what you never had in the first place
Never once to consider the cost

The cost of your own emotions
And the havoc they wreak on your soul
It's hard to keep track of your purpose
When you've already lost sight of your goal

So you continue to seek out the answers
That often lie right within your sight
Happiness comes from doing for others
Even when others are not doing what's right

You learn this is GOD's great wisdom
Do unto others as you'd have done to you
It's a lesson that's learned by repeating
As you seek in this world what is true

— May 13, 1997

~ CHAPTER 3 ~

The Itinerant Years OR *Seeking to Find*

I left New Orleans on a bright Friday afternoon in the fall of 1978. Sitting on a Greyhound bus, I began to reflect on the last seven years—where I'd been, what I'd done, and the people I'd met. I couldn't help but wonder what the future had in store for me. I was excited to be on the move again; it always gave me a sense of adventure when I was on the move. I savored the uncertainty of it all. The expectation of another place filled my soul with excitement. It was the quintessence of my nature, the way I was. Not knowing what lay ahead and the expectation of a new beginning was what this person thrived on. My existence depended on change, and in the next eleven years I would change often, not just personality-wise, but geographically too. My travels would take me from one end of the country to the other, north to south, east to west, and back again many times.

I would go through many changes myself. It is during these years where my sense of time does not always ring true to me. I lost a lot of memory. When it comes to time over the years, chronologically, I find it difficult to recall exactly, so please forgive me if you lose track. I did, long ago. But the people I met and the places I went are true to the best of my knowledge and recollection, so bear with me. I'll take you on a journey like none you've ever been on before, and through my travels, you'll begin to see the enchantment of it all, and even if you don't approve, at least maybe you'll understand why.

I arrived in Houston early Saturday morning. It was raining hard and very muggy outside. I had some money in my pocket, and as usual I spent it drinking at the local skid row bars in the area, getting the sense of what was happening where, and who was doing what. I had already learned over the years how to get the information I needed and to get it quickly. Although all places were basically the same, the attitudes and the physiology of a new place were always different, and it took a while to get these into perspective, and to arrive at a plan of action.

There was a bar right around the comer from the Greyhound station, just as there is in most places. I cannot recall the name of the bar, but it was typical of most bars that are close to bus stations and was frequented by the usual types—from gay to straight and those waiting to prey upon the unsuspecting. Not a place that even

I liked to hang around for very long. But from there I learned where the cheap hotels close to town and the labor pools were, knowing full well this is where I'd find the bars and hang-outs of the street people. This place turned out to be Congress Ave., in Houston, and it was only a few blocks from the bus station, another fact that didn't seem to change from town to town. Skid row never seemed to be far away, with few exceptions within walking distance.

The first place I entered was the Congress Bar and Hotel, the bar was downstairs and upstairs was the Hotel. You had to walk by the front desk, just a little cubbyhole in the wall to your left, with a desk clerk, if you can call him that, in attendance. As you walked through what they called the lobby, a short distance from the front door to the entrance into the bar, I could quickly see that I'd be spending a lot of time here in the months to come. The Congress Bar was one enormous room, with a bar that run the full length of the room on the left. The bathrooms were all the way to the back on your right.

Throughout the room were tables of the round, three-legged type, and around each table were four chairs. The floors were bare cement that had been painted to give the appearance of a floor that was not cement. Go figure. There was one barmaid behind the bar, and she was an older lady who turned out to be the owner of the bar and hotel. She had another girl working the floor.

One look around the room and the people in it and I knew I was in the right place. The people were of a wide variety—black, white, Mexican, and even a few Indians. There were as usual more men than women, although this wasn't always the case. There was a small area at the end of the room with a pool table, and a place set aside for dancing, with a jukebox in the middle. The jukebox was mostly country, but had a nice mix of oldies in with the country, with just a little touch of soul. Something for everyone.

I walked to the far end of the bar and ordered a beer, not really my choice of drink back then, but it was a beer bar—they sold no liquor. It didn't take me long to learn about the brown bag law in Houston, though. It was a law that allowed you to buy your own bottle of liquor, bring it into the bar and buy set-ups, something to go with the liquor, which usually cost as much as if you'd bought a beer. I don't have to tell you how I drank from then on—I'd bring in my own bottle and buy beer to chase it with. I wasn't going to waste my money on anything but alcohol. After my first beer, I bought a couple rounds for the house to warm them up a bit, if you know what I mean. I soon had many fair-weather friends, but that was all right. I needed information and this was one of the quickest ways to get it without any hassle.

I stayed in the bar all that first day until closing at two o'clock the next morning. I must have spent over a hundred dollars that first day. Back then my drinking capacity was unequaled. I could drink with the best of them and, it seemed, endlessly. I had no desire to waste any money on a room, so when I left the bar that night, I quickly used my experience to find a quiet out-of-the way place where I wouldn't be noticed, laid out my bedroll and went to sleep. By then it had quit raining, so I didn't have to worry about that. The little place I found was on Buffalo Bayou, not too far from the bar and right in town. As it turned out, it was close to where I would set up a permanent camp later. I had found a home for a while, and I was going to make the best of it.

As I said, Buffalo Bayou ran right through the middle of town, running mostly east to west. It was narrow in parts, only stretching three feet across in some places. It ran under many bridges throughout town, and through a couple of parks set up by the city for recreation for its many residents, yuppies for the most part. It had running trails and the lot that you'd find in most parks, and from time to time hosted city celebrations and festivals. Along the banks of the bayou there were secluded spots with thick underbrush, and in some places groves of trees. A lot of the street people lived along this narrow strip of ground that wove through town. It was convenient as well as private if you found the right spot.

I awoke the next morning feeling pretty good inspite of the wear and tear of the day before. It was Sunday and I learned another important lesson about Houston: If you wanted a drink on Sunday morning to take the edge off the night before, you'd better get it the night before, because unless you knew of a bootlegger (one who sells liquor and beer after hours), there was no getting a drink until after noon, and then it was only beer on Sunday. As I said, I wasn't too bad for the wear, so I figured I could get by until noon to get another drink. But after rolling up my bedroll and stashing it where it couldn't be found, I used that time to get a bite to eat and find out where the nearest bootlegger was. I surely did not want to drink beer all day Sunday, because as I said, that wasn't my drink of choice except for chasers.

There was another hotel a block behind Congress Avenue that had a restaurant under it that looked like a regular hangout for some of the locals I'd met the night before. I don't recall the name of the place, but right next door to the restaurant was a paper-hanging outlet: a place where you could pick up a few dollars a day distributing handouts—advertisements for local businesses—if you didn't mind the walking. This was a favorite source of income for the local winos, who couldn't get jobs anywhere else because of their appearance. Later the restaurant became a meeting spot for those of us who were lucky enough to know and work for a gentleman who owned various kiddy rides and rented them out to anything from private parties to church festivals.

The weekends were especially difficult to find work out of the labor pools, unless you had a steady ticket that worked on the weekends. And living the way I was, working and getting paid by the day, you almost had to work seven days a week to have enough to last you through the weekend. Otherwise by Saturday morning or at best early Saturday evening, you were broke. And when you're broke and it's a weekend, the days can be very long. To have a job where you could earn a few extra dollars on Saturday and Sunday meant you could drink all weekend. For those of us lucky enough, that made us an elite group; most of the street people were broke until they went back to work on Monday.

I met this man who owned the rides a couple of weeks after arriving in town through a person whom I met at one of the labor pools that I worked at. It was shortly after I'd established my own little camp on Buffalo Bayou, near the bridge that went over Main Street, by the local community college. The man who introduced me to the man with the rides was one of—if not the most—colorful characters I had met in my travels. His name was Calvin, but everybody called him Happy, a name befitting him well, because he was not only a comical-looking man, but he could make you laugh even when you didn't feel like it. I liked people like that because there were many times that I needed a good laugh, and enjoyed being around someone who seemed so positive most of the time. Happy was in his mid-fifties with salt-and-pepper hair and green eyes. He stood about five-feet nine, and wore the most outlandish clothes you'd ever seen. Only God knew where he came up with some of the combinations of clothes he wore, but that was Happy.

In years past Happy had been a circus clown—how befitting for a person like him. He had worked for one of the biggest circuses in the country for over fifteen years. From what I learned from our many conversations, he lost his job at the circus due to downsizing, if you want to call it that. The circus had to save some money so they laid off several of what they called "nonessential" personnel. Happy had until that time known no other way of life—he'd always been with the circus. His was the typical tale of a kid who run away from home specifically to join the circus. He bounced around for a long time from circus to circus, working as a clown when he could and even cleaning the animal cages, but was never satisfied. All his friends, and what he referred to as family, were still with the other circus and he missed them terribly. He had not only lost a job, he had lost his family, so to speak.

He left the circus route after a while and run with the carnival crowd for a few years, hoping to find what he had lost, but he never did and was never satisfied with anything else afterwards. He soon became part of the street life and roamed from town to town, looking for his elusive dream. Drinking was never a part of his life before, but became a part to help hide the sadness that I knew was inside him. With Happy, I knew, the outside never matched the inside, if you know what I mean. He presented a persona to the world around him that hid his true feelings—an ability that many of us could exercise at will. It was a mechanism that helped us survive the rigors of the streets.

Soon after I had met him, Happy came to live with me at my camp on the Bayou. There was safety in numbers when you lived that kind of life, but you were always careful that the numbers never got very big. One person was what I had came to like being around me all the time. More just created more problems. Happy stayed at my camp for almost the whole five months I was in Houston. Just before I left, Happy had a stroke while working at one of the many jobs he had out of the labor pools. He never fully recovered and had to be put in a nursing facility where he could get constant care. I missed his individualism a lot. He was one of a kind, and made me feel good just being around him.

Another person I came to know during my stay in Houston was "The Judge." His name was Lawrence, and he didn't like to be called Larry. Lawrence was in his sixties, I would guess; he never told me his real age. He was very distinguished looking, but you would never guess that at one time he had been a Municipal Court Judge in the very town that he now chose to turn his back on and live in the streets. Until about seven years earlier, he had a family, a home, cars, boats, and prominent social status in the community. He came from a blue-collar, working-class family, and had put himself through law school, working full time and going to school nights. It took him a long time to achieve his dream, but after many years of perseverance he became a lawyer. He often said he was never really happy as a lawyer, because they couldn't make a difference in the world. He became a judge because he felt in his heart that he could make a difference and make the world a better place to live. He put in a lot of hours at the courthouse, trying to do just that.

A couple of years before he gave up his judgeship, his wife divorced him. Now Lawrence will be the first to tell you that it was his own fault. In the process of trying to make this world a better place to live, he neglected the thing that was truly most important to him, his family. He never forgave himself for overlooking that significant part of his life. This was coupled with the fact that he was becoming disillusioned about the justice system. Over and over again he saw the same people come before him. He'd put them in jail, and the system would turn them loose. He often told me that his courtroom was like a revolving door, it never stopped. It got to the point where one day he just said to hell with it, walked out the courtroom doors and never went back. He gave up everything he had and took to the streets. He was fully convinced that he had failed. I never knew the Judge to take a drink. How he lived with his pain, I don't know, other than to reject the system. Instead, he wandered the streets of Houston with a shopping cart, picking up cans and whatever to make a few dollars a day to survive on.

He lived on the Bayou, just down from where my camp was, under the Main Street bridge, alone. He never associated with anyone, but from time to time would stop at my camp to have a cup of coffee, and bullshit for a while. I don't know for sure, but he may still be there. After I left Houston, I never seen him again. Although I did go back from time to time, I never took the time to try to look him up.

I left Houston after only four months. I had made a few enemies due to fights I had with other street people, and was beginning to feel uncomfortable with the situation. I hadn't managed to save any money up to this point, so I resorted to an old pattern: I hopped a freight heading north, with Dallas in my sights. Needless to say, I missed my mark by a few hundred miles and ended up in El Paso, Texas. It was difficult to get good information at the yards as to where exactly the train was going, so many times you had to take a shot and accept potluck. Even though El Paso wasn't where I wanted to go, I made the best of it. After all, it was a new place and any place was always better than the place you just left.

El Paso was a strange town to get to know. It had a very large population of Mexicans; being a border town that was to be expected, I guess. The Spanish population for the most part kept to their own kind. They were, as I found out, very suspicious of gringos—whites—and they weren't the friendliest people. Mostly they didn't bother you, and kept to themselves, but you got the feeling that they felt this was their town and you were an intruder. In order to hold any type of job that meant anything, you had to know the Spanish language, because they were the bigger part of the labor force. Don't get me wrong, I'm not demeaning them. They were for the most part lovely people. They just didn't associate much with anyone outside their own race, and if you think about it, that's pretty much the way we all are. The point I'm trying to make here is that the city itself was hard to get to know, because of the difference in the two cultures.

El Paso was beautiful, like an oasis carved out of the desert. It had mountains to the west and flatlands to the east, making quite a contrast. It was mid-February, and the nights were cold, though the days were mostly warm. There were days that were more wintry, but it didn't stay that way for long. I've spent winters in better climates, but this was at least livable. El Paso was also one of the what I call "party towns." How could it be anything else, with Juarez just across the Rio Grande? You could get anything you wanted in El Paso, but if you didn't find it there, you could go across the river to Juarez and get it. El Paso was basically a tourist town; many people came just to visit Mexico.

The job market in El Paso wasn't good, at least at that time; what jobs there were, were taken. The few that weren't taken were very competitive to get. For the time I spent in El Paso, which wasn't long, I stayed just south of downtown in a place they called Ascorate Park. It was a large park, with lots of places to be out of sight. It contained a large lake of the same name that was used by the locals for recreation. The only thing was that you had to keep changing your campsite to avoid being detected. The border patrol was always on the lookout for illegals, which made living there a hassle. I managed to get a few days work a week out of the labor pools, which was just barely enough to survive on if you chose to eat out of the many missions that fed the homeless there. It was while working at the labor pool that I met Terry.

Terry was a man in his early thirties, very tall and very thin. There was a reason for this that I'd learn from him later. He was well dressed and well spoken, leading you to believe he was an educated man. He had blond hair and blue eyes, and very smooth features. He drank, but was not what I call an alcoholic, more of a social drinker. I never seen him drunk, although he said he did get that way on occasion. He didn't live in the park where I stayed, but rather lived in an abandoned school bus in a field just north of the park. He'd been staying there now, according to him, for over a year. He'd been in the streets for only a year and a half when I met him, and was still learning the ropes. He was a trustful soul.

This is not advisable for a street person, but Terry liked everyone and it showed. There were those who took advantage of him from time to time, but he knew that, and didn't seem to mind. It was as though he were on a mission, and his time to complete it was short. Little did I know at the time how right I was in this perception. Terry was from another town south of El Paso, called Van Horn. He was a graduate of the University of Texas, in Austin, and had a degree in teaching. He came from a middle-class background, and was a very family-oriented person—a trait you didn't find often in street people—but here too there was a reason. After graduating,

Terry obtained a teaching position in Amarillo, Texas. He worked there for five years before leaving that position and never taught again. The reason for this, I learned, was that Terry was dying.

After a long bout of illness and many trips to the doctors, and an endless trail of specialists, he was diagnosed with inoperable cancer; exactly what type of cancer, he never said, only that the doctors gave him two years to live. When I met Terry he had already passed the two-year limit, and you could see he wasn't well. He was thinner every day, and there were lots of times that he was so sick he couldn't even work, and stayed in the abandoned bus all day. He chose to self medicate, by which I mean he treated his symptoms with over-the-counter medications. You couldn't get him to go to a doctor. Terry's family had a history of cancer, his dad and his grandfather both having died of it. Terry never knew his grandfather, but while growing up heard the talk of the pain he endured before he died and the medical bills he left behind. His father died the same type of death, only with him Terry had watched him die. His dad lingered on and on and suffered terribly before his death, to hear Terry talk.

Terry was never married, but was engaged to another teacher he'd met while teaching in Amarillo. They'd made plans to marry before Terry found out about his illness. When Terry first got the news, he didn't know how to react. All he could think of was the way his father and grandfather had died. His father's many trips to the hospital for treatments, according to Terry, only delayed the inevitable, and cost his family their life savings and everything else they had worked for over the years. Terry knew he didn't want to put his family through the same pain and be a burden on them. He also knew that if he stuck around, he'd feel obligated to appease his family and get all the help he could, thus draining them financially once again. He could not bear that thought. In order to save them from all that, he had to go somewhere that they couldn't find him and die like a man, as he put it, with dignity, and not put off the inevitable. He decided on his own to die when his time came and not prolong it any more than necessary. He knew if he stayed around his family, he'd not only be compelled by them to get all the help he could, but also by the law. He knew when the time came they wouldn't allow him to die if there were any means of making him last for a while longer.

I don't know what happened to Terry. I was only in El Paso for six weeks, and he was alive when I left, though getting sicker each passing day. But that was Terry's choice—he made it unselfishly and with his family's welfare in mind. Terry was a courageous man. I'm not sure I could have made the same choice. I loved life too much and would have probably hung on until all means had been exhausted. Who really knows for sure, but that's the way I felt at the time.

The streets contained a lot of death. I seen it time and time again, people lost in their own struggles to make a way in this world as best they could. There are many out there just like Terry who want something better, not for themselves, but for their families. Those who choose to leave the security of their families so as not to be a burden on them are truly courageous souls who deserve our respect, even though we may not agree with their decisions. Terry chose the right to die with dignity and honor. My hat is off to these people; they taught me a lesson in life I may have never learned otherwise: There are more important things in life besides myself. God bless you Terry, wherever you are.

As I said, I only stayed in El Paso six weeks, and on a mild spring day, I headed for a truck stop just north of town and began my quest again for that ever-elusive dream, whatever it was and wherever it lay, down the next road, around the next bend, or over the next hill. I headed west. Just exactly where I was going, I had no idea. I just had to go.

It didn't take me long to hustle up my first ride, and I was on my way. The driver of the truck was going to Tucson, Arizona, but going along with his advice that there was little work there, I continued west after we arrived in Tucson. He dropped me off at another truck stop along Interstate 10, and he went his way and I went mine. Still not sure where I was headed, only west, I started asking questions. From my inquiries, I learned that Phoenix was a good working town, so that's where I headed. If you want to know anything about the economy of a certain place, just ask a truck driver—believe me, they know better than anybody.

So now I knew my destination, and all I had to do was get there. I spent the whole day and night in that truck stop outside of Tucson before acquiring another ride. But this ride proved to be all I needed to reach Phoenix. I arrived in Phoenix with no money to speak of, so my tactics had to change. First, I had to find work as soon as I could, so that night I camped close to the downtown area. I knew this was where I'd find the labor pools, if there were any, and in most towns the size of Phoenix there is easily more than one such place. It was too late to obtain much information about the town, so I waited until early the next morning to find out what was happening and where. To do this, all I needed to do is find a restaurant near the skid row area of town, be there early and wait.

I got up around three that next morning, and started looking for the perfect spot. After only an hour of searching, I found it: a little hole-in-the-wall restaurant that looked like it couldn't get a health license to save its life. The name of the place was the Adobe Cafe, befitting a place like Phoenix. I ordered a cup of coffee and waited. It wasn't long before the street people started filtering in. One at a time I watched them come and go, looking for that perfect mark, a person I could extract information out of easily. After being in the streets for as long as I was, you learned who to talk to and who not to talk to. Certain people just had that look about them that said they didn't want to be bothered, and you'd better not bother them. I found that the older the person, the more likely they were to talk, and they came with a plus—they usually had the most accurate and honest information.

It didn't take long and I spotted him. He came in and sat right down beside me at the counter, what luck. His name was Andy, and I'm happy to say we hit it off. He was one of those people you liked from the start. He had an air about him that said, "I'm a nice person." You've seen them before. As it turned out, Andy did work at one of the local labor pools and was on his way to work. It's always best when going into one of these places for the first time to go with someone who is already established there, and Andy was. He'd been working at the same labor pool for two years now, and they liked him, a plus for me. Andy introduced me as a friend of his and from then on it was easy.

I got out that first morning and not only that, I didn't get stuck with a shit job. It was a job cleaning up a construction site and I enjoyed working outside, especially when the weather was nice, and it was. Not only that, but it turned out to be a steady ticket that lasted for over a month—as steady a job as you can get when you've only been in town for a day.

Andy got off work at 3:30 in the afternoon, and I didn't get off until 5:00. We made arrangements to meet at a local bar when we both got off, where else? You had to go to the bar anyways to cash your check, and being a drinking person where more appropriate a place to meet? Andy was one of those street people, just like me, that didn't approve of the missions to stay in at night, but preferred to live outside in the wide open spaces.

He had a camp just south of town, along an old wash (a dried-up river, except when it rained really hard, which wasn't often), called the Salt River. It was nothing but a sand and rock-filled dry riverbed with lots of shrubbery and clumps of trees spread throughout the wash. This seemed to be a popular place among the homeless. Because there were camps all up and down the wash, it was like a community in itself, but unless they knew each other, everybody kept to themselves and their own camp. Another plus is that the police didn't bother you there. Oh, they knew you were there, but as long as you didn't cause any trouble or they weren't looking for someone in particular, they left you alone.

The only thing was that when you left your campsite, unless there was someone staying behind, you had to take your valuables with you, the most important being your bedroll if you are a homeless person. Don't believe in that motto "honor among thieves." They'd steal you blind if they got the chance. It was survival of the fittest and most knowledgeable, every man for himself. If you were lucky you'd meet a person like Andy, who could share the watch with you. Now Andy was one of those street people who fit the stereotype that most have of the homeless. As I mentioned before, there are all types and any number of reasons for a person to be homeless, but to be faithful in relating these experiences, I have to tell all sides.

Andy was the stereotype: he was an alcoholic, he was in the streets because he chose not to be bothered, he'd lost everything he ever had to drinking—family, home, friends, jobs, everything. His own family didn't want anything to do with him, and besides he chose not to embarrass them anymore than he already had, so in a way, left home to protect them, because he knew the way he was. He always drank too much, often ended up in jail or detox—a place you either go to or are taken—to dry out from alcohol or drugs.

Andy wasn't into "drugs." His drug of choice was alcohol. He hadn't reached the point in his life where he wanted help, and maybe never would. At that time he chose to drink and to do it with as little hassle as possible. The streets gave him the opportunity to do just that. Even with all that against him, Andy was for all intents and purposes a good person. He was honest and wouldn't hurt a fly. He just wanted to be left alone to do his thing and not be bothered. Andy was the same age I was, thirty-three. He was average in every sense of the word. No distinguishing features set him apart from everyone else. For a street person, he was just about invisible, as many of us are until someone draws attention to us, or we do something wrong. No one ever sees the real person behind the mask; that would mean you'd have to get to know us. From Andy I learned where to go in town to obtain extra money.

It was Andy who turned me on to the plasma banks, where you could go and donate your plasma for extra cash, usually not very much, but when you were broke, a little seemed like a lot. I became a regular customer at the Salt River Plasma Donor Center. You could donate twice a week, and if you were a regular, got bonuses along the way, depending on how many times you donated during a set period of time. Andy also turned me on to the Salvation Army, a place you could go from time to time to get clean clothes, a warm bed, and not worry about the rigors of the streets for a while. The Salvation Army did help a lot of people get off the streets, if that's what they wanted, but most of those who used the Salvation Army regularly were just biding time, taking a rest until their next trip into the streets.

I learned a lot from Andy, and he continued to be a part of my education of the streets the whole time we run together. I knew a lot already, to survive, but in the streets you were constantly getting educated, and just when you thought you knew it all, something new would come along. I worked almost every day out of the labor pool, and spent my off hours either in a bar or at the campsite. I got to know a few others who shared the Salt River as a place of residence. Among these was Debra, and my book would not be complete if I didn't tell her story.

Debra was unlike anyone I'd ever met in the streets before, and how she came to live in the streets was one of the most bizarre stories I'd ever heard, then or since. Debra was a young black woman in her early twenties. She had gentle features, and always wore slacks or jeans and a man's shirt to cover her willowy frame. She said she liked the loose fitting look that a man's shirt gave her. She always wore tennis shoes with everything she had. I never seen her in a regular pair of shoes, or a dress. For most women who lived in the streets, a dress wasn't appropriate. Another of Debra's characteristics was that she didn't like or even hang around other women. She had a distinct distrust for those of the same sex. Later I was to find out why she felt that way.

Debra stayed at a campsite next to mine and Andy's, with an older gentleman in his late sixties that we all knew as Papa Smurf. With his beard he did look like the cartoon character of the same name. Everyone liked Papa Smurf, he was a real likeable person. Papa was on Social Security, and when he needed something at the store, Debra would make the run and get it. I came to know her because she would always stop by our camp on her way to the store to see if we needed anything. Papa also had a hard time getting around by himself—he walked with a cane—and Debra kind of took care of him and he took care of her.

There was nothing sexual about the relationship; in fact I never knew Debra to have any kind of a relationship with any man, other than just being friends. But she liked hanging around the guys, and could bullshit with the best of us. She was also quite a drinker, but usually furnished her own drink when she came visiting. She liked to drink vodka, with just a little bit of orange juice—a screwdriver, as they're called.

Debra grew up in East St. Louis. Her father was an alcoholic and abused her mother something terrible, although Debra said he never touched her. Her mother on the other hand, endured some horrendous beatings at her father's hand. When her mother finally gave up on the marriage, she moved out and moved in with a friend of hers, another woman, who by the way happened to be gay. Debra was only twelve years old when this transition took place. But she recalls the relationship between her mother and this other woman very well. They slept in the same room and in the same bed, and

Debra could tell you some horrific stories about things that took place in that relationship.

After her mother and the other woman had been together about a year, the other woman started coming on to Debra. This woman, as Debra tells it, was very domineering, and liked to play mind games with Debra. She would describe what she would do to Debra and her mother in detail if Debra ever told her mom what was happening. At this point I want to clarify something. Throughout the years I have gotten to know all types of people, from all walks of life. And if there's one thing I learned over the years, it was not to judge others. I have known lots of gay people, both male and female and let me tell you, they were mostly wonderful people. The biggest share of them don't mess with anyone who doesn't want to be messed with. They stick to their own kind when it comes to sexual matters and make some of the best friends a person could ever want. Their friendship comes unconditionally, with no strings attached. They can be true friends.

But like any other walk of life, they have their bad apples, so to speak, and this woman who sexually abused Debra was one of these, an exception to the rule. But as Debra got older she also got braver, and started standing up to this woman. In the end, to avoid any further confrontations and to save her mother any more unhappiness, at sixteen she decided to leave home. She wandered the streets of St. Louis for a year before heading west to Arizona. She caught a lift with a man she had met in St. Louis while in the streets there. He was headed for California, and that was Debra's original plan, to start all over in California.

But somewhere in Arizona, not far from Phoenix, the guy started trying to fool around with Debra. She would have nothing to do with him, so she left his company and ended up in Phoenix. Of all the females I ever came to know in the streets, Debra was one of the most street-wise. If Debra carried any pain from her experience, she didn't show it, either inside or out. She liked to laugh, and made you feel good just being around her and having her as a friend. She would go out drinking with us guys and was a lot of fun to be around. She would dance with you, so long as you didn't try to mess with her or make any sexual advances. She was a terrific dancer by the way.

I never knew her to have any aspirations to leave the streets. She seemed dedicated to taking care of Papa Smurf. I believe he was the father figure she always wanted and never had. I and everyone else knew as long as Papa was in the streets she would be, too. She was very devoted to him. And if you messed with him, or tried to take advantage of him in any way, you had to answer to Debra, and she was not the kind of person you wanted on your bad side. But here we are again, a story of two lives, messed up for whatever reason, following different paths; whatever the motivations, they made choices, right or wrong, that changed their lives.

Who's to say who's right or wrong in the decision-making process? Why do some of us choose to go one way, and others of us choose to go another? We can ask ourselves these questions over and over again and not come up with the same answers. That's just the way life is, we don't all have the same tools to work with when it comes to making important decisions.

I'm glad I met Debra and Papa. They were, in my mind, a match made in heaven: she needed him and he needed her. It was a perfect relationship. I never heard Papa's story; I wish I had. But Papa was a very private person, and never-but-never complained or discussed his past. You accepted him for who and what he was now, and the past had no relevance.

I lived and worked in Phoenix all the rest of that year and through the winter, but by March of 1980 I decided to move on. I headed to where everyone heads when they leave Arizona it seems, and that was L.A.—Los Angeles, the city of Angels. Arizona seemed to be a stopping off place for anyone headed west or even east for that matter.

I arrived in L.A. around the 15th of March 1980. It didn't take me long to locate the skid row section of town. With the exception of New York City, L.A. had one of the largest skid rows I had ever seen. It covered a wide area, from Main St. and 5th Ave., down Los Angeles St., all the way to Central Ave., then over to 7th St. and all the way back to Main. It was a street person's dream place—lots of work, a wide variety of places and things to go and do if that was your bag. It offered you many choices and opportunities to survive. There was something for everyone. It was one of those cities that I would visit many times over the years, and one of the easiest to get by in.

But it also had its downside. It was one of the most violent places I'd ever been, and this is where you put you street savvy to use the most. You had to be constantly aware of what was going on around you at all times or you could quickly become a fatal victim. I went through one of the most violent phases of my own life—like I'd never been through before. And even though I liked the life that L.A. offered, with its many choices, I didn't like what it had turned me into. I had to become one of them—the strong—to survive. I much preferred being one of the entities that was invisible, and lived in harmony with their surroundings.

I worked regularly out of one of the many labor pools that lined 7th Avenue. When you couldn't get out of one you went to another; you had lots of choices. One of my main hangouts when I wasn't working was a bar on 7th Street and San Pedro, not too far from downtown, called (what else) the 7th Street Bar. It was there that I met Chief, a Native American who would become one of my best acquaintances in Los Angeles. All Native American street people were called Chief, so it seemed. It fit and that's the way they preferred to be known—go figure, at that time it was politically correct.

Chief's story was not so different from many other Native Americans who grew up on a reservation and now lived in the streets, with little or no education, no work on or near the reservation, and wanting something better. Chief went looking for it. In Los Angeles, he found a workforce that didn't require a formal education; all you needed was a little brawn. Chief had left the reservation when he was twenty years old. He was now in his late fifties, and had lived the street life ever since leaving the reservation.

While Chief managed to keep a roof over his head most of the time, that roof only consisted of a bed in a large dormitory filled with lots of other beds that he shared with several others—a flophouse as we called them. There were many of these places on skid row that only charged a couple of dollars a night, and other than afford you a bed and a roof over your head, had no other purpose. Most who lived in these places carried all their possessions on their back, either in a backpack, or duffel bag, and where they went so went their possessions. And even though these people didn't literally live in the streets, I still consider them street people because other than what they could carry, they had nothing. Chief was always one of these people—he didn't have much on the reservation, so in a way he was used to the homeless life. He'd often tell me that the flophouses on skid row was better than what he had on the reservation. At least he had a job, if you want to call it that, and he had the freedom to choose where to go and what to do.

Chief was a drinking person, but he was not an alcoholic. It was only on an occasion or two that I ever seen him really drunk. His job was very important to him no matter how meager it was, and always came first. If he had to work the next day he drank very little the night before, and opted to go home early to get his rest. But by working out of the labor pools all his life, he was locked into a position that afforded no opportunity for change. At minimum wage you barely had enough for a bed and a meal, let alone the ability to save. Besides, Chief could neither read nor write; he signed his name with an X. Nobody would hire him because he couldn't even fill out an application, thus the labor pool became his life and his only means of providing for himself. This was a way of life that once you were locked into allowed little means of escape. You had to work everyday just to survive for that day, leaving no time to look for anything better, and even if something better did come up it was unobtainable because you couldn't weather two weeks without a paycheck. It was an endless cycle that so many of us came to know, and it wasn't just limited to the illiterate.

You might ask, "Then why did they (the street people) spend so much time drinking and spending what little they had?" My answer is that living and working on skid row afforded little opportunity for a variety of recreation or means of association with others—natural human needs—thus we gravitated to the only means readily available to us, the drinking establishments. There were always plenty of those. Not much of an excuse, I agree, but that's all we had and everybody needs something or someone to share their life with.

Another thing you may not realize, is that about a third of the homeless population that live in the streets are women and children, even whole families. No place was this so apparent as it was in Los

Angeles. The city seemed to draw people from all over the country and from all walks of life. When you're a single parent—especially a woman—with a child, and homeless, you spend your every waking hour wondering where your next meal will come from and where you will sleep that night. Who was going to take care of your child if you went to work? How could you even look for work with a child in tow? For these individuals, the street was a particularly harsh environment. If you didn't pair up with someone, your fate was sealed. And the streets teemed with what I call predators who preyed on people like these, who were naive.

Cindy was one of those naive people. She had a daughter, Ann, who was only four years old, and a son, Todd, who was eight. Cindy was a product of what most single parents, especially women, who lived in the streets were products of: domestic violence, another fact of life. We as a society (at least back then, I don't know about today) had few or no programs to help these families, and for what few there was, there was little room, and few resources. Cindy had come to the big city to hide. She was deathly afraid of her spouse. This left her with another dilemma: if she sought help, she was fearful her husband would find them, so she had to make it as best she could. To survive, she'd grab on to the first man who'd show an interest in her, just for her children's sake. Many of these men were users, and mistreated the women they were with something terrible. They would only have them around for their own gratification and nothing else. Consequently Cindy went through numerous relationships that never seemed to work out, but she would continually look for a new man when she had just left the one she had.

Cindy was not a beautiful woman in the physical sense of the word, but her insides more than made up for her physical appearance. She was as good as gold, had a beautiful personality and a big heart. She wanted nothing more than to have a life better than the one she had taken ten years to escape. And she was going about it the only way she knew how in her predicament, by trial and error. She figured that somewhere out there she would find someone who would take care of her and her children. The only thing was, her present environment was not favorable to achieving her goal. There just weren't many good men out there who lived in the streets that were of the settling down type, and of those that were, they too were in a situation that was difficult to get out of, if that was indeed what they wanted. But Cindy kept trying. She had no other choice. She didn't go to her family for help because her fear of her husband was so great. She was afraid of what he might do to them if he found them, and it wouldn't be hard for him to find her if she had chosen that route. So she was dammed if she did and dammed if she didn't.

It was just another vicious cycle like many others I witnessed during my time in the streets for women in similar circumstances. I'll not give you any other details about Cindy's past, because for all I know she is still hiding, and I couldn't do that to Cindy and her kids. I don't know if she ever did find what or who she was looking for. She just disappeared one day and I never seen her since. Hopefully she found someone, but more than likely she just went looking somewhere else. The streets are full of women like Cindy and they are mostly invisible, a part of the homeless that few people ever see, and as a consequence, don't even know exist.

Another family I met were the Truits. They consisted of a father, mother, and three children, and they lived—for as long as I knew them—in their only possession, a 1971 Ford Econoline van. His name was Jim, his wife's name was Judy, and I don't recall their children's names, except for their oldest boy, fourteen-year-old Jim Jr. Jim and Judy were both from a small town in northern Arkansas, somewhere near the Oklahoma and Missouri borders. They grew up together, were childhood sweethearts, and had been married for sixteen years.

Jim had worked in a lumber mill his entire adult life. His wife, as the children got older, worked at a local diner to help with the expenses. They always said they didn't have much, but they had each other. Even when they were both working there was just enough to go around but little to spare. But at least they had a roof over their heads, and food on the table, and their bills were paid. Then back a couple of years before I met them, and before they became homeless, Jim hurt himself while changing the engine in his truck.

For a while, Jim couldn't work because of his back, but they managed to scrape by with what little Judy earned at the diner. After a couple of months, long before the doctor wanted Jim to go back to work, he did. He had no choice; the bills were piling up, and they were getting so far behind they'd never get caught up. As it turned out, Jim went back to work too early and after only a couple of weeks on the job reinjured his back, bad this time. He injured a couple of disks in his back and because it was due to a previous injury his job wouldn't cover him under workmen's compensation—that in addition to the fact that he had returned to work against his doctor's advice.

They struggled for quite some time, but then Jim needed an operation, and was laid up for six months, during which time they lost everything and were staying in a local motel, living week by week on what Judy earned. It had been known for some time now that the diner where Judy worked was going out of business, and when they did and Judy lost her job, it was too much for Jim to handle. He was already upset because his wife had to support the family and he could do nothing—you see, Jim had a lot of pride. He wouldn't hear of asking his family for help, especially Judy's parents. Although both would have been happy to help, Jim would not accept what he called charity, which was another reason they stayed down so long. Now say what you like, but who of any of us have not felt the same way at one time or another?

For both Jim and Judy, being raised the way they were, pride was the one thing you hung on to that no one could take away from you when everything else was gone. The only thing Jim could think of was to relocate and start over again where no one knew them or about Jim's injury. Because of it, he couldn't find a job back home. Loading up the family and what possessions they had, he headed for California, partly because he had heard there was lots of work out there, and also because he had a brother out there somewhere. He thought it would give him the opportunity to locate his brother, as he hadn't heard from him for a few years. He wasn't sure exactly where his brother was, except that he was working somewhere in the Los Angeles area. Being from a small town, I guess Jim never stopped to realize just how big Los Angeles really was. Jim had no difficulty getting work out of the labor pools, but didn't like leaving his family in the van all day long until he could get out of work and get them something to eat.

Jim had it really hard, because what little he made had to feed a whole family, and he was barely making over twenty dollars a day, just enough to eat on and put gas in the van so they could go out of town far enough to find a place to park it and sleep where they would feel safe. Than back again the next day to repeat the same routine. I really felt sorry for Jim, because I didn't know how he was ever going to make it on what little the labor pools paid him. Neither Jim nor Judy drank. Their only vice I knew of was smoking.

I met Jim on a job we shared out of one of the labor pools I used to see him and his family around from time to time. Sometimes he brought them on the job with him, and they waited in the van until he finished. I ate lunch with them several times, and they were a very close-knit family. They stuck together no matter what. When they took their marriage vows, they took them literally, and it showed. Judy and the children never complained. They knew that Jim was doing the best he could. I couldn't see how they would ever get out of the predicament they were in. I'd run into Jim and Judy on occasion the first five months I knew them, then all of a sudden they were gone and I didn't see them anymore. I hope that somehow or other they overcame their dilemma and beat the streets. Not many succeeded, but I like to think they were one family that did.

Now in all fairness, I must interject at this point that there were some well meaning organizations and people out there like the Salvation Army, various church groups, missions, the Department of Human Services and other government agencies, as well as a very few alcohol and drug programs that catered to those without visible means of support. But due to the overwhelming numbers in the homeless population, the limited resources available, and the unwillingness of some individuals to follow through with the help offered, their hands were tied. No matter how well meaning they were, their job was made harder—there was just so much that they could do. I know of many frustrated social workers that tried their very best and had all the good intentions they could muster, only to be brought to an abrupt halt for lack of resources. Theirs was a difficult task, a path paved with good intentions that lacked the resources to do anything more than console and encourage a person to keep trying.

So I in no way want to demean these organizations. They done the very best they could with what they had, and the things that their own organizations would allow. They too, had rules to follow that at times didn't seem fair, but those were the laws they had to abide by. If you ever doubt the task they had and still have today, all I can say to you is try it sometime yourself. I always said don't judge someone until you've had an opportunity to walk a mile in their shoes. They did manage to help a lot of families and individuals, but they were so overwhelmed by the numbers that they barely scratched the surface.

It was somewhere around this point that my life was about to undergo a drastic change, and for the next two-and-a-half years, I would achieve some stability. It was early October of 1980, and I had been working some time on a steady ticket at a hospital in Culver City, called Brotman Memorial. Although I still worked on a ticket at the labor pool, my boss at the hospital was a man named John Russell. John was head of the hospital's maintenance department. He was a black man in his late fifties, and was quite a drinker himself. His wife owned a local mom-and-pop type grocery store. Through John I got a steady job at the hospital, and was able to move out of the city and into a hotel close to the work.

While working at the hospital, I met a nurse who was the head of the hospital IV therapy team. After knowing her just a few days, I moved in with her. I really cared about the woman a lot, and for two and a half years I tried hard to change for her and give some credibility to my life. I even checked myself into a local rehab program to try and overcome my alcohol abuse. In fact, before those two and some odd years were over, I went through three such programs. But no matter how hard I tried, and how bad I wanted to, I couldn't go more than a couple of months without drinking. By now I was going through all the symptoms of a typical alcoholic: sneaking drinks, hiding my alcohol, lying to Lena about my drinking, the whole nine yards. I even lost my job at the hospital, and went through a series of jobs, one right after the other, before even Lena gave up on me. I was beginning to realize that I had a problem, but wasn't sure yet if I wanted to do anything about it.

Now my life truly became itinerant. After returning home to Michigan briefly again, only to fail, I was back on the road, this time with a vengeance. My first stop after leaving Michigan was Chicago. It was early spring of 1983, and my life really moved fast from here on out, so please try to keep up.

The Problem

There became an important time in my life
When I knew there was something wrong
When all my world was collapsing around me
And I knew I no longer belonged

That somewhere out there, was an answer
To the problems I faced in my life
That somewhere there was a solution
'Cause the problem cut like a knife

But I was the cause of the problem
And it did not quicken to go away
I had become my own enemy
And my pride is the price that I paid

'Cause I lived in the sewers of the cities
While searching for the gardens of God
My mind was living in Eden
While through the bilge of the city I clawed

So I was not destined to find my answer
Until finally I made up my mind
That I was part of the problem
And my enemy was there all the time

I had to let go of the devil
Before I could see Heaven's Gate
'Cause I was my own worst enemy
And that's who I learned to hate

— May 14, 1997

~ CHAPTER 4 ~

The Troubled Years OR *The Problem*

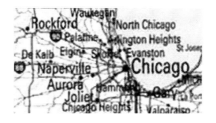

I don't know what there is about it, but it seems the moment you think you know that it isn't going in the direction you intended, things get worse. No matter what you try, no matter how bad you want it, until you actually accept the fact that something is wrong, nothing goes right. There's a lot of difference between admitting something is wrong and accepting it. The two are not one of the same; they require different actions on your part. This may be hard for some to understand, so if you've never been through a similar dilemma yourself you may not get it. This is what was going on in my life at this point: I knew I had a drinking problem, but I figured if the world would just straighten out things would get better. I never located the problem within myself.

During this time, I tried a lot of different things to fix my life, from rehabilitation programs to mental hospitals to Alcoholics Anonymous, and for a long time none of these methods worked. I tried to change my lifestyle, but that didn't work in the beginning, because I was only admitting the problem, not accepting it. I got into a lot of trouble during these years. I ended up in a lot of jails, and a couple of times was even put in mental institutions by the legal system. Still nothing worked. For a long time, I did believe I was going crazy. Anyway that is the point I had reached. As I headed for Chicago, I knew deep down in my heart that things were getting worse.

As I left my father's home in Lansing, I had every intention of going to an AA meeting, but somehow I got side-tracked and found myself in front of a convenience store not far from the meeting place with a bottle of bourbon in my hands. It was a cold spring morning, the temperature was near freezing and the wind was blowing hard. I didn't have much money, less than a hundred dollars at the time. I remember thinking, What the hell am I doing? I knew I dared not go back to my dad's place since I'd been drinking. I don't know what came over me, but as I stood there in front of the store, contemplating my next move, a man pulled up in his car, got out leaving the engine running and went into the store. Without a second thought, I got into his car and drove away. It was almost like a dream.

Not knowing what I was going to do at this point, I drove around town a lot longer than I should have because I knew the longer I stayed around, the better my chances of being apprehended were. Soon I came to my senses, and headed south, down Hwy. 69. I kept going until I crossed the Indiana border, then I noticed a sign that said Chicago, Hwy. 90, so I turned the car west, thinking that Chicago would be as good a place as any to start over again. I arrived in Chicago late that evening. I quickly determined where the local street people hung out, and headed for Madison and Halstead streets.

Once there, I parked the car with no intention of ever going back to it again, located the nearest bar, what else, and drank the rest of the evening until the bars closed. Then, still not having a place to stay, and not having a bedroll, my second mistake—I returned to the car, got in, started the engine to keep warm, and went to sleep. I awoke early that morning, with a tapping on my window. It was one of Chicago's finest, and I knew right then that I'd been nailed. I couldn't prove the car was mine, and the officer didn't accept my explanation. After a quick check on his computer, he found the car was stolen and took me to jail.

Now's where things get really strange. I had fully accepted the fact that I was going to prison. I had no doubt in my mind. But as it turned out, Michigan didn't want to extradite me, and said if I allowed Chicago to go through with the prosecution themselves, they would not consider bringing me back to Michigan.

Thinking, what the hell, I let them do it. Much to my surprise and due to the overcrowding of the Illinois Prison System, I was given probation. What a lark, hey? I stepped into a pile of shit and came out smelling like a rose. Things like this happened more than once to me over the next few years, and for a while I thought I was invincible.

I immediately returned to Madison and Halsted that day, and continued drinking with what little money I had left. That night I stayed in one of the local missions, something I didn't like doing at all. Early the next morning upon getting up, I headed straight for the nearest labor pool, and got out to work that first day. From then on I was established. For the first two weeks I didn't work every day, just enough to get by, and stayed in the missions off and on.

Then I got a steady ticket, working at a lumber yard unloading box cars, saved a little money, and rented me a bed at a local flophouse for three dollars a night. It was at this flophouse that I met the subject of my next story. His name was Fred. Fred was instrumental in showing me all the places to go and things to do in Chicago, giving me, in a sense, the lay of the land. I was always quick to adapt.

Fred was another of those many Vietnam veterans I told you about in the beginning, and his story was typical, though with a little twist. Fred was thirty-five years old at the time I met him. He had brown hair, brown eyes and what I call a ruddy complexion. He stood about five-feet, ten inches tall, and weighed about a hundred and ninety pounds. Unlike many I knew like him, Fred did not bring Vietnam home with him, instead he chose to forget everything about Vietnam. You couldn't even get him to talk about it unless he had a few drinks under his belt, then he talked about it with extreme repulsion. Except for abstract summaries he related from time to time, I know little about what happened to him in the war. Obviously it was not something he liked to discuss. He was proud of his medals, and carried them with him everywhere he went in a small display case the size of a large wallet. He had a Silver Star with two battle clusters, the Bronze Medal for bravery, three Purple Hearts, and the Presidential Unit Citation. How he received those medals was another matter he didn't discuss much, except that he won most of them in the Tet Offensive of 1967 in the battle of Saigon. He was there the same time I was, plus an extra six months that he volunteered for after his original hitch was over.

Fred came home like most of us, disillusioned about the war and why we were really over there, and hurt by the way he was treated when he returned. Before going to Vietnam, he was engaged to his childhood sweetheart. When he returned, for some reason or another, he never said, they broke up. He tried for several years to adjust, but couldn't hold down a steady job. The first two years he was home, he said, he had at least nine different jobs. So his problem wasn't about getting a job, just in holding one. He came back to the states hooked on morphine, like a lot of wounded veterans, especially those who had been wounded more than once, but he kicked that habit himself, cold turkey. He then turned to alcohol, and from what I could see, used it to forget.

His family, like many others of Vietnam veterans, couldn't comprehend what he was going through. They tried their best to understand, but their problem was compounded by the fact that he wouldn't talk about it. So they focused on the problems that were apparent to them: his drinking and his inability to hold a steady job. Soon, tired of being preached at, he left his home in Evanston, Indiana, and headed for Chicago. That was sometime in 1973, and he'd been in the streets of Chicago since.

I never knew Fred to be violent, like some veterans I knew, but I do know he had some horrendous dreams. Even after thirteen years, he was still having them. Usually the dreams only lasted a few years—at least mine did—and then they faded away, but no! Fred's dreams stayed with him. When he slept at the same flophouse that I did, I can remember him waking up screaming; in fact, because of that, they barred him from that flophouse because his dreams were too disrupting to the others. I truly felt sorry for Fred because he was like a man with a monkey on his back. He loved his family, and had always been close to them before Vietnam, but after, he was at a loss as to what to do. He wanted to put an end to all his troubles, but that recourse seemed to be—at that point in time—unacceptable to him.

He had been in the VA Hospital for a while just a few months earlier, and was one of the first to be diagnosed with PTSD (Post Traumatic Stress Disorder). The hospital's solution was to have Fred spend a year and a half in the hospital undergoing treatment. Fred would not hear of that, not just because of the time involved, but because he figured PTSD was just another way for the government to discredit their involvement with what had happened. He often said it was just another cop-out for those who wanted a free ride. Maybe he was right, who knows? All I know is that Fred didn't want to go that route. He insisted on being self-sufficient and not relying on anyone or anything to get by in this world. He'd say we made our own demons in Vietnam and each individual had to deal with them in their own way. He ruled out going home because he didn't want to burden his family with his troubles, even though he loved them and missed them terribly.

We often worked and drank together, and for the short time I was in Chicago, I got to know Fred probably better than anyone. He would talk to me when he wouldn't talk to anyone else, mostly because I'd been there too and he figured I'd understand better than other people. Still, Fred got by, didn't cause any unnecessary problems for anybody, minded his own business, and didn't ask for help, preferring to handle his own problems in whatever manner he chose without pressure from anyone else. When I left Chicago after a few months, he was still there.

Another sad story I came to know while in Chicago was that of Sebrina, not her real name, I'm sure, but that's what she preferred to be called. Sebrina was one of the many young runaways I came to know while in the streets myself. She was only sixteen, and had already been on the streets for two years. She came from a small town in northern Ohio. She had blonde hair, blue eyes, and a fair complexion, with that girlish look of a young schoolgirl. There are lots of people in the streets who prey on girls like Sebrina, so she grew up fast.

She went through a succession of men her first year in the streets, looking for someone to take care of her. She even prostituted for one of them for a while. Somehow or other she found a way to escape that life, but by then she was hooked on drugs and had to work as a stripper to supply her habit. It was the only thing other than prostitution that afforded her enough money. At one time she claimed to have a three-hundred-dollar-a-day habit. When I came to know her, she had already broken that habit, although I believe from time to time she still used, just not as much as before.

Sebrina left home not because of physical or sexual abuse, but because she felt she couldn't talk to her parents. They were career-oriented, and didn't have the time that a young girl requires at her age. And when they did communicate, she felt as though they were running her life for her. They wanted to pick her friends, and dictate her future. They often criticized her for her grades in school, and told her if she wanted to get into college she would have to do better. But Sebrina didn't want to go to college, not then at least. Maybe if her parents had been more understanding, and willing to listen to what she wanted, things would have been different. Now I'm not saying what she done, by running away from home was the right decision, but she believed it was the only choice she had if she ever wanted a life of her own.

She called once to tell her mother she wanted to come home, but right away her mother started laying down the law, telling her she'd have to do this and she'd have to do that if she wanted to come home. Needless to say, this turned her off immediately, and as far as I know, she never called home again.

When I knew Sebrina, she got by like many did in her circumstances, working in skid row restaurants and an occasional barmaid job. Over the years, she had somehow obtained some false I.D. that said she was twenty-one years old, although you only had to look at her to know she was much younger. But even if the people knew she wasn't old enough, they still let her slide because she had the I.D. Mentally Sebrina was much older than her years, the streets had a tendency to do that to people. She was a young girl with a woman's mind and body. She once tried a shelter called Covenant Place, but didn't last long because with all their rules it seemed too much like her parents' home. She just wanted someone to listen to her and allow her to make her own decisions when it came to things like her future and her friends. The only place she felt she could accomplish this was on her own.

Another sad story, but not unlike a lot of others in her age bracket that I met over the years. Not all of them were abused, just misunderstood—or so they thought—with no other place to turn. They felt trapped, and if you trap anyone, even a wild animal, it is going to break free any way it can and let's face it, a teenager doesn't have many choices. I knew of another individual in Chicago with almost the exact story. His name was Todd, and without going into the details, only to say, he was Sebrina in male form. The details of his life were almost parallel with that of Sebrina's, so much so it seemed uncanny, if you know what I mean. But it's a known fact that there are over half a million teenage runaways in the streets today, and the numbers are growing all the time.

I quickly grew tired of Chicago, not of the city itself because I loved the way it was laid out, with its Irish, Polish, German, Greek, Spanish and African American neighborhoods. They gave a person a wide variety of choices as well as a sense of belonging. You always knew where you stood, no matter where you chose to be. It had a strong sense of family and togetherness. I tired of Chicago because I was becoming too well known. I figured when you were walking down a street and someone from the opposite side of the street yelled out your name, that it was definitely time to leave. So in August of 1983, I headed southwest, with St. Louis in my sights.

I took a local bus out of town and rode it to the end of the line, as far as I could get out of the city, then caught Hwy. 55 heading southwest and hitchhiked the rest of the way to St. Louis. It wasn't far, and took me only the one day to get there. I can remember going through East St. Louis, still on the Illinois side of the river, and as I went across the great Mississippi River, seeing the Big Arch. It was quite a sight, especially in the early evening hours. I had a few dollars in my pocket, not much, but you know where I headed when I got there—where else?— the nearest bar—to gather information, I would tell myself.

And while this was necessary, I probably could have gotten it somewhere else. I felt more comfortable in a bar. Not wanting to spend any more money than I had to, I tried rationing what little I had, so I drank very sparingly that first night. I found out where there was a local flophouse that only charged four dollars a night for a bed. Even that was more than I wanted to let go of at the time, but it's not easy scoping out a safe place to stay in the dark, especially in a strange town. This is why it's necessary to get as much information as possible, as soon as possible, about the areas you need to avoid. The next day was Saturday, so I knew I'd have no luck getting out of the labor pool.

I spent the day gathering information and locating a secure place to lay out a bedroll. At least this time I had a bedroll, not like when I went into Chicago. There wasn't much to be found in the downtown area that looked promising to me, but a street person I had met briefly in one of the bars told me about a large park out on the edge of town that might serve my purpose. So before it got dark, I got on a bus going out Forest Park Parkway and got off at the entrance to the park. By the way, the name of the park was Forest Park, what a coincidence, yea. I had to be careful, and find a place in the park where I couldn't be detected because after a certain hour no one was allowed in the park.

I finally found a place over near one of the two big ponds in the park. It had some thick underbrush, and a small grove of trees around the backside of it, affording me a reasonable amount of privacy. Now all I had to do was be sure and save enough bus fare to get back and forth to the park each day—not always an easy thing to do when you live the way I did. More than once I had to find a place in town so I could make it to the labor pool the next day. I didn't like doing that because the downtown area was considered unsafe, but I managed. I was a survivor. St. Louis didn't prove to be that great a town for me—work was scarce, and I didn't particularly care for the way the town was laid out. All streets, it seemed, led to the same area downtown around the Arch.

After a month in St. Louis, fighting each day just to get by—and more than one trip to the city lock-up—I decided to check into a Salvation Army program in town that tried to help people get on their feet again. I spent twenty-one days in that program, and was moved into another graduate program to edge people back into the mainstream of society. The Salvation Army used me for their program now in an old hotel right in the downtown area. You were able to work there until you found another job and could make your own way again. They paid you a minimum wage while you were working to earn spending money while you searched for another job. I never did find another job, but managed to save enough money to finally get out of that place. I didn't care for it much. The first day I didn't get far—there was a bar just across the street from the hotel called the Red Door. I drank there all that day, and that evening got into a terrible fight with one of the locals, got arrested, and went to jail again. This was the fourth time since arriving in St. Louis that I had been a guest of the city, and I was getting tired of all this, fast. After cooling my heels for three days in the local lock-up, I was released.

It was an early weekday morning. I managed to get to a labor pool, and with a little luck and a lot of begging, got out to work. As it turned out it became a steady ticket that I was able to hang on to for three weeks. During this time, I saved as much money as one can save without being a complete hermit, and also met Cowboy, as he liked to be called. I had another run-in with the law, and once again came before the same judge I'd been before three previous times.

Labeling me as a chronic alcoholic, with over three arrests related to drinking, the Judge sentenced me to a program at the St. Louis State Mental Hospital. I remember that place well. It reminded me of something out of medieval times. It was a large complex, with old stone buildings that looked like they were built back in the time of King Arthur and the Round Table. All it needed was a moat around the grounds and it would have been perfect. They said when the hospital was first built, it was built with underground chambers, where they kept the worst of the mental patients, and that torture often occurred in these underground chambers. Those were the rumors anyway, and if you've ever seen the place, it was believable.

The program itself was a cross between an alcohol program and one for the mentally deficient; that is, they gave you medication to keep you under control while you were there. I always believed they were experimenting on us. That was my theory anyways. This is where I met Cowboy, a very unlikely place to take on an acquaintance, but Cowboy's story was much like mine. It seems that in St. Louis at that time, if you were constantly picked up for drinking-related offenses, they considered you unable to function in society and sentenced you to the mental hospital. This was not the last time or place this would happen to me, as you'll see later.

Anyways as I said, this is where I met Cowboy, and after we'd both been in the hospital for two weeks, we began to plan our escape. There really wasn't much to plan. In our part of the hospital there were no locked doors, the grounds were wide open, and we were often taken into the yard. We had to go outside our building to get to the chow hall that was located in another building on the grounds, as were the commissary and the recreation yard. All we had to do was walk off when no one was looking, and that's exactly what we done.

Cowboy had a plan. By then it was early November 1983, and the snow had already flew one time, and the days and nights were getting colder. The only obvious thing for us to do was to head south and get out of town as fast as we could before we were picked up again. Cowboy knew of this place in Florida where, if we could get there, we would have a place to stay and a job. The job being picking oranges. I'd never done this before, but remember thinking, how hard can it be?

Cowboy wasn't from Florida. He grew up in a small town in south central Oklahoma not far from the Texas border, but he had traveled around quite a bit like I had and had been to this place in Florida before. Cowboy was a tall, lanky man, six foot-three and on the thin side at about a hundred and seventy-five pounds. He had dark hair and dark eyes, and always dressed like a cowboy. With the hat, boots, belt, and denim vest, the whole shot, he looked like someone who had just stepped out of a Zane Gray western novel. He was a likable cuss about my age, in his mid-thirties. At times he seemed a little eccentric, but all and all he was a pretty nice guy who like me had a drinking problem, and chose to live in the streets to avoid all the hassle normal society laid on us. His story wasn't much different than mine, except he was never in the service, and had never done time in Vietnam.

He was unlike a lot of alcoholics of our type, in that he was an extremely honest person who wouldn't hurt a fly, and he was always sticking up for the underdog. He treated people the way he wanted to be treated, unless they abused his kindness. His family life hadn't been all that traumatic, although both his parents were alcoholics, and they didn't have a whole lot while he was growing up. He never said anything about any physical abuse, but admitted it was hard when the other kids picked on him because the whole town knew his parents were the town drunks.

But he survived that by getting tough—not on the outside, like you may think, but on the inside. You could not hurt Cowboy with words—they just rolled off his back— at least it didn't show. What was on the inside is anybody's guess. People like us were good at hiding our feelings—we had to be—in the streets you couldn't show any signs of weakness. If you did, you didn't survive long.

Anyway, we headed south out of town on Hwy. 55 all the way to Memphis, Tennessee.

Just outside Memphis, we took a more southeasterly direction on Hwy. 78. We traveled that road all the way to Birmingham, Alabama then caught Hwy. 65 south out of Birmingham and followed it all the way to Montgomery. We then caught Hwy. 231 out of Montgomery, south to Florida. Once in Florida we kept heading south until we hit Interstate 10, headed east on 10 to Interstate 75, then south on 75 until we hit a little town just northeast of Tampa called Dade City. This was our destination, where Cowboy knew we could find a place to stay and a job picking oranges in one of the many orange groves in that area. After my last episode in Florida I thought I'd never return, but here I was, so I tried to make the best of it.

Picking oranges turned out not to be my thing. It was hard, hot, backbreaking work, and made me appreciate those who done it all the more. I'd never berate the pickers of this world again, they could have that job. So two weeks after arriving, Cowboy and I parted ways. He found a girl and stayed behind, while I headed south, stopping in Tampa briefly to work out of the labor pools for a few days with the intention of moving on when I had a little money in my pocket. I had Miami in my mind, and wanted to check it out.

I had heard a lot of stories about Miami, and I wanted to see for myself. So after a few days in Tampa I once again was on the move. I caught Interstate 75 south out of Tampa and hitchhiked all the way to Naples, where I stopped just briefly to get something at a truck stop and ran into a truck driver who offered to take me to Miami with him if I agreed to help unload his truck when we got there. Of course I agreed, and soon we were headed across Alligator Alley. He had a short stop in Ft. Lauderdale to unload 10,000 pounds, then it was south on Interstate 95 all the way to Miami. We stopped at a truck stop just outside of Opalocka, Florida, and spent the night because it was too late and the place he had to unload his freight was nearby.

That next morning we went to our destination and I helped him unload his truck. Much to my surprise he handed me a hundred-dollar bill, much more than the job was worth and a hundred dollars more than I expected. Why he chose to do this, other than just being a great guy and knowing I was almost broke, I'll never know, but I was taught not to look a gift horse in the mouth. So I thanked him, we parted ways, and I headed for downtown Miami, just a few miles to the south. I was so close to Miami in fact, that I rode a local bus into town. It was early afternoon on a sunny and warm fall day. I was glad to be away from the winter in the north, and happy to be in Miami, even if it was located in Florida, the only state where I ever done hard time.

Miami didn't have much of a skid row, being mostly a tourist town. The area where the street people hung out was a mix of bars for the locals as I call them, and the downtown establishments frequented by office workers during the day and blue-collar workers and tourists at night. Most of the street people could be found in the area of N.W. 3rd St. and Miami Ave. where there were several bars that were less of a draw to those other than the local street people; also nearby were a couple of labor pools.

112

At this time I sought out one of these bars to get my usual feed of information as to where to go, what to avoid, and the best places to get out to work. I then done something that I didn't usually do: a man told me of a flophouse just a couple blocks away around 7th Avenue and 3rd Street above a dry cleaners that only cost twenty five dollars a week to stay at. As soon as I found out about the place, I left the bar and went and rented me a bed for a week because the beds went fast, especially on the weekend, and I wanted to make sure I had a place to stay. Living outside in the streets of Miami was dangerous. Little was I to know at the time how dangerous the place that I was staying would be.

I returned to the bar that evening, and continued to drink and collect information. I found out that the best place to get daily work was out of a labor pool called "The Labor Force." I also got to know this one gentleman well enough to have him put in a good word for me at this place, because he'd been working out of there for over two years, and was well-known and well-liked there. His name was Pete, and during the time I was there, I got to know him pretty well. He had a real interesting story.

Pete was in his late forties, from Pensacola, Florida originally, where he had been a policeman up until five years before. He had loved his job, but over the years it got the best of him. As many of us know, being a policeman is one the most stressful jobs that anyone can have and it takes its toll on the people in its ranks every year. Some are just not cut out for that type of work and it becomes too much for them. Many commit suicide rather than go on. Many lose their families over their jobs—there is a high rate of divorce among police officers. Many become alcoholics. I myself don't know how anyone can do that job and not drink. My hat is off to those who can. I'm glad it's their job and not mine; I would have killed myself long ago. So it was in Pete's case.

In the end the stress of the job took his family—he had been married for twelve years and had three lovely children—his home, his dignity and his job. He became an alcoholic, and he had reached a point where he couldn't take it anymore. The death, the violence, the inhumanity that he faced each and every day broke him and left him a hollow man who only wanted to be left alone. I felt that deep down Pete had a death wish but he didn't have the nerve to take his life outright, so was doing it slowly through his drinking. I never seen a man drink with the intensity of Pete. He was definitely trying to drown the pain and forget the past. His every waking hour was consumed with drinking; even when he worked, you knew a bottle wasn't far off. I always said if I ever got that way, I'd quit; little was I to know at the time but I was quickly headed in that direction.

I felt sorry for Pete though; you could see the pain and the sadness in his eyes. And while this alone would have been bad enough, he had also given up and didn't care anymore what happened to him. His family had given up on him long before. They had tried everything under God's earth to help him, but it all fell on deaf ears. Pete didn't want help; he just wanted to be left alone. Thank God I never reached that stage in my drinking. I knew many who had, and they were walking zombies waiting to die, or dead already. I came very close to that point before it was all over, but never crossed that final line that for many became utterly hopeless of ever getting the help they needed. One of my biggest fears when I finally realized I needed help was that people would give up on me before I had given up on myself. Thank God that never happened. A few in my family stuck it out with me to the end, until I finally did wake up and come to my senses, but now I'm getting way ahead of myself. This wasn't to take place for quite a few years yet.

The last I knew about Pete is that he had made a few trips to the hospital after throwing up blood and they had already told him he had cirrhosis of the liver. He was becoming very thin, but had a bloated stomach that made him look especially sick because his skin was starting to turn yellow. I left before he died, but I knew it was just a matter of time. Pete was a walking dead man, and surely also one of the Walking Wounded.

I almost died myself while in Miami, and although it wasn't due to drinking, alcohol certainly played a part in what happened to me. About two months after moving into the flophouse above the laundry, I had a confrontation with a Cuban gentleman who stayed at the same place. The altercation took place during an argument he was having with one of the many retired gentlemen who lived there with us. It was over a bed, of all things.

The Cuban wanted the bed that Pop, that's what I called him, had occupied for over a year now. Both the Cuban and myself had been drinking, and when he hit Pop that was just too much for me. I stepped between them to keep Pop from getting hurt, when out of nowhere out came a twelve-inch butcher knife. I never seen the knife, nor did I see it coming. He struck me in the belly, and at first there was no pain at all. In fact I didn't even know what had happened until I decked the Cuban and knocked him out. All of a sudden I could feel something warm running down my legs. I looked down and my shirt was soaked with blood as were my pants. I lifted my shirt, and there on the left side of my stomach was a big gaping hole, with something long and stringy hanging out of it—my intestines.

I gathered up my intestines in my hand, coupling them as best I could, and then for some reason, I'll never know why, I ran down the stairs and out into the street. I guess I was going into shock, at least that's what they told me afterwards. The desk clerk at the flophouse had by now called the police and an ambulance. They finally found me two blocks away, lying unconscious in a pool of my own blood on a sidewalk on N.W. 3rd St. They rushed me to the County Hospital, where I was quickly operated on and sewed back together.

It took over four hundred stitches to repair the damage the knife done inside of me, and as far as the hole went they left it pretty much open, to heal from the inside out. I had lost five feet of my large bowel, half of my stomach, and a small part of my spleen, as well as having a punctured lung. What finally almost killed me wasn't the injuries themselves, but complications from those injuries. You see, I had been drinking all that day, and before going back to the flophouse, had eaten a big meal. When I got stabbed and the knife pierced my stomach, everything inside of it went all over inside of me. I almost died from the infection and pneumonia that followed. At one point, I remember the doctor coming into my room and telling me very bluntly to get my affairs in order, because if they couldn't get my infection and the pneumonia—along with the fever that followed—under control I was going to die. I remember thinking to myself, this doctor doesn't know me very well, or he'd know I wasn't ready to die and that I wasn't going nowhere except out of this hospital as soon as I got better. Needless to say I lived to fight again, although for a while there it was touch and go.

I stayed in the hospital for seven weeks, at which time the police came to tell me they had caught the man who stabbed me, and to have me sign a complaint against him. I was supposed to go to his trial when I got out of the hospital to testify, but never did, so I guess they had to let him go free. All I wanted to do when I got out of the hospital was to get out of Miami, and I did just that. When I hit the streets, I headed north and in a day and a half ended up almost back where I first started out in Florida, in Tampa. I put Miami behind me and began all over again in Tampa, a place I came to like much better. I was never to return to Miami.

It was now early March 1984, still too cold to head north. I was what they referred to in Florida as a snowbird. I enjoyed the north immensely, except when the snow started flying. Then I had to head south. The south was more conducive to living in the streets; you had more options when it came to living conditions. In Tampa I once again became a literal street person, that is, someone who actually lives in the street. I was fairly familiar with Tampa, having been there briefly before.

There was a small area downtown that ran next to what I called the Hillsborough River. I'm not sure that's really what it was called, but that's how I remember it. This is what I referred to as the lower class skid row section of town, and was on the east side of the river. Another area that was frequented by street people was on Kennedy Blvd., just west of the river in the Hyde Park section of town. This also happened to be the location of the University of Tampa and this is where I took up residence. For a long time I lived under the bridge that separated the two areas, so I was kind of in the middle of both. It was also located right on the campus of the University.

Tampa was a good working town. It had several labor pools and a plasma bank all within walking distance. One of my favorite hangouts there was the Circus Bar, right on Kennedy Blvd., just north of the campus and near one of the labor pools that I worked out of regularly. It was also the place where I cashed my checks after work. The bar was owned by a man who had been a circus performer all his life, but was retired now, and ran the bar. It was typical of the local dives—small with a pool table and a jukebox. Its walls were lined with circus memorabilia: pictures, notices and the like, along with pictures of famous circus performers. Drinks were cheaper here than they were at other establishments that catered more to middle and upper class individuals.

I really liked Tampa, and for the most part worked every day that I chose too. The only problem was I was coming to a point in my drinking that I chose not to work some days. Sometimes I would just go to the Plasma Bank to get the few dollars I needed for that day. I was now drinking anything that contained alcohol—beer, wine, mouthwash, and an occasional bottle of whiskey when I could afford it. All the time I was in Tampa I lived in the streets, except for a brief stay in the Salvation Army Rehab Center to clean up my act for a while, and restore my wardrobe. I had a lot of acquaintances, but they were of the run-of-the mill type. Two people that I met in Tampa stick out in my mind, though.

Dan was from Green Bay, Wisconsin, where he'd lived all his life and been a die-hard Packers fan. In his early days he said he never missed a home game, but if you knew Green Bay, nobody in town missed a Packers home game. Football was a way of life up there. Dan was an outgoing person. He was five-eight and had red hair, blue eyes and a very light complexion covered with freckles. He dressed like most street people, wearing jeans and a sport shirt most of the time. He stayed in an old stable behind the University campus that hadn't been used for years. In fact I had heard that some of the students used that area too, for extracurricular activities, whatever they might be. I stayed away from there because I heard there had been some deaths back in that area that were not exactly Kosher, if you know what I mean.

Dan worked out of a couple of the same labor pools I did, and frequented some of the same haunts. Every once in a while, I'd run into him at the blood bank, too. Dan was an educated person, having graduated high school and gone to college. His family was very religious, and of course, didn't approve of his lifestyle. After high school, Dan got a job at one of the many dairies located in his area. He worked there for several years before finally succumbing to alcoholism and losing everything.

Dan was a little older than me, but when he was still very young married a girl he'd known all his life and started a family. He had two children. He had trouble with his family from the very start because of his drinking. Neither his mother nor his father ever touched alcohol. Dan had started drinking when he was sixteen years old and for a long time it was not a problem. But as time went on he got worse, as most of us did. He began having problems at home after he'd been married some time. That's the thing with alcoholism, it can take a long time and it sneaks up on you before you know it. Early on Dan realized he had a problem, and began seeking help the first time he and his wife separated.

Although it took him several tries, three rehab centers, and many stints in Alcoholics Anonymous, he finally thought he had his problem licked. In fact, he returned to school after his first year sober, and became an alcohol counselor, and from what I understand a damn good one. He even managed to get his family back, and was doing pretty well at getting his whole life back together. But you must realize, the life of an alcohol counselor is not an easy one. Especially if you care about people to the extent that Dan did. It is filled with many disappointments.

The fact of the matter is most alcoholics never stay sober for any length of time. This gave Dan, after a period of time, a sense of failure. He thought he'd be able to help everyone when in fact, only a small percentage of alcoholics make it in recovery. This is just a fact of life for the alcoholic. Dan put all his time into his work and when he wasn't at work, he was attending AA, and helping other alcoholics outside his work environment. This once again put a terrible strain on his marriage. Yes he was staying sober, but he never found a balance between his need to help others, and a healthy family life. His wife and children felt neglected, and no matter how much Dan tried to get them involved in the program they wouldn't. After three years of this, and all the arguments and disagreements, he and his wife again parted ways and she filed for divorce. This in itself devastated Dan, and that coupled with the fact he was becoming more and more disillusioned by trying to help others and failing, he soon succumbed once again to his disease.

Alcohol counselors have a higher rate of returning to their disease than do others because they are faced with it day in and day out, twenty-four hours a day. Dan tried several times, while still in Green Bay, to get back on his feet, but failed time and time again. His pride finally got the best of him, and he left town to avoid any further embarrassment, having once been a leader in his town in the fight against alcoholism.

He made several stops before finally arriving in Florida. In fact he was in the streets of Chicago the same time I was, though we never run into one another while we were there. It didn't take him long to return to form, and get worse. His drinking was progressing very rapidly now. And even though you'd think a person like him, knowing as much as he did about his disease, would be able to recover, as far as I know he never did. When I finally left Tampa he was still there, and still drinking. Maybe by now he's found his way back out, who knows? I can only hope that one day he did, because Dan was a beautiful person, and cared about his fellow man very much. In fact his feeling of helplessness is what inevitably led him back down that lonesome path of despair—he couldn't take it anymore.

Another person I'd like to tell you about is Joyce. I met Joyce at the blood bank, and hers is another sad story. Joyce is another of those people who had no business whatsoever being in the streets. She never asked for her fate, nor was I ever convinced she'd chosen it. Through circumstances beyond her control, she was thrust into a life where she didn't belong. Joyce was in her late forties when I met her and she'd been in the streets for over five years. She had brown hair, and green eyes, and looked even thinner than she was. Joyce never had a job the entire time she was in the streets. She was one of those street people you meet on the corner asking for change, one you would see rummaging through garbage cans behind restaurants for something to eat. She slept wherever her head might fall.

I was convinced that what had happened to Joyce was so traumatic it had caused her to have a complete mental breakdown and to lose all touch with reality. She had moments when you would talk to her and she made complete sense, then there were other times when she made no sense at all. She fluttered in and out of reality all the time, but she was completely harmless. I always felt that Joyce posed more of a threat to herself than she did to anyone else. I was always fearful something would happen to her. She didn't care anymore.

What, you might ask, can make a person like Joyce come to such a point in her life? I often tried to get her to check into a hospital and get some help, but whenever you mentioned hospital she went off the deep end. It was at these times when she was most harmful to herself, so I tried not to upset her any more than she already was. Joyce grew up in a small Midwestern town in Iowa, somewhere around Ames, but exactly where, she never said. She grew up and had a normal childhood from all I could understand, except that her parents died while she was in college at Ames—Iowa State University, I think.

She had a degree in teaching and for many years taught second grade in her hometown. She had met and married her husband right after college. She did say they went together for two years before getting married. They didn't have children right away, opting rather to concentrate on having a home and being financially secure before they took that step. Then after seven years of marriage, having bought a home and feeling relatively secure in their careers, they decided to have a family. She had two children right off the bat, two years apart. They then waited for three years and had two more, also two years apart. Joyce and her husband both came from similar backgrounds, both being single children, and both having lost their parents before they were twenty-five years old.

Then a tragedy took place, when her youngest children were one and two years old.

One day not long before Thanksgiving on a warm fall evening, Joyce went to the grocery store to get some things they needed for the house. Her husband stayed behind to watch the children. While she was gone, the best I can make out from what she had told me, the furnace in their cellar exploded and quickly engulfed the house in flames. Her husband was in the cellar when the explosion took place, for whatever reason, maybe he heard something or knew something was wrong, who knows?

At any rate he was killed instantly from all they can tell. All her children were upstairs in their bedrooms when the fire occurred. The house went up so fast, there was no time to react, even had there been someone there to respond to the tragedy. Neighbors called the fire department, and by the time Joyce returned from the store, they were already fighting the fire and there wasn't much of a house left. At first, Joyce hadn't any idea if her children and husband were safe or not, but soon realized that no one had made it out. She immediately went into a complete state of mental collapse. They took her to the hospital that evening and they admitted her to a mental ward soon afterwards.

She stayed in the mental ward for over seven months, and finally was released, but I am convinced she never recovered. She blamed herself for her children's death, saying if only she had taken them with her when she went to the store, if only she had been there, she could have done something. Whatever it may be, maybe her children would still be alive today if only she had been there. Now is where the details become clouded. When she left home or even how she came to be in Tampa is anybody's guess. From that point on I can only speculate that she had no family to speak of, nor did her husband, so she was all alone with no where to turn, and wanted to get away from the memories.

Joyce had periods of time in the streets when she was under the care of the Hillsborough Mental Health System, but they would just get her stable and back on medication, then turn her loose again. They had tried over the years to obtain housing for her, but she never stayed in those places—group homes, that is—where she could get help to stay on her medication and survive in this world, though nobody I knew at the time was more of a survivor than Joyce. It was her sense of reality that I worried about. I knew she could survive in the streets, but the conditions of her survival were the matter in question. Joyce is another of those people I knew who were still in the streets of Tampa when I left.

I have never seen her since, even though I've been back to Tampa a couple of times. Whatever happened to her I hope and pray was good, and that she finally got the help she needed so badly. But I can only hope, because too many times I have known the circumstances to get much worse and many did not survive at all, but died where they ended up among the Walking Wounded who never made it back home.

Sylvia was another story. She was seventeen when I first met her. At the time she was waiting tables in a local hash-house café. She was only working part-time and seldom had enough money to rent herself a room. She stayed with a group of other teenagers and runaways in an abandoned house that sat alone by itself, just off Bayshore Boulevard. There were at times as many as a dozen kids staying there. Sylvia was the only one I got to know. She often hung out at the same bars I did. Many of the kids were on drugs, but not Sylvia, although she did have a drinking problem. But then she had lots of problems. You see, Sylvia never wanted to be in the streets. She tried several times that I know of to get help from some of the local agencies, but their answer to her was to go back home, seeing she was underage. Well, she would have nothing to do with that, no matter what the cost. She wasn't going to return home.

Sylvia was a military brat. Her father was a career officer in the Army, a Lieutenant Colonel if I remember correctly. First you have to imagine Sylvia as she was. She was a very petite girl, only about four-foot-seven and eighty pounds soaking wet. She was blonde and blue-eyed and dressed like a Barbie doll. She looked all of twelve years old. How or why anyone gave her a job is anyone's guess. Maybe she had some false ID. Lots of kids in the streets seemed pretty adept at getting false IDs. They weren't hard to come by if you knew who to talk to. From the time Sylvia was old enough to walk and talk she had to answer to her father. She described him as one of the strictest disciplinarians I ever heard of. He literally brought his work home with him and expected the same excellence from his family as he did from the men under him at the base. I can only imagine how a child as young as Sylvia might have taken this treatment over so many years.

She often said she'd come home looking for a father and there wasn't one, only a drill instructor. Her clothes had to be folded a certain way, her room cleaned and kept to her father's standards. She went through regular inspections where her father would tear everything up and make her do it all over again. She had to be home from school at a certain time, and God forbid she should be thirty seconds late. She said every morning she and her brothers had to synchronize their watches with their father's so they would have no excuse. The whole house had to be kept a certain way and nothing could be out of place, or they would face punishment by their father.

And while he was never physically abusive to his kids or wife, you can imagine the extent of the mental abuse they must have endured. I cannot fathom the damage he done them. Here is a young girl who only wanted her father to love her, and tried her best to do exactly as he wanted, but nothing was ever good enough. She said she never knew her father to put his arms around any of the children and tell them he loved them, or even to give them a simple hug. My God, what that must have done to young minds!

In fact as strict as he was, I don't know where Sylvia ever came up with the courage to run away; things had to be a lot worse than we can realize. But at fourteen, this wonderful, charming, and likable young lady felt in her heart strongly enough that anything was better than home, even the streets. She had no one to turn to because her mother and brothers were as deathly afraid of her father as she was, but she was the one who mustered the courage to run away. Having traveled from base to base ever since she could remember and never having much contact with family other than her immediate one, she didn't even have any roots to return to. Her father was stationed at a base in California, Ft. Ord, I believe she said, when she finally got the courage to run away.

She went to Florida right away because that was as far away from her father as she could think of at the time. And also, she said, because that's where her fondest childhood memories were. It seems while her father had been stationed in Florida, she had made some friends at school that she for some reason felt would still be there after all the years. Needless to say she never did locate any of them, I don't even know if she tried. She got so wrapped up trying to survive in the streets, I don't believe she ever found time. She became so frightened of trying to get help getting off the streets, out of fear her father would find her and make her come home, that she gave up even that.

Then one day a call came into the police that shots had been fired at an old abandoned house on Bayshore that runaways were known to frequent. Upon responding to the call, they found Sylvia in an upstairs bedroom with a few bedrolls in it, shot once in the head. They said she died instantly. As far as I know the police never found out what happened, or even who done the shooting, and last I heard had written it off as a drug deal gone bad or some other type of retaliation.

Now here truly was a young lady who not only didn't want to be in the streets, but shouldn't have been there in the first place, a young girl forced to make a choice that she was much too young to make. A young girl who only wanted a father's love, and couldn't find it. Too young to be so old, too young to feel unloved, and far too young to die. Caught between an unkind world and an environment where love comes with a cost, she never learned what real love could be. She was too busy trying to survive and even then she didn't make it. Sylvia was a good friend, probably one of the few that I considered a friend and not just an acquaintance. But I couldn't give her the love that she was seeking. Even though I had the feeling she considered me a father figure, I couldn't give her the love that only her real father could give.

Outside of caring about her and what happened to her, I couldn't change her mind about what she should do to get help. The fear that she felt about having to return to a home that was void of all feelings and had nothing to offer was too strong. There was nothing I could do to change her mind, no matter how hard I tried and believe me I tried and my words fell on deaf ears. I miss Sylvia. She was without a doubt one of the Walking Wounded and she made an impact on my life. I learned that some circumstances are beyond our control and that sometimes the damage is so great that even the best intentions are to no avail. But even armed with that knowledge, you couldn't help but try, time and time again. So it was with Sylvia and me.

I went through some difficult times in Tampa myself. I started to binge drink, and I would go days without stopping or even sleeping. I'd go to work only long enough to amass money for my next binge. Many times rather than go to work, I'd stand on a street corner and panhandle to get enough money to drink on. What I couldn't get panhandling, I'd get from the blood bank, donating sometimes four times a week at two different blood banks under two different names. A very dangerous situation, let me assure you. The safe period for donating plasma was twice a week because it takes your body at least forty-eight hours to replace the white blood cells you've given up. Donating more than that was putting your life at significant risk, but I was rapidly approaching the point of not caring. All I could think about was my next drink and where it was going to come from.

Then, one evening in late May I was picked up wandering around downtown Tampa in a blackout, not knowing how I came to be there or even who I was. The police took me to the Hillsborough Mental Health Facility where I stayed for over two weeks. I was becoming a danger to myself and I didn't care. I met a girl there, and when I first got out went to live with her briefly. This was a mistake from the get go. It was the blind leading the blind—she was in as bad a shape as I was. I thought at first that she would fix me, but she couldn't even fix herself.

When I left her, I headed for the streets again and was soon right back into my old life. Feeling sure that a change of scenery was the magic pill I needed, I put together a bedroll and a few essential supplies and headed to a spot in north Tampa where trains were diverted north. With only four quarts of water—an absolute necessity—a carton of cigarettes, two loaves of bread, a large jar of peanut butter and one of jelly, I hopped a freight heading north, not giving a damn where it was going. I figured wherever it ended up would be better than Tampa, and maybe there, wherever that may be, I could put my life back together. But I forgot one important thing. I was taking my enemy with me, myself.

Just four days later, on an early summer morning in late June, I got off the train in, of all places, Hoboken, New Jersey, just across the Hudson River from New York City. This was only the second time in my life that I'd been in this area, having been here once before while still in the Army, stationed at Carlisle Barracks in Carlisle, Pennsylvania. But this time I was about to see more of New Jersey and New York than I ever seen before, and I was only there for five months.

Alone in a Crowd

There is nothing more dangerous in this world
Than a man who has nothing to lose
When within his life there is nothing more
And he is left with yesterday's news

When all about him is emptiness
And the walk has lost its power
The steps he takes, he took before
And the minutes change to hours

Hours to days he cannot face
Because the pain he can no longer bear
The world has ceased to be his shell
And the lion has lost his lair

When all about him, nothing seems
As the realm that he once knew
And death has become an alternative
And one and one is no longer two

It's the loneliness that one man feels
When in a crowd he is still alone
The heartache he faces each day of his life
Is the sorrow that is still unknown

When he knows not where he'll lay his head
Nor where his next meal will come from
When each day is filled with uncertainty
And he knows soon the end will come

Because tomorrow is not a promise
And today is already gone
Yesterday is just a memory
And he knows that he doesn't belong

Belong where his life has led him
He doesn't care what tomorrow will bring
Lost in a world, no one sees him
He's heard the fat lady sing

— December 1988

~ C H A P T E R 5 ~

Bowery Days OR *I Loved New York*

I spent only three days in Hoboken, just long enough to work out of one of the local labor pools and obtain enough money to move over and settle in New York City. I had stayed in Washington Park for three days while working in Hoboken, and got rousted by the local police six times. The police were starting to get aggravated with me, so it's probably best that I didn't stay longer than I did.

When I left New Jersey, I crossed over into Manhattan and stayed just long enough to have a few beers and decide I wasn't ready for Manhattan yet. That same day I caught a local and crossed over the Brooklyn Bridge into Brooklyn. I immediately headed for Flatbush, which was said to have a large concentration of street people and labor pools to work out of. For the first couple of days I stayed in Prospect Park, but quickly learned it was too hot there to stay for any length of time. I then moved up to an area around Flatbush Avenue and 7th Avenue, where I found an abandoned school bus behind an old burnt-out building. I stayed there for over a month.

Flatbush was a unique place with all its brownstone tenements and the many local shops that lined its streets. It had a sense of belonging about it, that's the best as I can describe it. I felt comfortable there. Flatbush was mostly a blue-collar working community, with lots of family values. It was also dotted with places where a street person could find haven—abandoned tenements and buildings that just sat unoccupied and open. Work was no problem—there was plenty to be had and lots of places to go to find it. For a couple of weeks, I done pretty well. I drank only moderately and seemed to be keeping a handle on staying out of trouble, but I continued to stay in the abandoned bus. Nobody bothered me there, except for one time that another street person tried to move in on me. I quickly put a stop to that by acting like I was out of my mind. He wanted nothing to do with me, so he moved on quickly. Looking back, I realize now how close that was to being the truth. You had to be crazy to live like I did in Brooklyn, especially with all the cheap flophouses you could stay at in the area. But I was tiring of flophouses and didn't like the crowds, preferring to be by myself.

I did meet one person in Brooklyn that I took a liking to right away, his name was Johnny. Johnny was from southwestern New York, Buffalo to be exact. Over the years, I ran into a lot of people from Buffalo, so much so that I began to wonder if anyone lived there anymore. Johnny had red hair, blue eyes and a fair complexion with lots of freckles. He was proud of his Irish ancestry, and talked about his parents having come to the United States from Ireland before he was born. His parents were hard working, with very strong family values. According to Johnny he had a great childhood. His family didn't have a lot, but they had all they needed and never went without. Johnny's dad had worked for the city of Buffalo in the parks department his entire life until retirement and his mother worked at a local manufacturer that made children's clothes.

Johnny graduated high school in 1965, just one year after me, which made him about my age. He was a thin lanky man, and stood all of six feet tall. He used to make me laugh; he had a way of saying things that sounded funny, whether they were or not. I think it was his brackish accent that made him that way. Johnny had done a three-year stretch in the Navy, and a year in Vietnam.

That was another reason I took to him so quickly; I had a special feeling for Vietnam veterans. He spent all his time in Vietnam on a ship off the coast in the South China Sea. He was a fireman on the ship. Vietnam hadn't done to him what it had to so many others I knew, and I was glad to know not everyone came through it so messed up.

Upon returning home, he met a local girl and got married. Johnny applied for and got a job with the local Fire Department. He had to go to school for six months to get it, but had no problems because of his Navy experience. He and his wife didn't start a family right away, but opted to concentrate on their careers first. Johnny worked while his wife went to school and got her nursing degree. The first five years of their marriage, according to Johnny, were great. But after his wife started working she started becoming very independent. She acted as though she didn't need Johnny anymore, and arguments ensued. They became more and more intense, until one day Johnny came home from work unexpectedly and found his wife in bed with his best friend. Johnny immediately packed his bags and left. Even after all that Johnny was making it fairly well.

He moved back in with his parents for a while and everything was fine. The straw that broke the camel's back for Johnny was a fire he attended to in the winter of 1976. It was around Christmas time and the air was festive. The call came into the department in the early evening hours, and they responded in minutes. By the time he got to the fire, a single family dwelling, it was already engulfed in flames.

Johnny recalled hearing screams coming from within the house as soon as he pulled up. He and another fireman tried desperately to reach the area of the screams, but were unable to because of the intense flames. When the fire was finally put out, and they went into the dwelling to check on the inhabitants, they found an entire family, all huddled together in one of the bedrooms and all dead. A mother, father and three children, ranging in age from six months to seven years. The mother still had the baby clutched in her arms, and the rest of the children were covered by their parents, who had been trying to protect them. Johnny snapped. This wasn't the first time he had experienced death in his job, but he said it was the first of this type and magnitude. And it was compounded by being a holiday. A Christmas tree was said to have started the fire.

A week after the fire, Johnny had a complete nervous breakdown, and ended up in a mental ward. He spent three weeks in the hospital, and upon returning home, never worked at the fire department again. He tried several other jobs, but none of them panned out. He couldn't get the sight of the baby in its mother's arms out of his mind. Up to this point in his life Johnny had never taken a drink, but when the drugs from the hospital could no longer take away the pain and the memories away, coupled with his broken marriage, he started drinking and drinking heavily. He had many stints with the local law enforcement agencies, and had gotten to the point where no matter what he done he was constantly in trouble with the law. In Johnny's mind this was too much for his aging parents, so he decided he had to get away. He went to New York City and had been there ever since.

This was in the spring of 1977 and it was now July of 1984, so he'd been in the streets for over seven years. Johnny used to make light of things, but I believe that was just one of his coping systems to hide the pain he felt. He liked to make others laugh, I think, because he found it hard to laugh himself. Johnny and I were tight, all the time I was there. We were together often enough that I got to know him pretty well. He was like a brother to me. When I finally left New York, he was still there. I don't know if he ever let his family know where he was, he never said. But I have a feeling if he had they would have come and got him and took him home. He loved his family very much, and was only doing what he was doing to protect them. Johnny was another of the Walking Wounded who had found a pain he was unable to bear and was coping with it the best way he knew how. He wasn't a bad person, just a very sick one, like many of us were. We were sick and we thought we were bad. I can't explain it any better than that.

New York was a smorgasbord of inhabitants. When they say that the city is a melting pot, that's exactly what they mean. I know of nowhere in the world that had such diversity. Although I didn't find it to be one of the friendliest places I'd ever been, I can understand why. New York was so big, and everyone seemed to have their own agenda. Even the native New Yorkers seemed to be overwhelmed by the size and the numbers. There was so much to do in New York you could easily find something different all the time.

It was also an easy town to get around in. You had the subway as well as the local buses that afforded you transportation anywhere in the city, seven days a week. I often when bored would take a day and go to Coney Island, right on the southern tip of Brooklyn. You couldn't find a better hot dog anywhere, unless you were at Yankee Stadium. Then you had the Bronx to the north, and Queens in-between. Staten Island to the southwest, and then there was Manhattan, the hub of the whole city. If you couldn't find what you were looking for in New York, you just weren't looking. I truly loved New York. Had it been farther to the south I would have stayed there year 'round, but winters in New York were anything but friendly. They reflected the mood of the people. New York had its share of snowbirds, those who summered in New York and wintered in Florida, not only among the street people, but the locals too.

I often enjoyed singling out certain people, especially among the street people. I was drawn to those that most had nothing to do with, the untouchables as I called them. These people often had the most fascinating stories. I loved hearing about their lives, and what brought them to be where they were. I'd do this several ways, depending on the circumstances of the meeting. Sometimes I would just take them out for a drink, or even a small bite to eat, depending on my own finances. I seemed to be drawn to these individuals. Maybe it was through my own need to know that I myself didn't have it so bad; there was always someone who had it tougher than me.

One of these people was Sadie. Sadie was a bag lady, and typical of a lot of her type I came across over the years.

I met Sadie in Flatbush. Her territory was between Ditmas Avenue and Avenue P. She liked to trade at the many second-hand shops that monopolized that area. She'd find the damnedest things in dumpsters, and could always turn junk into money. Sadie was sixty-four when I met her and she'd been in the streets, according to her, for twenty years. She had been a career woman in the military, having spent twenty years in the Army. She had worked as a clerk in finance, and worked herself up to department head before she retired—this being why she was so good with figures, and knew how to make something out of nothing.

Sadie was a small, very stout woman, and a more street-wise person you couldn't find. She'd been through it all, knew just where to stay at night and not be bothered, where the best spots were for obtaining anything from food, to clothes, to collectibles. If you wanted to find anything, or know the gossip of the streets, all you had to do was ask Sadie. She was always in tune with her surroundings, and knew when to stay and when to go. She lived in the streets of Brooklyn, year 'round, even in the winter. She was adept at keeping warm no matter what the weather. She always wore several layers of clothing, and always had extra in her shopping cart. She kept everything in that cart from personal cleaning items to lots of blankets, as well as her items for trading.

Sadie was a real trader at heart. Had she lived in the times of the Old West, I'm sure she would have been a fur trader or something along those lines. Sadie was a real sweetheart; she could find good in everyone. And how she loved to talk. She often spoke of her days in the Army. Having joined in her early twenties, she knew right away that would be her life. Sadie never married, and didn't have any children; the service was her life and her family.

She was forced to take an early retirement because of her health, although I cannot imagine what could have been wrong with her. She never said. It was always a sore spot to her, and she didn't like to talk much about it except to say she resented that they made her retire before she was ready. After her retirement, she tried doing several things to fit into civilian life, but couldn't adjust. It was almost like she had been institutionalized, and in a way she had been. As I said, the Army was her life and her family, and when she was forced to retire it was like her family divorced her. At least this is how she related it to me. She felt abandoned and alone, unable to adjust, and she chose the streets. Her days were highly regimented in that everything was a routine, a habit left over from her years in the service. For a street person, her life was better organized than anyone I'd ever known. If you knew her routine, you could always find Sadie, because she was at the same place, the same time, doing the same thing at any given time of day. If she ever had to deviate from that schedule, it really screwed her up, and she had trouble getting back on track.

Sadie was one of those people who chose the streets because they were more comfortable to her than "real" life. She never bothered anyone and never asked for anything. She was very independent, and made it on her own. That's the way she was. Many times she helped me out, when it should have been the other way around. Sadie liked people and never had a bad word to say about anyone. Everyone who knew her liked Sadie, too. And if anyone ever bothered her—someone new to the area—they had the whole of Brooklyn to answer to.

I know of many people Sadie helped out, one way or the other. She was like a mother to all the street people, and was always ready to listen or lend a helping hand whenever she could. I don't look at Sadie's situation as being a sad one, because she was happy. She had lots of friends and got by without help from anyone, which is the way she liked it. I believe had you taken Sadie out of the streets, she would have died. In the streets she felt alive and useful. She was after all the ultimate recycler. She not only recycled goods, she salvaged people by letting them know they had a least one friend who really cared about them. She had to have saved a few lives when they were fragile and ready to give up—she could always give you a reason to go on.

Sometimes even today, I miss Sadie and could use one of her gentle hugs. She was a touchy-feely person who thought a hug could cure a lot of ill feelings, and she was right. Many times that I felt bad, a hug from Sadie brought me back to reality and gave me a desire to continue when all I had wanted to do was give up. The streets to Sadie were like the Army: her life and her family, and she felt comfortable doing what she was doing. One of the Walking Wounded? Maybe not. She was, after all, where she wanted to be, doing what she wanted to do, and was happy in that environment. If you're still out there Sadie, I love you, and I miss you very much.

Another person I met in Brooklyn was Pat. Pat was another redheaded Irishman with bright blue eyes. It seemed there were a lot of Irishmen in New York, and if they weren't policemen or firemen, they were politicians or ex-politicians. So it was with Pat. In his heyday he'd been a career politician who became disillusioned by society and his inability to make things better, or to change the process by which politicians operated. He often referred to politics as one of the most corrupt professions in society.

Pat was originally from New York City, having grown up in the Elmhurst section of Queens. He got involved in politics after he'd been an official with the Longshoreman's Union. At a young age he got involved in local politics, first becoming an alderman as they were called back then. He went on to hold higher offices within the borough, but in order to protect his anonymity, would not reveal just what office he finally held that brought about his demise in politics, and ended with him living in the street.

I really liked Pat, but for a street person, he was too idealistic. He wanted a perfect world, and we all know that is not possible. His desire for perfection was his ultimate downfall. He lived in a dream world, that's the best that I can describe it, and he couldn't get it through his head that he couldn't change things by himself. It takes more than one person working towards the same goals to effect significant change. He finally reached the point where he became so frustrated that he could cope no longer, living the lie he felt he'd been living.

Pat was a drinking man, but I have to say it never interfered with his life. He worked every day out of one of the many labor pools, and was as self-sufficient as one can be on minimum wage. He was funny to be around, and had a lot of good stories about local politics that made you think he must have been in the middle of things to know what he knew. He could tell you some stories that could get you killed if you spread them around, I'm serious. Every once in a while Pat would disappear for a week at a time and I'd wonder if he'd gotten into trouble.

I never found out where he went or what he did during these absences. It might have had something to do with his kids. He had been married three times and had five children, ranging in age from eleven to twenty-six. But he never told anyone, that I know of, about his frequent disappearances. Pat was a proud man but always felt like a failure, not only to his profession, but also to his family. He was another of those street people who didn't ask anyone for anything, determined to be self-sufficient, and make it with no one else's help.

He always kept a bed in one of the local two-dollar flophouses, preferring to know each night where he would lay his head. He seldom ate at the missions, except for maybe holidays like Thanksgiving and Christmas, when a traditional meal was served and work was scarce. Pat never bothered anyone, and wouldn't hurt a fly. He was another one of the invisible people you knew were there, but never saw. Never a burden to society even in his hour of need, he made it on his own, the best way that he could.

In August of 1984 I moved to the Bowery on Manhattan's lower east side. The Bowery was an area well known as skid row, and was home for some of the most hardcore street people. I was working at a construction site on Delancey Street in the Bowery and happened into a small mom-and-pop restaurant at lunchtime to get a sandwich. As I entered the restaurant, I noticed a sign in the window, "Help Wanted, Cook." Sid was the owner of the place, and his wife's name was Molly. They ran the restaurant by themselves. It just so happened Molly had taken sick, and Sid decided to take on someone to help him until she got well. I explained my situation to Sid, and told him of my experience as a cook, and he hired me right on the spot. He felt my experience with Cajun dishes would add a little flare to his modest east-side establishment. I told him I had no permanent place to stay, so he set up a cot in the back storage room, and I became the night watchman as well. I wasn't a very good one, though, because when I wasn't working I was drinking most of the time. But Sid didn't know that, and anyways, I was better than what he had before: an aging dog with most of his teeth missing. And yet that old dog was good company, and I enjoyed having him around.

His name was Butch. I took to the restaurant right away, and Sid and Molly both kind of adopted me as the son they never had.

They were in their early sixties and never had any children, and although neither Sid nor Molly ever said why, I felt it wasn't out of choice, but rather a matter of inability. They both loved people, all people, and enjoyed the contact they had with the street people as well as their regular local customers. A lot of retirees lived in the area, and Sid's prices were cheap enough, and the meals nutritious enough, to warrant their business. Besides, Sid's food portions were always so big, I questioned how he could ever make a living the way he operated. Very seldom would he turn anyone down who really looked like they needed a meal. That's the way he and Molly were. I had only worked at the restaurant for four days when I met Doc.

Doc was a regular street person in the area. He mostly stayed in one of the many nearby missions. When he couldn't get a bed at one of the missions he stayed wherever he could. He came into the restaurant every morning about five o'clock for coffee and two homemade biscuits with jelly. The whole time I was there he never had anything different. He worked, when he could, out of one of the labor pools that provided dishwashers for other restaurants in Manhattan. When he couldn't get work there, he hung paper— advertisements—all around the city for a few dollars a day, usually less than minimum wage.

Doc, like many of us, had a drinking problem, so he didn't work on a regular basis, but did manage to keep a couple of dollars in his pocket, for medicinal purposes, as he would say. Doc was a likable man in his early fifties with gray hair and gray eyes. He was a heavy-set five-foot-eight. He always dressed in a suit without a tie, and although it was never very clean, he managed to get another when the one he had got too bad. The only thing was they all appeared to have come out of the thirties. All he needed was a chain and a pair of spats and he'd look like one of the wiseguys, a local hood.

He very seldom shaved, and when he did, he cut himself a lot. Unusual I'd say, for a man of his original profession. You see, at one time, Doc was actually a doctor, with a lucrative practice in Queens. He had been married and divorced twice, and one of the reasons he was in the Bowery was that he was hiding from his second wife. Doc told me he'd left his practice nine years before, a direct result of the death of a child under his care and the malpractice suit that followed. He had insurance as most doctors had, so it wasn't the money that made him leave his practice, but rather that he blamed himself for the child's death. The child had been only three years old when he prescribed some medication that killed it. He often told me that in all honesty, he felt he was doing the right thing by prescribing the medication he did. It's just that it turned out not to be the right medication for this child. And even though he felt he had done the right thing in his heart, he believed if only he'd known more about the medication and the possible side-effects on certain individuals, he'd not have prescribed it. He never made any excuses, and accepted full responsibility for the child's death, but afterwards made a conscious decision never to allow anything like it to ever happen again. So he gave up his practice, went broke over the malpractice, and found himself penniless and in the streets with a wife hunting him for more alimony and child support.

Now I'm not saying what Doc done was right, but I think his decision was pretty responsible, as far as his practice went. If he couldn't give the best possible care to his patients and was putting them at risk because of his own shortcomings, it was better for all concerned if he just gave it up. He didn't want the responsibility of ever causing someone's death again, especially that of an innocent child. As far as his wife was concerned, maybe he wasn't so responsible, but he was penniless and had nothing more to give. She had gotten everything else, and to avoid going to jail he chose to hide instead. And believe me, there was no better place to hide than the Bowery. People who lived there seemed to disappear. They were just faces in a crowd of shattered humanity.

Most people who lived in the Bowery became transparent to those around them. Doc was a good person, and many times I saw him help another homeless person out when they were sick; he'd miss work sometimes in order to help another human being. He never treated anyone for anything more than an occasional abrasion or cut, but rather got them to a place where they could receive proper treatment, and could often tell you what was wrong with you, before it got too bad. He was in a way the Bowery's own personal nurse and consultant to the homeless, and believe you me, the Bowery could have used many more like him.

I seen a lot of deaths in the Bowery, too numerous to mention, and lots I never even got a chance to know. The Bowery seemed to be, for a lot of its inhabitants, the last house on the block. Many just went there to die, I know. Maybe not consciously, but that was the inevitable result. Hardly a day went by when the sun came up that you didn't find someone in an alley or a door stoop, dead, many as a direct result of their drinking, or victims of the rampant crime that took place down there. The Bowery could be a violent place, yet at the same time mean security for those who anywhere else would be outcasts. Death was a fact of life that you came to accept in the Bowery; it was around you everywhere.

Now on a lighter side, I'd like to tell you about one other person I came to fall in love with while living in the Bowery. Not all of these stories are sad; some people were better off in the Bowery than the place they came from originally. One such person was Don. I met him at the same place I had met Doc, the restaurant where I worked. Don was a street person only in the sense that he had no permanent home; he paid his rent by the day at a local hotel, and worked for minimum wage in one of the local labor pools. Don was only twenty-two years old with an average build and brown hair and brown eyes. He was originally from Paterson, NJ. and grew up in foster homes, his mother having abandoned him when he was just seven years old. Don was never adopted because he had some medical problems, not physically, but mentally. He wasn't retarded, but he was very slow, as I called him. I don't know how else to describe it. He was far from dumb, in fact quite intelligent; it just took him a while to catch on to things. He went to special classes while growing up that were designed to prepare him to be able to make it on his own one day, and in my estimation, had done a damn good job.

Don couldn't get the type of job that required split-second decisions, or for that matter, any decisions at all. He excelled at doing what he was told, as long as the task was physical and not mental. He was strong as a bull and not afraid to get dirty. This made him pretty popular with the local labor pools because he never complained, like a lot of us would, about some of the menial tasks we were sometimes asked to perform. Don was perfect for the labor pools—no one else would hire him and no one else really liked working for the labor pools like he did. Don loved that he had a job and he was making it on his own. He didn't have much to show for his efforts but at least he wasn't a burden to anyone, let alone society.

He enjoyed a drink from time to time, but I can honestly say I never seen him really drunk. He paid all his bills on time, and if he owed you anything, he'd pay you back promptly. He'd often charge a meal at the restaurant when he ran a little short, but always paid you back the next day, if not the same day. Don had no family, but everyone who'd been in the Bowery for any length of time looked out for him. He was pretty gullible, and could be taken advantage of real easy. Don had a lot of friends. He had a child-like attitude all the time; it was like he was always looking at something for the first time. He loved life and he loved people, and was real proud of himself for being able to live on his own. Some of the foster homes he'd been in as a kid were not all that nice—some were, but some weren't. All he knew was that he didn't ever want to have to rely on anyone else ever again to take care of him.

Don wouldn't hurt a fly, and often you'd find him wandering the streets with some animal following him around. He adopted every stray. They'd stay with him awhile, then disappear as quick as they had come. Then a couple of days later, you'd see him with another one in tow. The Bowery was a perfect place for Don. He could afford the rent, and the prices in the restaurants were cheap enough to afford him a good nutritional meal at a reasonable price. He had enough money to survive, but not much else. The important thing here to remember was that Don was happy, and after all, isn't that what we all desire out of life? Maybe Don could have made it somewhere else, but would he have been as well accepted by his peers as he was in the Bowery? I think not. Society can be cruel at times—at least that's been my experience.

There were a lot of people like Don all across the country, male and female, who, had it not been for the acceptance you find in a community like ours on skid rows across the country, would have no other place to go where they could feel welcomed for who they are and not what they are. Let's face it, in normal society people are a little afraid of people like Don, and somewhat distrustful of them because they're different. That's the way things are in the real world.

I enjoyed my stay in New York City. It was a lot like Chicago in the way the neighborhoods were set up. But it was getting late in the year, and I could feel winter in the air. It was, by now, early October of 1984. While my usual choice for the winter was Florida, I decided instead this winter to hold up in Louisiana, New Orleans to be exact. New Orleans was one of those towns you just kept going back to; it got in your blood. Besides, I knew the area already, knew I could find a job without much trouble, and knew I could find a place to stay until I got on my feet. So on October 12, 1984, I'd managed to save enough money for a bus ticket with a little extra pocket change, and I was on my way back to New Orleans.

But other things in my life were rapidly evolving, too. I was getting worse with every passing month. Because of my deteriorating mental state, my life was changing. I worked less, and drank more. My methods of obtaining the money I needed to keep up my drinking habit also changed, as did the choices of where I stayed.

Although I had often lived literally in the streets before, my choices became less prudent. I was beginning to sleep wherever I passed out, even on doorsteps, something I said I'd never do. My priorities changed as my drinking progressed. I'd say to myself, "When I get that bad I'll quit drinking," then when I reached that stage, I'd say "No, I meant when I get that bad," the next step down the ladder, until finally I was like all those I said I'd never be like. But even at my worst, I was still drawn to others and their stories. I was fascinated by what had made others make the choices they made. I couldn't help myself. I felt that somewhere in life I had a mission, and without realizing it back then, I realize now, this must have been it: to let others know that everybody who lives under these circumstances is not there by choice. I mean they may have made a conscious decision to get to that point, but that decision was based on circumstances beyond their control. Not like me.

While some might consider me one of the Walking Wounded, I never put myself in that category. Yes, there was my disillusionment in Vietnam, and other factors that contributed to my choices. I still feel that I had decided to be where I was. I was intrigued by how others came to be there along with me. My drinking and my curiosity led me to make my choices, along with my nomadic

140

spirit. I went searching for my purpose in life, and found it in the very place I went to search.

As I left New York, I couldn't help but feel some regret because somehow I knew I'd never be back. I loved New York, but it wasn't conducive to my attitude at the time. I didn't want to die in the Bowery, though I always figured my life would end alone and in the streets somewhere. But for now I wasn't ready to go. As the bus headed south, I had an air of anticipation, as I did with most of my moves. I always thought, this time it will be different. When I reached New Orleans, I had little in my pocket—just enough for a few drinks—but I was confident that some of the people I knew from my last stay in New Orleans would still be there and would help me out.

I was both right and wrong in this assumption; some were still there, but many more had moved on, just as I had. Not only that, but some of the places that I was so familiar with were gone too. Places have a way of changing—just like people, they never stay exactly the same. The first place I headed for was the Dixie Bar and Hotel on Crondelet Street. When I arrived at that location, much to my surprise, it no longer existed. I panicked briefly, then realized there were other places I knew as well. Besides the Dixie, Irene's Zoo Review was also gone just across the street, so I went around the corner to the Mansion, Radar and Lulu's place. Although Radar was no longer around as much (he and Lulu had broke up), she still ran the place and there at the end of the bar was Barbara, an old and familiar face, as were a few others I recognized from before.

As my investigations continued, I ran into more and more of the people I knew from before and who knew me. But somehow things didn't feel the same, I couldn't put my finger on it, I just knew it wasn't. As it turned out, I was what was different. I just didn't realize it at the time. The first night I done something I very seldom had done in the past, I stayed at the mission on Camp Street. The next morning, I got up early and headed for the labor pool. I needed some money to get by. I didn't get out the first day, so I spent the remainder of the day at the plasma bank, donating blood to get twelve dollars for a couple of bottles of wine that night.

In the past I very seldom drank wine, but my money was funny, and I needed something, so I chose the path of least resistance, and a method to stretch what little I had. The next couple of days I got out of the labor pools and had a little more. When the weekend came, I headed for the area of town known as Uptown. I had heard that the man who use to run the Dixie now ran a place—just a flophouse, no bar—down on Annunciation Street. When I arrived there I immediately recognized several of those people who use to live at the Dixie when I had been there before. The man who ran the flophouse was also one of the regulars I'd gotten to know. They were still in the business of getting people offshore, and knowing my background and me personally, let me stay until I could get on my feet and pay them back. I wasn't there very long before I was headed back offshore again. Even here I somehow felt things weren't quite the same. I'd only work long enough to pay my bills and hang on a good drunk, then when I was broke and in debt—and only then—would I go back to work. Things were seeming less and less permanent.

While staying at this place, I made an acquaintance named Eddie. He use to work offshore like the others and me, but he was now on SSI. He'd hurt his back real bad in an accident, and could no longer work. I spent a lot of time with Eddie, drinking and sharing experiences. He was about twenty years older than me and had been around the oil fields longer than I had, although mostly he'd worked on the boats. Eddie was not very heavy, but he was always in a lot of pain. His back bothered him most of the time. He drank a lot, I believe to relieve the pain. It seemed the only time he felt comfortable was when he had a good buzz going.

Eddie was where he was out of necessity. His SSI only went so far, and he had to live as cheap as he could in order to get by. He had a daughter who didn't live far away, somewhere around Gulfport, Mississippi. She came to visit him often, and she would bring him extra money. But she could never get him to come live with her. He tried a couple of times, but didn't like having to depend on his daughter; he was too independent, and insisted on not being a burden. He made frequent trips to the doctor. Sometimes he'd get so bad that he couldn't even walk and the ambulance had to come get him. He couldn't move otherwise. Eddie bought me many a drink, and even from time to time slipped me a few dollars when I needed it. He was very good to me and I could never figure out why, because to most of the others he was pretty antisocial. If you worked regular and made your own way, you were all right to Eddie but if you were a bum, as he called them, he wanted nothing to do with you.

Eddie was Irish, his father having come from the old country before Eddie was born. His mother was of an Indian background, from the Choctaw tribe in Mississippi. He was very proud of his Irish-Indian ancestry, and spoke of it often. Eddie looked older than his years, and had more wisdom about him than most his age. I would sit and listen to him for hours. I guess if I ever had a friend, Eddie was it. He asked nothing of me, except my company, and expected nothing from me except respect. I liked Eddie a lot. He was an oasis to me when I needed someone only to be there and listen. We had many good times together, and never left the confines of the house. I use to make all his runs for him. He didn't get around very good, even though he tried the best he could to get out himself from time to time. But he never wandered far—just to walk to the store a block away was a chore for him. If he went anywhere else, he'd call a cab or get someone to take him.

I began to work less and less, until finally I couldn't even afford to stay at the flophouse, so I moved out and moved under a highway overpass just a few blocks away. I was going downhill fast. I turned to giving plasma as often as I could, and even started to panhandle a little to get the money to buy another bottle. It was during this time that I met Sam. Sam's story was another sad one. I don't know why, but those people were either drawn to me or I to them, I'm not sure which; maybe a little of both. I only know wherever I went, they would appear.

Sam was a mirror image of me at that time. He was in almost the same stages of disease as I was. He was only two years older than me, and at the time it gave me a wake up call that I noted, but didn't act upon. Sam wandered into my area one day, very down and despondent, unable to even work steady out of the labor pools, not having a place to stay, and not knowing where his next meal was coming from, let alone his next bottle. This was the same state I was in; little else mattered to me except that next drink and how to get it. Sam had been in this state a little longer than me, so his panhandling skills had progressed better than mine. When he went out to get some money for a bottle, he always came back with one.

During this period both Sam and I let ourselves go terribly. We were lucky to take a bath once a week, though sometimes more. Our clothes were dirty most of the time, and we didn't care—we were obsessed with that next drink. I can understand how people become so irritated with panhandlers; we were really persistent at times. How people even put up with us at all is a mystery to me. I know had the shoe been on the other foot I would have surely been agitated. I'll take this time to apologize to anyone I may have offended, and to thank those who took pity on me and helped me out. I never wanted to reach that stage, but it seemed like a natural progression for an alcoholic who lives on the street as long as Sam and I did. Sam had a background like many I came to know in the streets who didn't seem to fit the kind of person you'd expect to find there.

Sam was a Vietnam veteran but didn't have the usual symptoms that some of us had. That is to say, he had accepted what had happened, and the way society was, rather than trying to fight it. In fact, after he came home from Vietnam, he enrolled in college where he studied finance and got a degree in Investment Banking. He never really worked in the banking industry, but rather opted for a career on Wall Street as a broker. Sam was from Albany, New York and moved to Manhattan after graduation to pursue his career. Just from the looks of Sam, he was someone you'd expect to see in a three-piece suit; someone you'd find behind a desk at a bank, dealing with other people's money. Even when Sam was disheveled he looked important, he just had that air about him.

He stood about six-foot tall, and weighed about two hundred and twenty pounds in his heyday. Then however, he only weighed around a hundred and fifty pounds, making him look very thin. This was due of course to our lifestyle: we'd rather drink than eat. If we hadn't eaten in over three days and were starving and only had a few dollars in our pockets, you can be sure we didn't waste it on food, but rather got a bottle. Sam started out on Wall Street while he was still in college. During term breaks and summer vacations he worked on the floor, buying and selling stocks with a flick of the hand. Sam told me this took a terrible toll on him, both physically and mentally. But when he graduated, he secured a job with one of the big brokerage firms in New York. He told me which one, but I have forgotten. In the beginning he often spoke of the power he had, the ability to make or break someone in a split second. Working with other people's money, not having to risk any of his own, this is what gave him his feeling of ultimate power, and for a while he thrived on it. But after working on Wall St. for over sixteen years, and being very successful at what he done, he began to be disillusioned about the role he played in the lives of others.

At first he was only drinking socially, but as time progressed so did his drinking. He began to make a lot of bad decisions, and his partners were becoming less and less confident of his ability. They began to give him extra time off to regain his composure. He'd check into a rehab center, get to feeling better, go back to work and be all right for a while, then the walls would crumble again. Over the many years of pressure, coupled with his drinking, Sam developed ulcers and other physical problems, in addition to becoming more and more mentally unstable. Then one day he had a complete mental breakdown, was put in a sanitarium and never regained his composure enough to return to work. Sam had been married once, and had two children. His wife had divorced him years before his breakdown.

The one thing Sam always said that he done right during all the time he was into investments was to set up a trust fund of stocks and bonds that would take care of his children throughout their childhood, through college and even beyond if they were handled right. The law never came looking for Sam for nonsupport; his children were already provided for. But Sam missed them terribly. He loved his children very much, but couldn't stand to have them see him the way he was, so decided to stay out of their lives for everyone's sake.

One day Sam had been out most of the day, hustling a little bit of money and returned to camp with a bottle, but very tired. Sam usually made the runs to the store to get another bottle if we needed it, but for some reason, I don't recall why, this one particular time I made the run. Sam stayed back at the camp and rested. Between us we only had about twelve dollars; I had four, and Sam had eight. So I told Sam I would get this bottle and he could save what he had to get us a much-needed drink the next morning to get us going again. I couldn't have been gone more than ten minutes—the store was only a few blocks away—and when I left Sam he was alone and resting.

When I returned to the campsite, I found it all in disarray: our bedrolls had been torn apart, and our knapsacks had been gone through. At first I seen no sign of Sam, and I could only wonder what had happened. It was obvious someone had been there and was looking for something. As I continued to search the site for things that were missing, I glanced over near some brush, just to the left of the campsite, and noticed something that looked odd, but that I couldn't make out.

As I walked closer to the brush, the scene became clear. There was a hand sticking out of the bushes, and it was Sam. He had been beaten severely about the head, and a bloody two-by-four was lying next to him. I didn't have to examine him very much to tell that he was dead. His pockets had been turned inside out, and his back pocket was completely ripped off. It was obvious he had been robbed and killed for the eight dollars that he had in his pocket.

I called the police, and for a while I thought they believed I was the main suspect. But after questioning me, and talking to someone else who had seen two suspicious men walking out from that direction, one with blood all over his shirt, they finally believed me. I don't know why it was that all my years in the streets, I seemed to be around a lot of death. I could never figure out the reason for this, other than to blame my lifestyle. But I can tell you I experienced more death than I ever wanted to. I figured when I left Vietnam that I had left all that behind me, but it continued to follow me wherever I went. I stop to think now how close that came to being me. Had Sam and I stuck to our usual routine, I would have been there in camp when those men arrived, and I would be the one who was dead. And to top that off, my reasoning told me not to bother to move to another spot, because it was unlikely that lightning would strike in the same place twice. How insane can you be? I continued to live in the same place for a while longer, and kept to my normal routine.

I told the police all I knew about Sam and where he came from, and I guess they got hold of his family and they came and got him. When I inquired about the arrangements, they told me he had already been claimed and taken back to New York. Here was a man who not only wouldn't, but couldn't hurt anyone or anything, just trying to get by as best he could under the circumstances, being as little a burden to his family as possible, dead before his time. Another victim of the environment we lived in, an accepted fact of life, that you could only hope and pray wouldn't happen to you. Sam was one of the Walking Wounded no more.

The Long Road Home

From out of the wilderness and into the light
Out of the darkness of one's own soul
A long and tedious journey begins
It's a long road to travel home to hold

A journey that begins with disclosure
Of the knowledge that hasn't been there
That your life had taken many wrong turns
And your heart has been left bare

Bare for all to see the misery
Of a life that once was aware
Of better ways and better things
But not in much need of repair

It's a desperate journey, but one you must make
If you're never again to roam
Each journey begins with one small step
As you travel the long road home

Because somewhere in this world there lies
The happiness you've been searching for
Your paths have crossed, like ships in the night
You just never opened the right door

So take that step to find your way
Each ending has a brand new start
If your heart is genuine, your journey begins
And you have done your part

—May 15, 1997

~ CHAPTER 6 ~

A Cry for Help or *The Long Road Home*

About a month after Sam was killed, I moved from under the overpass to an old abandoned factory about three blocks away. The area really wasn't any better, but it afforded me more shelter when the weather was bad. It was also more secluded, and a less traveled area; not many came back that way, and if they did they were usually only passing through. It was not the kind of place that even street people were drawn to. Besides it was over on Tchoupitoulas Street and really off the beaten path. I was becoming more and more of a loner. But throughout this stage of my life I still met many street people, although most of them were already in recovery when I got there, or entered before I left. It would still take me eight years before I found my magic pill and I finally quit drinking. I feel it's important that you know my progression through my battle with alcoholism, and the many paths it led me. It wasn't a change that took place overnight—as I said it took me over eight years after I finally decided to get some help before I finally got the message, and found something that worked for me.

It all started one morning in early January of 1985. I woke up like any other morning, and reached for my bottle. I had gotten two the night before, and started drinking like any other morning. I finished one bottle, and was starting on the second, when it hit me: I thought, I can't do this anymore. Not knowing what I was going to do right then, I left the camp and what was left in the second bottle, and started walking. As I sat on a bus bench at Lee's Circle, a lady came by and handed me a pamphlet of a religious nature. I read what it said, and other than the fact it said that Jesus loved me, I cannot tell you anything else that was in the pamphlet. And just like that I decided religion would fix me. I knew of only two missions in town who took in street people and had a program to get them back on their feet again. One was a Catholic Mission on Camp Street, and the other was a Baptist Mission, further down the street, close to Canal. The Catholic Mission was closer so I went there first, but there was no room at the inn. The program was full, a reality that struck many when they finally decided to get help. Many give up after the first try, and just go back to drinking. It's not hard to concede to your disease again; it's very subtle that way.

One of the most important things, I always said, and this has been my experience, is when an alcoholic finally decides they need help it is imperative that you get him or her out of their environment as soon as possible, before the disease takes over again. It is virtually impossible for an alcoholic to recover in an environment that is conducive to his or her disease. You must remove them from the temptation and put them into a sober environment if they are to have half a chance at recovery. Believe me I know, I've tried it the other way; maybe for some it worked, but if you drank like I did, I think it's impossible.

After being turned down at the Catholic Mission, I almost did give up. I needed help now, and I knew the longer it took me to get it, the less chance I had of making it at all. As I sat and contemplated my next move, I remembered there was another place just a few more blocks away that offered a program that might help, the Baptist Mission. I decided to give it one more try. If that didn't work, I wasn't sure what I'd do. I said a little prayer as I headed down the street, I wanted help that bad. I hadn't talked to God in a long time, so I knew I was serious. Don't get me wrong, I had nothing against God, I just thought he'd given up on me. Still, I thought a prayer couldn't hurt. When I arrived at the mission, an old hotel in the downtown area, I walked up to the front desk and expressed my desire for help. They sent me back to talk to a lady who I think was in charge of the place, and after a short interview, was admitted into their program.

The program consisted of Bible studies, church services every night, and twice on Sunday and Wednesday, plus you were assigned a task that helped keep the place going. Besides the program, they also offered meals to the homeless, and a place to stay occasionally. I thought sure I'd be assigned to the kitchen, with my cooking background, but to my surprise I was given a front desk job, assigning beds and doing paperwork for the people who sought to only stay the night. I dove head-long into the program. I was a model participant all the time I was there, though that didn't prove to be very long. But while I was there I met Tim.

Tim was about twenty-two, but much older in street years. He was typical of a lot of young people who chose the streets at a very young age. Tim had been there since he was fifteen. He had blond hair and blue eyes, stood about five-foot, eight inches tall, and weighed about a hundred and sixty pounds. He liked wearing baggy pants and shirts, the bigger the better. He walked with a limp, the result of an operation after an automobile accident with his parents when he was only six years old. Tim didn't come from a broken home, and for that matter was never abused, not in the physical sense anyways. But from the time he was eight years old, he and his two older sisters were left alone to fend for themselves.

Both Tim's parents were alcoholics, and when they weren't working, you could find them at the local bar. Tim grew up in Muncie, Indiana. By the time he was ten, he was already smoking marijuana and experimenting with pills. At twelve he was running with one of the smaller gangs in town. Growing up he didn't know much love, and very little discipline; he was free to do whatever he wanted. By the time he was thirteen he had already been in trouble with the law several times, mostly for minor offenses.

At fourteen he quit the smaller gangs, and joined a group of skinheads who, besides their far-out ideology, were heavy into hard drugs like cocaine and heroin. Tim said all he ever wanted was to feel like he belonged, that someone cared about him and would watch out for him, and help him along in life. Well he found what he was looking for, but it was all in the wrong places. Tim only lasted with the skinheads for a year; he couldn't accept their ideology. Somewhere along the line, growing up, he developed a conscience. I don't know where or how, but he had one—most unusual, considering the way he was raised and the people he hung out with.

Anyways, at fifteen Tim hit the road, and first he went to Los Angeles to try and find his way. Los Angeles proved to be a rough town for a small town kid like him, and he had a lot of trouble adapting. For a while he said he worked as a male prostitute on Hollywood Boulevard, hustling tricks for money to get by. He didn't like what he was doing, but felt it was the only way at the time. I honestly believe most individuals who choose this type of life don't like what they're doing, maybe with the exception of a very few. Anyways, this didn't last long. It was just too distasteful to him. He eventually met a young girl who also was a street person, and only sixteen years old. But she had a regular job as a waitress in a restaurant just down Sunset a ways, where a lot of young street people hung out to pass the time. Her name was Angela. She lived with a group of other young runaways in a closed, rundown hotel with a fence around it, next to Grumman's Chinese Theater on Hollywood Boulevard.

Tim moved in with her almost immediately. He thought he'd finally found the love he'd been searching for all these years. As it turned out Angela was into drugs, a lot deeper than even he was. She dealt drugs to supply her habit, and she turned tricks once in a while when she was short of money. Tim really believed in his heart that he loved her, and this tore him up. But then what did Tim know about love? He'd never experienced it himself, so anyone who showed him any affection at all was to him the only form of love he knew. His stint in Los Angeles didn't last long though, his girl Angela was found dead of an overdose only three months after they started living together. Confused and hurt, he felt he had to get out of town. It was too violent for him.

For the next six years he wandered around the country looking for a place to belong and be loved, and as young as he was, he'd been everywhere. Then at the age of twenty-two he ended up in New Orleans. Down and dejected, tired of running and being used, he checked into Covenant House, a drug rehab center mostly for young people. He cleaned up his act, at least his drug abuse, but before the program was complete he moved out. He couldn't deal with the strict rules they had. Back in the streets again he soon took up drinking, something he said he'd never do because of the way his parents had been. But in no time he felt he had become as bad as them. Hurt and disillusioned again, not knowing where to turn, he checked into the Baptist Mission one night, just to get a good night's sleep, and had been there ever since. That was over a year ago. He now was working for the powers that be, and was on payroll as a regular employee. For him religion was the answer.

Tim was happy, and talked about never leaving, and as far as I know he's still there. It was the answer for many who chose to go that path; some found it but some didn't. Who knows why it works for some and not for others? I guess it had to do partly with your expectations. There's something that will work for everyone if they live long enough to find it, but one thing didn't necessarily work for all. You had to find what worked for you. That's the way it was with me anyways; for me religion by itself didn't work. Now don't get me wrong, there's nothing wrong with religion. It worked for a lot of people; it just didn't work for me. I was looking for something different. I only stayed at the mission for about a month and a half when I decided to leave. It was too stifling; I needed more latitude. I left the mission at the end of February 1985 and decided it was time to leave town. I headed for Texas. Like always, I thought that a change might be just what I needed to get my life in order again.

I started out hitchhiking across Louisiana on Interstate 10. I didn't want to go back to Houston, but short on money, I decided to stop there long enough to earn enough money to get me somewhere else. As it was I ended up staying in Houston for three months. I concluded that the weather was still too cold to head north, so I would stay in Houston until the weather broke. For the first month in Houston I lived under the Pierce Elevated, a highway overpass on Pierce and Main streets, almost right in downtown Houston. A contingent of homeless had taken refuge there and it was like a little community in itself.

Between panhandling, working in the labor pool occasionally, and twice-a-week visits to the plasma bank, I quickly returned to my old habits. I can remember thinking, How the hell did this happen again? I really wanted help but my disease was still too strong. But then around the first of April 1985, I walked out Washington Avenue and checked into the Salvation Army Adult Rehabilitation Center, intending to stay until my life got straightened out.

I really liked the Salvation Army. Over the years they done a lot for me—they took care of me when I needed taking care of, they fed me when I was hungry, and clothed me when I had none to speak of. For a while they gave me some direction in my life, and hope— hope that a person could make it out of the depths of their sorrow and become a useful human being again. They gave me a job, and returned my self-respect. They loved me when I was not so lovable, and they never turned their backs on me in my hour of need. They were always there; they didn't judge me; they accepted me for who I was. I honestly believe had it not been for the Salvation Army and the many times they took me in when nobody else would, I would have been dead long ago. And even though I really never got sober through them, it was my experience with them that helped me get sober in the long run. Because little by little they restored this once broken human being to believing that one day I would make it. I cannot put into words what the Salvation Army has meant to me over the years, and to the many others who did make it as a direct result of their compassion and care, and to their insight to see the need for a place like the Adult Rehabilitation Center. I owe them my life. While I was staying there I drove truck for them, picking up their donations all across Houston, and it was during this time that I met Dwight.

Dwight was thirty, dark, tall and thin. He was born and raised in Minneapolis, Minnesota where he had a normal childhood, with wonderful parents; to hear him talk, he loved them very much. He had never been married, but did have one son from a relationship he was involved in for three years when he first got out of high school.

Dwight was a musician, and I don't believe there was an instrument he couldn't play—he was extremely talented. In fact at one time in his mid-twenties, he had played with one of the biggest rock groups of that time. It was then that he got involved with drugs and alcohol. It was such a part of society back then, and being in a rock group meant a lot of pressure. The long road trips, playing in different towns every night, not getting a lot of rest, and the pressures of being famous had its drawbacks. He said it started out innocently enough, just taking a few pills to be able to perform under pressure. But the demon continued to grow until it engulfed his whole being. In the end it got so bad that he couldn't perform at all, and was soon without a job.

It didn't take long and not only was he without a job, but he was broke, and found himself in the streets and penniless. Too proud to return home and allow his family to see him the way he was, he stayed in the streets for four years, stealing to buy drugs, and hustling in any way he could to get by. Then one day he'd had enough, heard about the program at the Salvation Army, found out where it was and checked himself in. For the street person, it was one of the few places around that offered help and asked for nothing in return, except that you be responsible for yourself. Dwight stayed in the program for almost a year, then right about the time I left, he felt ready to return home to his family. As far as I know, he is still straight and with his family, one of the many success stories from the Salvation Army Adult Rehabilitation Program. They saved a lot of human beings, but for some reason my time hadn't come yet. I still had places to go and people to meet before I would finally get the message.

I left the Salvation Army in late May with a little money in my pocket and headed for Dallas. I made it as far as San Antonio before I got too drunk to continue, ran out of money and had to start all over again. In San Antonio, I quickly returned to my old form, back in the streets. I bounced around San Antonio, living in an abandoned school bus not far from downtown and the convention center.

After being in San Antonio for just a month, I was picked up by the police, wandering around downtown, dazed and incoherent. The alcohol was really taking a toll on me. Believing me to be a danger to myself, if not society, I was taken before a judge and committed to the San Antonio State Hospital. Even I started to believe I was losing my mind, to the extent that when my hearing came up for review I didn't contest it when they wanted to keep me for a while, for my own good they said. I believed them and I stayed there for almost four months, at which time I met Carmen.

Carmen and I became quick friends and even though she was gay, we shared a special bond the whole time I was there. Carmen was only twenty-six. She was very butch, if you know what I mean, but had a gentle side to her once you got to know her. She put up a front to the other women, but to me, she was an entirely different person. I grew to love her very much like a sister. We were buddies, and virtually inseparable while we were there in the hospital together. I got to know Carmen probably better than anyone else had ever gotten to know her. Carmen came from a broken home and at a very young age she was sexually abused by her biological father. After her mother divorced her father and he disappeared, she went through a succession of men, two of whom also sexually abused her. At a very young age Carmen got into drugs and alcohol.

She finally ran away from home when she was fifteen. She lived in the streets for a while, and even worked as a prostitute when she was just sixteen. Many times she told me of stories where she was physically abused by the men she was with. It's no wonder she turned out the way she was. She'd been to hell and back already and was still only a young girl. She told me that when she was with a man, in the physical sense, it literally made her sick.

Why in hell we got along so well, I don't know, except for the fact that she loved my poetry, which I was into very heavily at the time. My poetry showed a lot of compassion and pain in

156

my own life, and she said she felt almost kindred to me. At any rate we were the best of pals. She had taken to one of the other girls, Andria, and I became good friends with her too. Andria had almost the same story as Carmen. But it was Carmen and I who confided in one another all the time. Many times we would just sit, hugging one another and crying over our stupid lives and where they had taken us. Here we were, at the last house on the block. We felt, after all, how much lower could you go than a mental hospital? The time I spent there was one of the most enlightening times I'd ever known and also the happiest since I'd been in the streets, if you can believe that. I don't know why, but for one of the first time in a lot of years, I felt safe and protected.

Then in September of 1985 Carmen was released from the hospital and went home to Victoria, Texas. Once again I felt all alone and sad. I had lost my best friend and it was devastating to me. I went into a deep state of depression, and the hospital almost put me in a ward much worse than the one I was already in. Fearing the worst and not really caring anymore, I walked away from the hospital one day and never went back. I stayed in San Antonio just long enough to get enough money to get up the road as far as Austin.

Once in Austin, I wasted no time and checked into the Salvation Army there. It was there that I met a counselor who would make a difference in my life, and would ultimately help me back on the road to recovery. Her name was Elaine, and even though she was not then, nor had ever been a street person, I feel it necessary to tell you a little bit about her. She was one of the many unheralded people who work tirelessly in the background to unselfishly help people like me. I fell in love with Elaine. She was not only a beautiful person on the outside, but her beauty inside was unmatched.

Elaine was just a few years younger than me, and stood all of five feet tall; she had brown hair and dark eyes. She worked as a counselor at the Salvation Army Adult Rehabilitation Center in Austin, Texas, and was herself a recovering alcoholic. She was one of the first women I met that truly cared about others, especially other alcoholics. She walked the talk as we use to say.

 She'd spend hours of her own time to help another alcoholic. Elaine was one of the first people that I opened up to honestly. We shared many an intimate moment in her office after working hours, just talking. She was one of the first to help me understand the inner workings of Alcoholics Anonymous, and even though it still took me many years after I met her to become sober, she planted a seed that stayed with me.

She was the first to tell me that I was a sick person, not a bad person, and make me understand that philosophy. When she put her arms around you, gave you a hug when you were in pain, and said she loved you, you knew she meant it. Never before had I met a person who worked so hard helping others, asking for nothing in return. She taught me what unconditional love meant. I stayed longer in this program than I had in any others because of her, and I learned a lot about myself through her. She had a way about her that made you want to open up to her and be honest.

So I'm just taking this time to thank Elaine—not her real name, but she knows who she is—for the time she loved me when I was unlovable and no one else would. At a time in my life when I didn't know which direction to go, she led me. I know in my heart, had I never met Elaine, I would still be wandering the streets today. So I thank all those out there like Elaine. I know there are many who work in the background, unnoticed, who give of themselves to help other human beings in pain. Without people like her, there would be many more casualties in the disease of alcoholism. Wherever you are Elaine, I want you to know I love you. Through your efforts you gave me back my life and you taught me what real love was. Up to that point, I had no idea at all. I could say the words, but I didn't know what it was like to live them. God bless you, wherever you are.

Another person I met in Austin this trip was Rick. Rick was yet another Irishman who was proud of his ancestry. I don't know why it is, but I seemed to meet a lot of Irishmen in my life in the streets. Rick was from Ada, Oklahoma. A cowboy type, he wore western garb every day and everywhere he went, from the hat on his head to the boots on his feet. Rick was in his forties, and had that Irish red hair and blue eyes. He wasn't big—about a hundred and fifty pounds—but he walked with a swagger in his step. He had a sense of humor that made me laugh at a time I thought I couldn't. Again I drove truck for the Salvation Army, and he was my helper, and a damn good one at that. I got to know Rick really well.

158

Rick had been in the streets for over fifteen years. He never completed high school, but was nevertheless very intelligent. When he was younger he worked on a ranch, and was as close to a real cowboy as you can get in this day and age. When Rick was twenty-four his parents were killed in a car accident, and he took over the ranch that had been in his family for many years. It wasn't much by today's standards, only a thousand acres, but he was determined to make a go of it. His father had died owing a lot of bills, and Rick worked feverishly to pay them off. It was always his dream to have a place of his own, and being an only child, knew one day he would end up with the family ranch, but he surely didn't want to do it in the way it happened, and would have gladly waited a lot longer to take over the reins.

But it happened the way it did, and he was determined to make a go of it. He done the best he could. He invested what little savings he had on a top bloodline of two steers and one stallion, and was going to build on these bloodlines. At first it looked as though his gamble would payoff. But two years into the project, he had a few setbacks, and was once again deep into debt, owing the bank a lot of money. The second year he lost his crops to a drought and one of his top breeders, shot by some kids who were out for some fun. He tried his best to recoup his losses, but the money just wasn't there, and the bank would not help anymore. At first he tried to sell off some of the land, and to auction off some of his assets to pay the bank, but still several thousand dollars short with a bank note due that he couldn't make, his family's ranch was taken over by the bank and auctioned off to the highest bidder.

This proved more than Rick could handle. Penniless and not a roof over his head, he turned to the streets and had been there ever since. Before that time Rick didn't have a drinking problem—he drank, but it didn't interfere with what he was trying to accomplish. But in the streets it didn't take long to overtake him and drag him deeper and deeper into despair.

Feeling himself a failure, and at fault for having lost the family ranch—a very significant factor for someone like Rick—he continued on a downward spiral until he ended up in Austin, at the Salvation Army, beaten to the point that he didn't want to go on. Unlike many of us, who fight rehab for years, Rick was one of the lucky ones who took to it right away. He lost a lot of years in the streets, but in the end, was determined to get his life back. His dream was to return home someday and somehow start all over again, and as far as I know that's exactly what he done.

I stayed in Austin, worked hard on my program, and was saving money to be able to return to society and make a go of it again. But somewhere along the line, I became too self-confident, and once again thought I could do it on my own. BIG mistake. I left the program in March of 1986, got a job and an apartment, and even got me a car, the first I'd had since I got out of the Army. I continued to go to AA meetings, but more and more I was going less and less. I was getting cocky, and thought I had the bull by the horns. It wasn't long before I fell flat on my face and was back to drinking, this time worse than before. In short order I lost everything I had worked for, including my home, and was back in the streets. Thinking like an alcoholic, I figured a change of geography was what I needed, so in April of 1986 I headed for Dallas, flat broke.

I arrived in Dallas late the next evening and found a place to stay behind the farmers market, just east of town and close to a labor pool. The next morning I was sitting in the labor pool, and hoping I could get out. I needed a drink bad, or at least I thought I did. I continued to work out of the labor pools and drink for a couple of months, during which time I met Allen.

Allen was thirty-four, a big heavy man who always wore work clothes—old uniforms he'd purchase at a local second-hand shop. Allen at one time, before he was thrust into the streets, owned his own business, a small body shop in the town where he grew up, Tucson, Arizona. He never finished high school, but went to trade school and was very good with figures. He was an honest and hard working man. He quickly built his business up to a modest state. He wasn't getting rich, but he was getting by quite well. Because of his character, he had a lot of repeat business, and word of mouth got around that this was one man you could trust with your car to do what he said he would do, and do it well. Three years into the business he took on a partner, who was a mechanic. They bought a larger building, and divided it up, half a body shop, the other a repair shop.

Now as good as Allen was with figures, his partner was even better, and had a better business sense about him, so Allen turned control of the financial end of the business over to him. While this man was good in business matters, he was not the man Allen was. He lied to his customers, and made repairs that didn't need to be made. He didn't complete the work on time and you couldn't count on his word that he'd do what he said he'd do for the price he said he'd do it for. Not only that, he was dishonest, and over a three-year period, gradually siphoned off large amounts of cash that should have been divided between him and Allen.

Allen wasn't dumb by a long shot, but he was a trusting person, and his partner was a top con man and could always explain the discrepancies. Allen always believed the best of people, and that was his downfall. Allen had been married once when he was young, but had no children, and his wife had died of cancer four years into the marriage. Not wanting to take a chance of going through that again, he never remarried.

It only took his partner five years to run the business into the ground and go bankrupt. Allen lost everything. He sold everything he had—even his home—to pay creditors and was left with nothing. And it's as I've said before, pride was the downfall of many of us. I'm sure Allen had many friends that would have helped him out in his hour of need, and even some family members. He was too proud to ask for help, so he ended up in the streets. When I left Dallas in August of that year, Allen was still living in the streets and working out of the labor pools, but I have to believe he didn't stay there very long. Allen was one of those people who didn't belong in the streets, and still had the fortitude to change his life.

He drank, but it wasn't a problem. Yet. You got the feeling, knowing Allen, that he was just passing through, but even then it was taking him a long time. He'd already been in the streets several years, and the streets had a way of getting hold of you and not letting go, at least not for a long time. It was always easy to get there; many people are only a paycheck from being in the streets themselves. But once there it was hell fighting your way back out. Some tried again and again, only to give up, it was so hard. Anyways in August of 1896, I was on my way out of Dallas, and on my way back to the West Coast, with a few stops along the way.

Late one evening, I gathered my bedroll and a few necessary supplies, walked out to the rail yards and hopped a freight train headed west—my first stop, Salt Lake City, Utah. My every intention was to go to Los Angeles again, but as it often is when you ride the rails, best intentions are often replaced by potluck, and Salt Lake City is where I finally got off the train. It wasn't cold yet; it was still early in the year, so I decided to stay for a while and check the place out. Salt Lake was a wild town—at least it had a lot of wild women, the reason for this I can only guess. Salt Lake being very religious-oriented, its children lived all their adolescence years under the control of their parents. After coming of age they decided to let their hair down, so to speak. Now don't get me wrong, there was nothing wrong with the way the parents raised their children. In fact, Salt Lake City was the most family-oriented city I'd ever known—the family was a very close-knit unit and always came first.

The Mormon religion is the foundation of this ideal, and in my opinion we would all be better off if we shared some of the same tenets as the Mormons and put the family and our fellow man first. Salt Lake City is one town that you could never go hungry in. The church had a large warehouse just off the downtown area where a person could go, and for a little bit of work, walk away with enough groceries to last a week. Sometimes the task they asked you to perform was one that really didn't need doing in the first place. They believed you felt better about yourself if you earned the groceries yourself, and they were not a handout. You know something, they were right, when you walked away you did feel better about yourself.

As far as being a good working town, I didn't consider Salt Lake to be one of the best. They didn't have any labor pools as I knew them, but rather, you'd go to the State Employment Office, just off State Street, and they had a room you would sit in and perspective employers would come by and choose people to go out on temporary jobs. In a way this was good, because you usually earned more than minimum wage, but you were often lucky to get two or three days of work a week out of there.

Salt Lake City was a strange kind of place from what I was used to. It was the first place I'd ever been where the State ran the liquor stores, and you had to fill out a form to get a bottle of liquor. Unless it was a private club, no hard liquor was sold in any other establishment, bar or otherwise. You could however, like in Texas, buy a bottle from the liquor store, and take it to the local tavern and buy set-ups, mixes to go with your booze. The bars were really big on punch boards, a form of legalized gambling. You bought a card, punched out the appropriate places, and maybe, but very seldom, won a cash prize. The odds were with the cards, not you. I believe even this was state-regulated, but if I'm wrong, I apologize to the state of Utah.

I found a place to stay in a storeroom behind a local bar near the Convention Center in exchange for cleaning up the bar every day, and a few drinks, no cash. Between that, two or three days of work out of the employment office, and regular trips to the food warehouse, this is how I lived for the next couple of months. This is where I met Cappy.

Cappy was an older gentleman who always showed up at the bar as soon as the doors opened; in fact sometimes he'd be outside waiting for you to open the doors an hour beforehand. Cappy was all of sixty years old, although I never did learn his exact age. He had salt and pepper hair, and gray eyes. He stood about five-seven, and was close to a hundred and ninety pounds. He always wore coveralls— I don't believe he had any other kind of clothing. Cappy was from southwestern Wyoming, where he'd worked all his life as a sheepherder. His job had been an arduous one. It required him to live for months at a time in the mountains with the sheep he was entrusted with. In all this time he lived in virtual solitude, often going a whole hitch without seeing another human being.

Every six months, he was given a leave of about a month or so, at which time he went to town to sow some oats, and spend the money that he had saved while working. Then he would go back and repeat the same routine. Cappy done this for over thirty years until his health got so bad he had to give it up. He'd spent a lot of time in and out of the hospitals since then. I believe he had cancer. Although I never learned the cause of his illness, I could see that he wasn't getting any better. Cappy got a check every month, I believe it was SSI; sheepherders didn't have much of a pension plan. He lived in an abandoned, one-room shack next to the railroad tracks. He lived from month to month on his little SSI check, and when he ran out of money, he had a small bar tab that the owner of the bar used to let him run. Occasionally you'd see him on a street corner towards the end of the month, panhandling. Cappy drank only beer and never got really drunk. He was a gentle man, although he had a way about him that told you he wasn't to be reckoned with.

I never knew him to get into any trouble, other than an occasional argument with a drinking buddy over sports or politics. He was very opinionated when it came to politics. As far as sports were concerned, he was an expert on everything. He had a memory that stored all the pertinent sports information there was. He was a fanatic when it came to sports, any kind of sports. Cappy bought me many a drink, and we used to sit for hours and talk. Cappy was like me in that he liked people, but he was a lonely man. His years of solitude had taken their toll. It was like he was trying to catch up for all the years he spent alone in the mountains with no one but sheep to talk to.

Cappy had spent his first year in retirement in group homes around town as a guest of the county while waiting for his SSI to begin. He could have stayed, but when he finally got his SSI, and all his back pay, the county took most of what he had from what he'd built up over that past year. This really pissed him off. He felt they could have left him something, but they took it all, leaving him without enough money to even get a room. He stayed another month, but when the home then took over three-quarters of his check, he said to hell with that, and left. He felt he could do much better on his own. I don't know how long Cappy had been in the streets, but I know he was happy, and he didn't bother a soul. As far as family was concerned, he was never married. He had no children, and he never talked about anyone else. As far as I know he was alone.

Cappy died in the streets and was buried by the county in an unmarked pauper's grave. Another victim, you may call it, but I'm a little mixed in those feelings. I would like to point out that Cappy worked all his life and he earned his SSI. He became a street person because for him, he was suited, but he died alone and ended up in an unmarked grave. Cappy never had anything better, and lived the way he did because that's where he was happiest. I believe Cappy had a lot more than many of us had—he was content within himself, and he caused nobody any harm. Surely God has a special place in heaven for people like Cappy.

One day while sitting in the employment office trying to catch a job, a man walked in and asked if anyone was interested in a live-in job that would last through the winter. I really didn't have any intention of staying anywhere through an entire winter, especially in the north, but after talking to him, and no one else being interested or qualified, I accepted the job. It was a job cooking and part-time bartending at a restaurant in Cheyenne, Wyoming called the Jolly Roger. So the man bought me a one-way bus ticket, told me when to show up and where to report when I got there, and where I would be staying. In one week, I was on my way to Cheyenne, Wyoming, knowing only that I'd be paid one hundred dollars a week, and room and board.

It was early November, and the weather had already started getting cold, and although Cheyenne itself didn't have any snow on the ground, you only had to look to the mountain ranges all around to know that the snow was coming. You could see it inching down the slopes, farther and farther everyday. I can remember riding on the bus to Cheyenne, and saying to myself, what the hell are you doing going north? When I finally arrived, I went straight to the hotel where Mr. Perry had told me I'd be staying, and much to my delight, it was right over a bar—how appropriate. After settling into my room I asked how I could get to the Jolly Roger Restaurant and Bar, and was pointed in the right direction. When the bartender told me it was within walking distance, I figured what the hell, what's a few blocks.

As it turned out it was about three-quarters of a mile from the hotel. In warm weather this would not have been a problem for me, but I was in Wyoming, it was winter, and believe you me, you have no idea what a winter is until you spend one in Cheyenne. Now don't get me wrong, Cheyenne was a beautiful town, in a rustic kind of way—they still tied up horses to hitching posts on Main Street. I loved it; it was a drinking town, and the people were very friendly, outgoing and fun-loving—my kind of people. I never got to see much of Cheyenne, though.

My area of interest stretched from the hotel and bar to the restaurant and back again. I can't even remember the name of the bar or hotel, or even what street it was on. It seems like Main Street, but I'm not sure. I only know that right across the street from the hotel and bar was a train depot, and of course the railroad tracks. I remember thinking I could have hopped a freight, cashed in my bus ticket, and got off right across the street from where I needed to be. But considering my luck lately on getting on freight trains, I probably would have ended up in Florida somewhere. Not a bad scenario but unrealistic for what I needed to do. It's just my luck with freight trains had not been good of late.

Obviously, Cheyenne was a cowboy town, and I liked that aspect of it. The bar below the hotel was an old country bar, and I liked that, too. There were several other establishments within walking distance, a few feet in Cheyenne in the winter is what I consider walking distance. God, it was cold, and the wind never stopped blowing. There were a couple of restaurants near the bar, although I ate all my meals at the Jolly Roger—they were free after all, and part of my pay. I spent a lot of time at my place of employment, and whenever I did go home, I tried my best to get a ride.

Most of the time it wasn't a problem except when I had to stay until closing. Then I usually had to walk, an experience that will live with me forever. I believe it never got above zero the whole time I was there, and many times much lower than that. With the wind-chill factor, it felt like sixty below. Had Cheyenne been located in the south, it would have been the perfect town for me. I enjoyed the people I worked with; they were exceptional individuals, and easy to get along with, with the exception of the cook that I relieved. He didn't like me, and I knew right off the bat that I didn't like him. He was one of those know-it-alls, and you know about know-it-alls—they're very irritating to those of us who actually do know it. There was a strong personally conflict there.

I went to Cheyenne thinking that I could work all winter, save some money, and get a brand new start when I left. Wrong! The management of the Jolly Roger had no problem giving me a bar tab, after all they could take what I owed at the end of two weeks and deduct it right from my check. Between that bar tab and the one they let me run at the bar below the hotel, I believe I left Cheyenne owing them money. I had only enough to get me a bus ticket out of town when I did leave. There were not many street people in Cheyenne. The weather was not conducive to that way of life, although there were a few living from paycheck to paycheck, with nothing left in-between, like me. I did manage to get acquainted with at least one of them. His name was Bull.

And guess what he had done for a living most of his life? You guessed it, rodeo was his game. In Bull's heyday, he'd ridden with the best—Larry Mahan, Tex Watson, and all the rest. He knew them personally, and could go on for hours talking about his days of riding bulls, the worst of the rodeo professions by far. Bull had started riding in rodeos when he was just a kid of twelve.

By the time he was eighteen, he turned professional and traveled the rodeo circuit all around the country. He never reached the status of being the best, but he said he'd reached the top twenty at one time. Bull's main problem was this dark cloud that followed him around. He said he had the worst luck when it came to injuries. At one time, to hear Bull tell the story, he had broken every bone in his body, right down to his fingernails.

Bull was forty-four when I met him, and hadn't ridden a bull since Cheyenne Rodeo Days of 1971 about fifteen years before. It was there that he had the accident that ended his career: he was gored in the back by a bull, almost died and was left partially crippled. Bull was from Boise, Idaho originally, but after the accident, he stayed in Cheyenne. He never spoke of any family or being married and having children, so as far as I know there wasn't any. Bull was a tall, thin, lanky man with jet-black hair and dark eyes. He walked with a limp, an old rodeo injury, he use to say. He wore western clothes—fancy shirts, jeans, and cowboy boots, with a western hat that looked like the one Gabby Hayes use to wear in the old westerns with the front and back brim of the hat turned up.

After his rodeo days were over, he obtained a job as a bartender. All retired cowboys are bartenders, at least it seemed that way to me. At first his drinking was not a problem. He could function well and still drink.

But over the years, his drinking got worse. He couldn't hold down a regular job and was soon reduced to cleaning several of the bars along the strip—as I called that part of town—to get by. He lived in a room behind the bar and hotel where I lived. You'd always find him in one of the bars, most of the time bumming drinks from the many people he knew. He didn't eat very often, at least not that I knew of. When I came in from work I would often bring him a plate so he would have something to eat that day. Bull was a proud man, as were most real cowboys I knew. Except for asking for a few drinks from time to time, he never asked anyone for anything else. He could have drawn SSI if he wanted to, I'm sure, but he wouldn't hear of it. He considered it a free ride, and he wanted to make it on his own as much as he could. For the most part, he got along well; at least he seemed satisfied.

But he was never happy to my way of thinking. He missed the call of the rodeo and being around the action all the time. It hurt him deeply when he couldn't ride anymore. For a long time all he did was feel sorry for himself, and in a way, he still did. But he was in a rodeo town, and as time went by that proved to be enough. From time to time he'd run into one of his old riding buddies, and they would have a good time drinking together and sharing old experiences. But when his friend left, Bull always went into a deep depression, sometimes taking days to pull himself out of it. I liked Bull. He'd had a lot of bad breaks in his life and I mean that literally! He didn't accept the fact that he'd never be able to ride again, and often talked about going back on the circuit. But not only was that physically impossible for him, he was getting up in years, and his age worked against him.

As far as I know, Bull didn't have any physical problems outside of those caused by his profession, and for all I know he is still in Cheyenne to this day, doing the same thing now that he was doing back then. I couldn't imagine him changing. There was no desire in him to do so. He appeared content and was beginning to accept his lot in life, at least to the extent that it wasn't doing him any more harm.

I managed to make it through the winter in Cheyenne, and why not? It took me the whole winter to save enough money to get out of town. I was beginning to believe I worked for the company store, and would never get out of Cheyenne unless I walked. By April of 1987 I had enough money for a ticket and I gladly left, vowing never to spend another winter in the north, let alone Cheyenne. I had a good time while I was there, and even though my drinking was still a problem, I faced no real setbacks and managed to maintain. I was glad to leave—I knew I'd miss the people, but not the weather. After all winter lasts for eight months a year in Wyoming, a little too long for me.

I had heard from some of the people passing through town that Seattle, Washington was a good working town, and having never been in that part of the country for any length of time, I decided to go there. I'd also heard it was a lot like Cheyenne, very beautiful, and the people very friendly. Besides that's as far as my money would take me. Even though I was happy to be leaving Cheyenne, there was a little bit of apprehension in my heart. For one of the first times in my life, I wondered what the future had in store, and where my life would lead me from there.

I arrived in Seattle two days later and went to the nearest bar to get my bearings and find out where the street people hung out. I hadn't thought about getting help for my problem for quite a while now, but all of a sudden it became an option again if I ran into any problems. Right away Seattle reminded me of San Francisco and Oakland, the way it was laid out with Bellevue right across Lake Washington from Seattle, you had to cross a bridge to get to the other side. Everything I had heard about Seattle was true.

It was one of the most beautiful places I'd ever seen, anywhere. The locals called it God's country, and they weren't far from right. If there was a garden of Eden surely Seattle was as close to it as any place could be. And the people were everything I'd heard about them; I could have easily made Seattle my home. I still sometimes miss the place a lot. With the beauty of Puget Sound to the west and Lake Washington to the east, Seattle was almost completely surrounded by water, with the exception of the north and south boundaries of the city.

The only beef I had about Seattle was the rain—it falls about three hundred days a year. The winters are mild by northern standards. But even the rain added beauty to the city because it kept everything so green, and the green in Seattle and northern Washington State is a green like none other you could see anywhere in the world.

I located the area where the street people hung out, and I must say, compared to other parts of the country even the skid row section of town—if that's what you really wanted to call it—was clean looking. At this particular time there was a lot of work in Seattle, and I had no problem getting day labor. I first tried to stay in Jefferson Park around Beacon Avenue, but that didn't work out. The police were very adamant about this, but I got lucky and found an abandoned house just off Beacon Avenue to stay in. Actually I stayed in a shed behind the house; it was in better shape.

I met Janet in a coffeehouse on Fourth Avenue; she was only sixteen and a runaway. She had already been in the streets for two years. Janet was from Tacoma, just south of Seattle. She didn't travel far from her home because she still had a brother in a foster home there, and from time to time would sneak and visit him when he was in school. Janet was short and a little heavy, but she was still a very pretty young lady.

Janet's parents had abandoned her and her brother when she was ten years old. From that time on it was an endless series of foster homes for them. Janet said she always felt responsible for her parents having abandoned them, because she didn't feel she was good enough for them. She had very low self-esteem and was always putting herself down. I used to get upset with her because of it. I'd tell her not to do that, because there were enough people in this world that would do that for her; she didn't need to do it to herself. Besides, I often told her she was a very good and beautiful person, with the personality of an angel.

Janet liked everyone, and trusted everyone—not good for a street person, especially a sixteen-year-old girl. Many of the foster homes she had been in, while they didn't physically abuse her, told her she was no good. I guess she had a discipline problem, and they put her down something terrible.

There was one home she was in for about four months that she really liked, but for some reason the powers that be decided to move her. She said they were the only people she'd ever known that treated her like a person and not a piece of trash. She often thought about going back there herself, but thought better because she was afraid of what the authorities would do if they knew. So she opted for the streets, and done whatever she had to do to survive, though I never learned what that was. She had had a series of boyfriends since being in the streets, and for a while I guess they took care of her, but they too had a tendency to use her. Janet didn't take drugs or drink alcohol, at least never around me.

We would sometimes on the weekend go to Alki Beach Park in West Seattle and sit by the lighthouse and watch the ships in Puget Sound go by. We talked for hours on end. She was good company and we became good friends, often meeting for coffee in the morning before I went to work, and maybe an occasional sandwich after I

170

got off. There was hardly a day went by that I didn't see her at least once. But we remained strictly friends. She was very young and I had this thing about messing with young girls—to some it didn't seem to matter, but to me it didn't seem right. Besides, I think she viewed me as a father figure. She use to share intimate things with me that at times made me feel a little awkward, and were hard for me to respond to. She was really having a hard go of it.

I tried to get her to check out some places that might help her, but she didn't trust anyone in authority. There were a couple of places she used to stay at night where there were other teenage runaways and she felt safe. How she never managed to fall victim to drugs and alcohol, I'll never know, because it was all around her. One day Janet came to me and she was crying really hard and couldn't stop. She said she had gone to visit her brother and he wasn't there; the county had moved him, and she didn't know where. He was her only family and not knowing where he was she felt more alone than ever. I tried to comfort her, but I was no replacement for her brother. Then Janet disappeared for about two weeks, and I didn't see neither hide nor hair of her. I assumed she was looking for her brother.

I then heard that the police had found the body of a teenage girl in a house that was known by authorities to be frequented by runaways. I was scared for Janet, and I tried to find out if it was her, but the authorities wouldn't give me any information, and the word on the streets was silent too. No one wanted to be involved or associated with the incident. I hoped and prayed that it wasn't Janet, because I never seen her again. Maybe she found her brother or someone who would take care of her, and she was all right and happy. But it was unrealistic to think along those lines. I knew the streets only too well, and knew how cruel they could be. If you're out there anywhere Janet, I hope you're well. You gave me some happy times just knowing you, because you were such a kind and gentle lady. I miss you.

Another person I came to know well in Seattle was Blue. Blue was a young black man about twenty-eight years old. He was another tall and lanky one. I cannot give a detailed description of Blue, nor can I tell you exactly where he was from, except that it was a large city in the Midwest. If I told you any more about him, it would not be hard for you to figure out who he is, and I have to protect his anonymity. You see, Blue was drafted by the NBA when he was twenty. He opted to give up his senior year in college in order to be eligible for the draft. Blue had had a real hard time of it growing up—he'd lived in the projects all his life. He had three sisters and two brothers.

His father worked in the service industry until his death, when Blue was thirteen. His mother done the best she could keeping the family together, raising the children with good values, and she done a damn good job. All her children managed to stay away from the many pitfalls of the ghetto, and the peer pressure that came with growing up in the projects. She managed to instill in her children a sense of pride, and a belief that if they applied themselves, they could accomplish anything.

 Blue told me she was a constant source of encouragement to all her children. She allowed them to make their own choices about their future, and stood behind them as best she could. It's bad enough trying to raise six children alone, and being there for them all the time, under normal circumstances. But to do it under the adverse conditions she and the children faced every day, having to scrape out a living, must have seemed impossible. But she never gave up on herself or her children.

Blue spent his every waking hour—when he wasn't in school or helping out his mother whenever he could—on the basketball court. In high school he played varsity ball in his freshman year. He was very good at what he did. Besides his mother, Blue said his coach in high school played an instrumental part in his growing up, teaching him discipline and teamwork.

At fifteen, Blue had one run-in with the law, when he chose briefly to succumb to peer pressure and ran with a gang that was into stealing cars and selling drugs. But a policeman, who saw a young man with potential and not a career criminal, helped steer him back in the right direction. Besides his mother tore his ass up when she found out. Blue said he knew from the beginning that gang life wasn't the kind of life he wanted to be associated with, but being a kid of fifteen and wanting to belong he was sucked in as so many other children are today. But few have a mother like Blue's in their life, or the other role models that turned Blue around before it was too late.

I have to give Blue's mother a lot of credit: It must have been very hard on her, but she was a strong woman, with good values, and an outlook on life where she found the best in every situation. She never complained, according to Blue, and she always found the time to listen to her children. "Can't" wasn't in her vocabulary. She never offered discouragement—only encouragement—to her children, and wouldn't let them expect less of themselves. Nor would she allow them to make any excuses. She taught them that they and they alone controlled their destiny. Truly, Blue's mother was a super woman, and her sense of family and values rubbed off on her children.

In Blue's senior year in high school he was all-state, and by the time he graduated, he had his choice of colleges and a full scholarship. Blue dreamed of playing professional ball, and he never lost sight of that goal. One thing his mother and his other role models instilled in him was the need for a good education, and although Blue wasn't a great student, he managed to keep his grades average, and got by. Blue chose a college in the Midwest, not far from home, so he could be near his family. He quickly rose to stardom, and by his junior year was being sought by all the major teams in the NBA. It wasn't a matter of if he'd be drafted, but rather a matter of by whom.

By the time Blue was in his junior year in college his priorities started to change. His mother became very sick, and was having a difficult time making a go of it for her and the remaining children at home. She couldn't work anymore, and the doctor bills were piling up. Against his mother's wishes, but given his need to help in any way he could, he opted to give up his senior year, and petitioned the NBA to be eligible for the draft. Because of his family's circumstances, matched with his ability to play, they granted him a deferment, and allowed him to be drafted. He was taken in the third round of the draft, and was given a contract that reached seven figures.

As far as Blue was concerned, his family's problems were over. He paid off all his mother's doctor bills, bought her a house in the suburbs, and provided her with an income so she wouldn't have to work anymore. Blue had hit the big time, and his dreams were coming true. All the things his mother and others had taught him were paying off.

Now I'd like to say this is the end of the story for Blue and his family and they lived happily ever after, but this is real life. For the first couple of years everything went well for Blue, and even though he wasn't considered the best in the NBA, he was talented enough to play in the starting line up. Blue's strength came from his belief in teamwork, and while he wasn't a headliner, he topped the league in assists his first year. He never considered himself a star, only a part of the whole, putting the team first, rather than pursuing his own agenda. For Blue, it was family first, and team second. If there was room left for him, fine.

By the time Blue was twenty-three he was on top of the world, his family was well taken care of, his future was secure, and everything seemed to be going great. Then Blue started taking time out for himself, and treating himself to some of the luxuries of his labor. He started drinking and running with the fast crowd. In the off-season he was in an automobile accident, and only by the grace of God, no one, including himself was hurt. This didn't deter him in the least, and his problems escalated fast. He started getting involved with prostitutes and with them came the drugs. Now here's a kid who all his life never had anything, and had to grow up early to take care of his family. I can almost understand how he fell into the trap that fame sometimes leads kids to now days; he got too much too fast. The pressure of providing and being responsible for his family at such an early age, coupled with the pressure of staying on top of the game, were too much for Blue. In a way, he had a breakdown, and lost track of his priorities.

By his third year in the league, he'd already been suspended twice, and had been in three different rehabs for his addiction. He couldn't get a handle on his life, and by his fourth year in the NBA, he had lost everything, including his job and his bank account. As far as Blue was concerned, his life was over, his dreams crushed. He had let himself and his family down, and he was devastated. For a while Blue dropped completely out of sight, and no one knew where he was. Then when he emerged again he was on skid row in Seattle. He had kicked the hard drugs, but now alcohol had taken over his life. I can only imagine the pressure that Blue must have felt that led him down this path—it had to be beyond anything I ever knew.

When I met Blue he had been in the streets for three years, and was getting worse by the day. He was a good man; he never bothered anyone, and only wanted the best for everyone. He never put anyone down, and treated people the way he wanted to be treated. He was friendly and outgoing, but inside he was in a lot of pain. He tried not to show it, like we all did, but all you had to do was look into his eyes. He felt alone and a failure and no amount of talking could change his mind about himself. I know he could have gone home and his family would be behind him all the way to help him straighten himself out, but once again, pride reared its ugly head and claimed another victim.

Blue was a victim of the pressure kids face today, not only to succeed, but the peer pressure they face everyday from the people around them is more intense than anything we knew when we were growing up. I can't see how any of our children get by today unscathed. All we can hope to do is what Blue's mother done—the best we can—and hope for the best. This world today claims a lot of our kids, and there doesn't seem to be any relief in sight.

So it was with Blue. He only wanted in his heart the best for himself and his family, and why not? They had paid their dues. They lived in hell, and had fought their way out, only to fall victim to today's pressures. Anything less than improvement was to Blue a failure, and that was something he couldn't accept. He gave up, like so many of us have, to live a life less than what God had intended us to live. Blue never learned to handle failure, so life handled him. I only knew Blue for four months. I left Seattle in September of 1987, and he was still there. I pray, as I do for so many others, that he'll find his way someday and be able to return to God's plan.

In September, I left Seattle and headed for San Francisco. The winter was fast closing in, and even though it didn't get that bad in Seattle, I wanted to be farther south. I was getting restless again as I had so many times before. I was still looking for my answer. Instead I found in San Francisco a new education, just when I thought I had seen it all. San Francisco showed me things that strengthened my resolve to climb out of my own hell and become a useful member of society again.

In the Tenderloin District of San Francisco where I lived for another three months, I saw a lot of misery, and experienced it firsthand. The Tenderloin was the skid row to beat all skid rows, including the Bowery in New York. Here they not only came from all walks of life, but from every aspect. There was more concentrated pain in the Tenderloin than any other place on earth I had been.

San Francisco was a hard time for me. I was living in the streets and they were not so kind. When I first arrived in San Francisco, I tried one of the many missions in the Tenderloin area, the skid row section of town. It was like the Bowery of lower east side Manhattan, only worse, if you can believe that. It was cleaner, but because of its location and the weather, it was a melting pot of misery. I saw more families in the streets than any other place I had yet been.

One family that I came to know well were the Burches. They consisted of Brad the father, Ruth the mother, and their two children, Brad Jr. and Becky. Brad Jr. was eight years old and Becky was eleven. I met them living in the courtyard of a church in the Tenderloin where I was staying.

It wasn't much; you had to sleep outside and bring your own bedroll, but it was much safer than the missions. You had to be inside the courtyard by six o'clock in the evening, because that's when the priest locked the front gate and didn't allow anyone else to enter. The people who stayed there were the same every night with the occasional exception of one or two new people. We got to know one another and watched each others' backs. We were like a family that had bonded out of necessity, for protection. You see, in the Tenderloin there was safety in numbers. Anyway Brad and Ruth had both grown up in a small town in Iowa. Brad had worked for over twenty years in the same plant, and had looked forward to retiring from there some day. Ruth had been a homemaker all her life, and had never done anything else.

Outside of being a high school graduate, that's all she knew. Brad had dropped out of school when he was seventeen, after failing his senior year. The plant where Brad had worked for so many years employed almost the whole town—it was the town's main source of income. If you didn't work for the factory, you worked for one of the places in town that supported the populace in some way or the other. Like so many small towns, they were unable to diversify, and put all their eggs in one basket believing the plant would be there forever. Brad and Ruth were looking

176

forward to buying a house soon. They were tired of living in an apartment and wanted their own place.

Then one day, before that could happen, Brad went to work, only to find a notice with his time card that the plant was closing in thirty days, moving its operation to Mexico where the labor was cheaper. The economy was bad, and they said if they didn't do something they were going to go bankrupt. Brad was devastated, and scared to death. He wondered how he'd be able to support his family, not to mention the years he had wasted working towards retirement.

He waited a long time before he said anything to Ruth. He didn't want to worry her unnecessarily, and thought he'd be able to figure something out by the time he told her. They both had families in the area, but Brad said they were all worse off than they were. The nearest town that offered the possibility of another job was over one hundred miles away, and even those prospects didn't look good. It seemed everyone who had jobs in Iowa at the time were hanging on to them for dear life because the economy had gotten so bad, and jobs were few and far between.

Brad lived on his unemployment until he was unable to keep up with the bills, then out of desperation he decided to go somewhere, anywhere. Thinking the prospects would be better in Northern California, he loaded up his family and what few possessions they could carry—and that they hadn't sold for the trip—and headed for California in his stationwagon. With a few hundred dollars in his pocket and a tank full of gas, they set out. They arrived in San Francisco the next day, having driven straight through. Upon arriving, things quickly got worse for them. They had stopped at a store and gotten something to eat for themselves and the kids, and had driven to a park just outside San Francisco to sit down and eat.

While they were sitting at a picnic table, someone, somehow, stole their car and everything in it. Brad called the police and made a report, but they didn't give him much hope of being able to recover his belongings. He explained to the police his situation, and they directed him to a mission in the Tenderloin that might help him out until he could get on his feet.

They rode the Bart (San Francisco's subway system) into the Tenderloin district and sought out the mission the police had told them about. By then it was late in the evening, and dark. For a family from a small town in the Midwest, in the big city for the first time, this was not a good idea. There were a lot of predators in this part of town, and they could spot a mark (easy hit) a mile away. Before they ever got to the mission, right in front of his wife and kids, someone pulled a gun on him and took all his money—if these people didn't have bad luck, they'd have no luck at all. Brad almost lost it right there; had it not been for his wife and kids, I believe he would have. He called the police again, made out another report, and again didn't get much hope of recovering his property. Locating the mission, they stayed there that first night, at which time he got into a fight with one of the regulars, who was hitting on his wife.

Completely disillusioned now, he didn't know what he was going to do. The next day, he and his wife and children left the mission, and never went back. Even for a single man, the missions were a battleground, and the strong preyed on the weak and helpless. You were far better off in a park somewhere, to my estimation; at least the numbers weren't so great on the outside. Brad was quickly learning the same thing.

Not knowing what to do, only that he had to find a safe place for his wife and kids off the streets so he could look for work, they started going to the churches in the area asking for help. They all had the same response: go to one of the missions, they were set up to help better than the churches. Besides, most of the churches in the area supported the missions in one way or the other. Finally he settled on the courtyard at the church down by the Bart System. At least his family could stay there in relative safety during the day, and wouldn't be bothered by predators while he looked for work.

There was lots of work in San Francisco, but the only work that would afford you money on the spot, a day's pay for a day's work, were the labor pools. Well I need not tell you, by the time he spent his day's pay buying his wife and kids something to eat, and the few other necessities they needed, he was broke and right back where he'd started. That was life for the street person; it wasn't hard to get down, but it was near impossible to get back up again, especially if you were penniless and had a family to look after.

That's the way it was for Brad and Ruth. It is typical of the families I met living in the streets—they had a run of bad luck, and were struggling to survive. They didn't ask to be put in the situations they were in, but there they were nonetheless. They sought a better life somewhere that they were unfamiliar with, often getting in over their heads. And I kid you not, there still are many like Brad and Ruth in the streets today. This led me to realize that many families in this country are just one paycheck away from being in the streets themselves. And these people are your neighbors, your friends, relatives and acquaintances. I can safely say if you've ever known a family who had a run of bad luck and one day packed up and disappeared, look to the streets. You're likely to find them there.

Another family I got to know in San Francisco I met at a small park frequented by locals living in the Tenderloin. It had swings for the kids, a basketball court for older children, and a lot of benches to sit on and relax. Right in the middle of the Tenderloin, it was a favorite hangout for street people when they had nothing better to do. The park was full on the weekends, when work out of the labor pools was scarce. Everyone just hung around the park, waiting for the day to go by. This family, the Ramseys, were in different circumstances than Brad's family, but no less demoralized.

Benny and Toni Ramsey were migrant farm workers. They had three children, Rebecca, Max, and Chastity—twelve, nine, and seven, respectively. Benny was in his early forties and Toni was a few years younger. They were born and raised in a small farm community just south of Omaha, Nebraska. Benny grew up on a farm, but when he was fourteen his father died, and he being the only child, he had to quit school to run the farm. He had known Toni all his life; she grew up on a farm not far from his own. Toni also had to quit school early to help with her brothers and sisters when her mother turned sick.

Now Benny's father wasn't much of a businessman, and that, coupled with a few bad years and bad crops had left the farm on the brink of bankruptcy. Benny did however manage to keep the farm going for quite some time, but having inherited his father's lack of business sense, in a few years the farm was claimed by the government for back taxes. Not knowing anything else and having no formal education, he had difficulty getting any kind of a job to sustain his family.

To provide for themselves they went on the migrant circuit, following the seasons to harvest other farmers' crops. This is what brought him to the San Francisco area. At home in Nebraska the work was seasonal, with not much to be had in the winter. In northern California, the Salinas Valley provided year 'round work. When it was slow around Salinas, they went a little farther south to the Napa Valley and found work there.

I don't know what you all know about migrant farm workers, but you probably think of illegal aliens from Mexico when you think along those lines. But there are also a lot of migrant workers who are people just like you and me, but who haven't enough education to obtain a job doing anything else, especially when farming is all they've ever known. Many migrant farm workers are treated very badly by those they work for. They live in substandard conditions with substandard pay that ties them to their profession without any hope for improvement. They make just enough to get by, and sometimes not that.

This got Benny in trouble. He had tried to start a movement to improve the living conditions and pay of farm workers, and he was black-balled from the circuit. Everybody who hired migrant workers knew about his activities and wouldn't hire him. This is what brought him to San Francisco. Broke, with only the possessions they carried in their car, Benny needed to support his family. He knew about the labor pools in the city, having worked them when work was slow on the farms. He knew he wouldn't be much better off, but at least it would be better than what they had, nothing. They use to drive out by the Presidio, an old Army base overlooking the Golden Gate Bridge, and sleep in their car, unable to afford a room, let alone an apartment or house. They lived that way for as long as I knew them. It was impossible for them to get ahead, especially with a family to take care of. Damn, it was hard enough for me to get by. I know how much harder it must have been for him. I met Benny at the labor pool where I worked from time to time, and a few times even rode out to their campsite to sleep, when I wanted to get out of the Tenderloin for a while.

Neither Benny nor Toni drank. All his money went to feeding the kids and his wife, not leaving much to save. They were good people, not very smart, but they cared about other people and did not tolerate injustice. I seen Benny go without many times so his children and wife would have more. He tried hard to provide for his family, and even got the children into school from time to time. This is what hurt Benny most: having to move around as much as they did, he knew his children wouldn't have much more of a chance in this world than did he and his wife. At one time he even thought about giving them up, to be raised by a normal family. But he loved his family so much, he couldn't bear the thought of being away from them. Besides the children loved their parents, and probably would not have gone peacefully, preferring to take their chances with their parents rather than without them.

Benny's pride was also a drawback. He wouldn't ask for "charity" as he called it; if he couldn't provide for his family, he'd rather be dead. As a result he chose to go it alone, and asked for help from no one. He was locked into the only lifestyle that would allow him to provide for his family. He didn't have any other options if he didn't want to break up the family and I knew he would never do that. They were his life. He didn't ask to be down and out like he and his family were, but it was all he knew and he was doing the best he could to provide for them.

There are many families like the Ramseys in this country of ours, who only want to provide for their families and not be a burden to society. I run into them all the time. They didn't belong where they were, but were there because there was no other place for them in today's society if they wanted to do it themselves. These, too, I consider the Walking Wounded. Before I left San Francisco, Benny and his family were headed for Florida to work in the citrus industry down there, hoping they could find something better. I hope their car made it, and they found something better than what they had. At any rate, I myself left the Tenderloin in September of 1987 and headed once again to Los Angeles to spend the winter. It was a bit warmer down there, and once again, I was familiar with the area and knew I could find work.

I arrived in Los Angeles a couple of days later, and immediately felt at home. It was like I had never left, and I immediately got back into my old life. Not much had changed, except for the names of a few of the bars where I used to hang out. Everything else was the same: a bee hive of activity—lots of work and plenty of bars.

I only stayed in the central part of skid row a few days, sleeping in parks and wherever I might find a fairly secure place to lay my head without being hassled. I got work the first day out of one of the many labor pools I was familiar with from before. This allowed me to seek out some of my old haunts, and get familiar with the subtle changes that had taken place since the last time I was there. On the third day, a Saturday, I looked for another place to stay, away from downtown and a bit safer. I headed out Central Avenue towards Glendale. About halfway between Glendale and downtown, with easy access to both places, I found a one-bedroom trailer in a fenced-in lot next to St. Vincent DePaul's warehouse, a Catholic charity. It was in a secluded part of the lot and afforded reasonable security from the streets. The only thing was, I had to come in late after the people in the warehouse left, and leave early before they came in to work.

Except on the weekends. Then all I had to do was be careful that no one spotted me going in or out during the daylight hours. There was no running water, of course, and no electricity, but who needs those things when you are living in the streets? I put a plastic trash bag in the toilet, and done my thing in the bag, being sure to take it out with me when I left in the morning, and replacing it with a new one. As far as showers were concerned, there was a water hose next to the warehouse building that I use to use after it got dark—the showers were cold, but I managed to keep fairly clean. There were a few bars in the area, some stores and restaurants and it was easily accessible by bus. Seven days a week, all I had to do is manage to save bus fare to get to and from work at the labor pools, downtown everyday. This was especially hard on the weekends, but I managed. Only a couple of times did I have to walk in to work because I had spent all my money that weekend and had no bus fare on Monday morning.

I was living in the trailer when I met Kate and David at one of the local bars. They were living in a burnt-out house just a few blocks away from where I was staying. David was working in the labor pools, just like I was, and was getting there by bus, the same as me. In fact I had seen him on the bus a few times before I actually met him and Kate. Both David and Kate were young, and both were runaways. They had met in a juvenile facility, where their parents had put them because they were too hard to handle.

I'd say Kate was about seventeen and David was nineteen when I met them, but they had already been in the streets for two years. They were both from the same place in northern California but until they met in the facility, they hadn't known one another. Kate's mother was divorced from her father, who was a guitar player in a well-known band and traveled a lot. David's mother and father were still together, but his father was anything but faithful to his mother. Kate was a manic-depressive, and you could tell at times that she wasn't on her medication, because of her pronounced mood swings. Sometimes I don't know how David could put up with these swings because she'd get completely out of control when they happened.

David himself was OK, but he liked taking prescription drugs, and had somehow found a doctor in the area that would give him what he wanted, when he wanted it. Kate had tried to go to her father for help when she and David first left. She believed he would do anything to help her because he understood her better than her mother did. But when she went to her dad, he was completely preoccupied with a new girlfriend, and all he wanted to do was send her back to her mother. This made Kate go ballistic, and now she was sure that neither of her parents loved or wanted her.

With David it was a little different—his problem was his temper. It got him in a lot of trouble in school and with his parents. He knew his father was cheating on his mother and this aggravated the matter. I think in their own way they still loved their parents very much, but they both felt that their parents had abandoned them. Kate thought her problems were because of her medication, instead of the other way around, and didn't like taking it. They were a couple of mixed-up kids. About a week after I met them, the house they were living in was torn down, and they moved in with me. I wasn't really crazy about this situation, I preferred staying alone, but couldn't turn them into the streets. I agreed to let them stay for a while, until they could find another place of their own.

This worked out for a while, but three weeks after moving in, David was picked up by the police for having illegal drugs and wasn't about to get out of that for quite a while. Kate went completely mad for the first few days, ranting and raving that we had to get him out, no matter what it took. But the reality finally hit her that David wasn't coming back for quite a while and she settled down a little. But it was short-lived. She had no money of her own, so I took care of her as long as I could. She had no skills and was too mixed up to work herself.

The problem was all she wanted to do was drink, and I could barely afford my own vice, let alone support hers. For a month I managed to get by. I bought everything at the store, and didn't go to the bars; we both drank at the trailer. This arrangement was getting old fast, and I tried to get her to call her parents and go home. After a week of badgering her, she finally did call her mother. I don't know how the conversation went, and she didn't discuss it when she came back to the trailer, but she was a little calmer after that. Then about six weeks after she and David had moved in with me, she never came back one time after I gave her some money to get us another bottle. I like to think she used the money to get back home. The money wasn't important, although at first I was pretty mad because it was my last twenty-dollar bill, it was Saturday and I couldn't get any more until Monday night when I got in from work. In a way she and David were good for one another, they kept one another from doing anything more stupid than they were already doing, and David did manage to control her when he was around—something I could never do.

I was glad they were gone, but in another way I was kind of sad. I had gotten used to having them around and now I was alone again, and when I was alone I was my own worst enemy. I started drinking more and more, and was myself getting totally out of control. I wasn't going to work regularly, and was obsessed with alcohol. I really didn't want to drink anymore, but also didn't want to feel the pain of loneliness I felt. Then one day I just got sick of it all and I checked myself into the Salvation Army downtown. I stayed there for almost three months, during which time I met Jarvis.

Jarvis was an older black man who had been in the streets since his wife died, twelve years earlier. Jarvis was the worst kind of drunk—at least in the minds of those who didn't know any better—because he drank only wine and was considered a wino. He'd check into the Salvation Army from time to time to get well, save up a little money and go back out again on another drunk. Jarvis was a small man, with salt and pepper hair and dark eyes. He only stood about five-feet-four, and weighed about one hundred and twenty pounds. He had the smallest feet for a grownup that I had ever seen. Jarvis was a friendly person, at least when I knew him. There were those who knew him when he was on the wine, and according to them, he wasn't a nice person to be around then, but I never knew him that way. Jarvis's one other vice, besides his drinking, was he liked to gamble and would bet on anything.

During the time we were both at the Sally, there was a bingo game in the *Los Angeles Times* every day, and Jarvis played it religiously. The first thing he done every day was to get him a paper, he was so obsessed with the game. This went on for the first month that I knew him, then one day the unthinkable happened, at least for a street person, and a wino at that. He hit the big one, and won ten thousand dollars in the game. It took him two weeks to collect his money but when he did, he was gone like a shot. I say this was the worst possible thing that could happen to Jarvis, because a wino, loose on skid row with ten thousand dollars in his pocket was as good as a dead man. I knew if he didn't drink himself to death, the jack rollers would get him. And they'll kill you for two dollars, let alone ten thousand.

Just one week after Jarvis left the Salvation Army he was dead. The jack rollers didn't get him, but the wine did; he literally drank himself to death in one week, a fate that was inevitable. We all knew that when he left it was just a matter of time, one or the other would get him, and it did. I stayed another month at the Sally, and then left myself.

Feeling well again I thought I could do it on my own once again, and once again I was wrong. It wasn't long before I was as bad as before, and maybe even worse. I couldn't get it right, and once again was pulled into a state of despair that was worse and worse each time. It wasn't long and I found myself in another mental institution, the Norwalk State Mental Hospital in Norwalk, California. By now I was despondent and wanted to die. I didn't want to live like I'd been living anymore, but didn't know if I would ever find my way out of the hell I had created.

The Process

When you search for change but cannot find
That which you're searching for
When all seems lost and times not right
What is it that opens that door

You know you really want to change
But change is just not there
No matter what you say and do
Your life just seems unfair

So on and on you seek to find
You cannot give up the ghost
You want the change, but change don't come
It's what you want the most

So try again, 'cause try you must
No matter what the cost
Change don't come to those who wait
And those who wait are lost

So desperation leads the way
And eventually the change will come
But until it does, the search goes on
Until the job is done

And when it's done and finally over
You know the search was worth the wait
Because the search was part of the process
And the process was your fate

—May 1, 1997

~ CHAPTER 7 ~

Years of Despair OR *The Process*

It was now early March of 1988, and my desperation was reaching critical proportions. I had to get help in order to survive. I didn't know how much longer I could go on the way I was living. I realized that no matter how good the intention, the outcome depended on me staying out of my own way. I had been independent for so long that in the back of my mind I figured if I only knew the steps to take, I could then go out, apply them to my life, and everything would be all right. Wrong again! I was about to learn what many who finally seek help for the first time learn, that it takes more than just knowing; your whole life has to change.

When I entered the Norwalk State Hospital, I decided once and for all to do everything that they told me to do no matter how ridiculous it might seem to me. I was determined to make it.

The program they put me into was a combination of an alcohol program and one that treated my mental condition. A doctor gave me the name of a condition that he said was the cause of my behavior, put me on medication, and proceeded to treat the real problem, my alcoholism. Now I'm not putting these professionals down; they were doing what they thought was best, according to what they knew at the time, but in reality it felt like they were just giving me an excuse for being the way I was. In truth I was the way I was because I drank too much, simple as that. Anyways, I went along and I stayed in the hospital through the whole program, which consisted of several steps. First you became stable on your medication; then you went through a twenty-one day alcohol program; then you moved on to the next step that integrated you back into society, all in a matter of a couple of months. They didn't keep you any longer than necessary because of funding cuts going on at the time. It seemed like a big processing station that treated the symptoms, and expected you to take care of the rest.

While I was still in the hospital, I obtained a job driving truck and was making more money than I had made in many years. I saved my money until I had enough to get my own place, then struck out on my own to apply what I had learned. There was just one problem with this scenario: knowing and doing are two different things. Now that I had an excuse for the way I was, I could blame my condition on something other than myself. It wasn't long before I was right back where I started. I had tried to do too much too soon, which was typical of my attempts to quit drinking over the next few years.

There is the key word that says it all, MYSELF. I still believed that, armed with the knowledge of what was wrong with me, I could correct it MYSELF. It took me a long time to realize that this was not true. I wasn't to learn that lesson for quite a while yet—a mistake so many of us make—you cannot go it alone. Soon it was the same old pattern: I lost everything I had gained in a short amount of time: my job, my home, even the car I bought, the first one I'd had in many years, was gone the first night I was back in the streets, stolen behind a bar where I had parked it on Central and 7th, in the farmers market district in downtown Los Angeles a few blocks from skid row. It was on this run—as I began calling them—that I met Preacher.

I don't know how I never had run into Preacher before; he had been in the streets and on skid row in Los Angeles for eight years. Preacher was just as you'd expect him to be, a defrocked Catholic priest. He was a gentle man, and the harshness of the streets hadn't changed him much. Preacher was thirty-eight, and all his life had wanted to be nothing else but a Catholic priest. He grew up in the church with devout parents who were very supportive of his goals. He entered the seminary right after graduation from college, where he had obtained a degree in business. Preacher came from a small town in northern Oregon. He went to college at Washington State, and on to seminary school in northern California.

I never realized it until listening to Preacher's story how stressful being a priest must have been. Listening to everyone else's problems, day in and day out, trying your best to do what's right, and all this coupled with the restrictions the priesthood put on a person—in my expectation—could lead to nothing but a drinking problem. This was Preacher's first downfall, which ultimately led him to have a complete mental breakdown in just a few short years. I believe it to be as Preacher always said: no matter what the intentions and desire may be, some people are not cut out for that kind of life, or for any life one may choose for that matter.

You have to have more than desire and good intentions to make it in any endeavor. You must also be prepared mentally for the consequences of your choice, whatever it may be. There are consequences for every choice we make in life, good and bad, and you have to be prepared for both if you expect to survive. This is something they didn't teach him in seminary school, nor did he learn it growing up. The church was good to Preacher, they never gave up on him, tried everything at their disposal to help him, and stood by him until the end.

The end was when Preacher gave up on himself; it had nothing to do with the church. He labeled himself a failure, couldn't bear to face his parents or his peers any longer, and after a long stint in a mental institution, turned to the streets and the only thing he knew for relief: alcohol. I would often see Preacher on the corner of 5th and Los Angeles, panhandling. He was too far gone to work; he couldn't stay off the alcohol long enough.

Many times the money he came up with went to help someone else rather than himself. He still put others first in his life, as though their needs were always greater than his own. I never seen anything like it, at least not on skid row, where someone was more concerned with others than themselves. Almost always it was the other way around. I was of the school "every man for himself first"; it was a point of survival, but one Preacher never learned. It wasn't in his makeup, and he couldn't ignore the pain of others. This was his mechanism for coping with his own position. He could always believe there was still a part of him that wanted to do good, even in a bad situation.

I know of many people Preacher helped out, and believe you me, on skid row he was an asset. We could have used more like him in that environment. When I left Los Angeles in October of that year, he was there doing his thing, and as far as I know, is still there today. It was during this time that Preacher introduced me to another person that didn't belong down there. She was Laura, and a special project of Preacher's. He use to look out for her because, you see, Laura had serious mental problems.

I met Laura while having a drink with Preacher at one of the local bars, the King Eddie, on 5th and Los Angeles. She came into the bar because she had seen Preacher come in. He was one of the few people she trusted in the streets because he didn't make fun of her or judge her, and treated her as a friend, not a freak. I often saw Laura on the street, and I couldn't understand why society would allow someone as sick as she was to be on her own. She obviously belonged in a hospital somewhere, if not some sort of group home. She couldn't take care of herself, and how she survived the streets, I'll never know. Surely God was looking after her, and I know he put people in her life, like the Preacher, to watch after her. She couldn't do it any other way; this lady was in bad shape.

It took Laura a while to trust me, too, by seeing me with Preacher and from the way I treated her like a person and not a freak. Laura was the type of person that most people would see on the street and would walk to the other side to avoid. She had a habit of talking to herself, waving her arms around and walking in circles—you knew to look at her that she wasn't all there.

I remember seeing her on the streets being teased by a group of local youngsters. They were throwing things at her, and had hit her in the leg with something that had cut her really bad. She was bleeding so badly her sock and tennis shoe were soaked in blood. I chased away the kids, took her to a coffee shop, and called an ambulance to hopefully take her to a hospital and get her some help. The ambulance came and treated her wound, but she wouldn't let them take her to the hospital no matter how hard I tried to convince her.

I later learned from Preacher, who knew more about her story, why she was that way—she had been in a lot of hospitals—both mental and regular—in her time, and had been treated badly in more than one of them. She never wanted to go back, under any circumstances. She had even been sexually assaulted by one of the staff at a group home.

I could see why she preferred the streets. Laura had been treated bad all her life, her parents gave her up to the state because of her condition. They hadn't been able to control her, and then the state drove her off by the treatment she received in their institutions. The streets were her only alternative; she had no other place to go. I know there were a lot more like Laura out there that society had created, but could do nothing about, because they had slipped through the cracks and disappeared. Laura was another of the Walking Wounded who didn't belong—under any circumstances—where she was. Like with so many others, I don't know what happened to Laura. Maybe Preacher is still there looking out for her; she needed someone. I don't know how long a person like her could survive in an environment like that otherwise.

I soon tired of my life and decided once again that a change of scenery would fix me—if I could only get away from this area, I would be all right. So in October of 1988 I headed east. Two days later, I found myself back in Phoenix, another old hangout of mine, and right away I headed for my old stomping grounds, the Salt River flats just south of town. Much to my amazement, when I arrived at the flats it was completely vacant; no one was staying there anymore. You could see where the old campsites had been, but no one was there. I later found out that just a few days before, the police had come down there and told everyone to leave or they would be arrested for trespassing. They said they were doing it for everyone's own good because conditions were getting bad there, and who knows, maybe they were.

Things have a way of changing overnight when you live this way; at any rate, everyone was gone. I couldn't find any of my old cronies. They seemed to have disappeared, or moved on, whatever the case may be. When you live in the streets, nothing is permanent. I headed north towards town to find a place of relative security, where I could establish a foothold, when I ran across an old, half burnt-out house. I stayed in the half that wasn't burnt. The next day I sought work in one of the labor pools I use to frequent. I was soon back into my old routine. I didn't stay that way very long though; the desire to get help was still strong, and it seemed to me that my excursions were getting shorter and shorter.

One morning I found myself in a daze in a back alley downtown, behind a bar I used to go to all the time and had been at the night before. The police drove up and took me to detox—where they take drunks to dry out. Back then in Phoenix they didn't put you in jail unless you became a problem, they instead took you to detox. I spent seven days in detox, and during that time they tried to place me in a program where I wouldn't have to go back into the streets again. They found me a place on the east side of town that was operated by the Salvation Army. It was near the state mental institution, and was in what had been a motel at one time. It still could have been for that matter; it was in good shape. I stayed there for a month, at which time I met Sissy.

192

Sissy, believe it or not, was an old Hollywood actress. At first I didn't recognize her, but when she spoke I recognized her voice right away. She was not famous by any standards; she played mostly supporting roles, always the dumb blonde. She was in a lot of movies in the 40s and 50s and if I told you her real name, you probably would still not recognize it. The characteristic that identified her most was her voice—it was a man's voice, very deep and mythical. She supported herself fine in Hollywood, doing bit parts and supporting roles, and was in a position where she had plenty of work, but not the recognition.

Her downfall was drinking. She got involved with the fast crowd of Hollywood and in ja few short years was one of the statistics. She was a bright lady, but too trustful, and people took advantage of her. Most of the money she earned had been mishandled by a bad business manager, or spent on her addiction to alcohol. At first she went to all the best treatment facilities—though there weren't many at that time. When her money ran out completely, she found herself in the streets, hopping from bar to bar, grabbing on to anyone who would buy her a drink, or better yet, take care of her for a while. She had been doing this for three years when I met her.

She had had a long period of sobriety at one point, and was an avid member of Alcoholics Anonymous for a long period. What put her back in the streets after so many years sober is anybody's guess; she never said, although it did have something to do with a man. Sissy was a delightful person, and still had a sense of humor, and after all it was nice having sort of a celebrity around. She stayed the whole length of the program, but left two weeks before I did. I never seen her again, even after I returned to the streets, so maybe, just maybe, she was one of the lucky ones who made it that time.

After leaving the program, I was sent to a halfway house, where I quickly found a steady job and started getting my life back together. Once again I was saving my money, had bought a car, and finally had me a place to stay. I continued to work at my job for another month after moving out of the halfway house. Then one Friday night, after getting paid, I found myself in a bar, wondering what the hell I was doing there. For the umpteenth time, I lost everything: my job, my car, my apartment, and was back in the streets.

About a week later I was on a bus bench north of town with no place to go when I waved down a police car, thinking they would take me to detox. Instead, they found out I was a veteran and took me out to the V.A. Hospital and dropped me off. I went in and told them who I was and what my problem was and they admitted me right away to the mental ward, and listed me a danger to myself.

It so happened that at that time a new program was getting started for Vietnam veterans who had what they called Post Traumatic Stress Disorder. In fact the foremost authority on that disorder was running the program at the time. He run me through a battery of tests to see if I might be one of those veterans who suffered that affliction. The tests came back positive. But me, being a know-it-all, didn't buy it. I thought the diagnosis was just another cop out, and wanted nothing to do with their program. Besides, it would have required me to make a one-year commitment, and at the time I could not see past tomorrow. So I ran, and I mean that literally. They didn't want to let me go, but I busted through the security doors and left against their wishes with a couple of guards on my tail.

I didn't know what I was going to do at the time, just that I didn't want to be in the streets again. So the next morning I went to the Salvation Army Adult Rehabilitation Program, just south of town, and checked myself in. By this time I was pretty well-known in the Salvation Army Centers of the Southwest, and I didn't stay long before a Major who ran the program and knew me from Los Angeles asked me if I wanted to do him a big favor and take over the Houseman's job at the Tucson Center. They had no one in the center down there at the time that knew as much about the operation as I did, so he thought I was a good candidate. I immediately accepted the position, and was on my way to Tucson the next day.

The position was high up in the ranks and gave me the run of the center. I answered only to the officer in charge. I was responsible for the smooth operation of the living and eating quarters of the center, and was in charge of everyone living there. The job also came with a generous salary. I saved my money, and the first thing I did was buy a car. It was late January of 1989. I stayed at the center until March, at which time I became overwhelmed with the responsibilities required of me, and went back to the streets and drinking. I didn't stay in Tucson though. Work there wasn't any good. So with the money I had saved, I turned my car east towards Houston. Before I got through New Mexico, my car broke down, and not having the money to get it fixed, I sold it to a mechanic in a little one-horse town that I happened to be near at the time, and bought me a bus ticket to Houston.

Every time I started doing good and had a few possessions, I lost them all when I returned to drinking. I quickly came to know the meaning of the Lord giveth and the Lord taketh away. It was almost as if I had a self-destruct mechanism so that every time I was doing good, I would self-destruct. I really didn't want to live the way I was living anymore, but I couldn't help myself.

I arrived in Houston almost broke. I was beginning to believe I would never get things right, and deemed myself a failure. Right away I headed for the Pierce Elevated, an overpass on Pierce and Main in Houston that was a well-known hangout for the homeless. I had stayed there before. I found a thick cardboard box, the kind they sell those big refrigerators in. It was almost half an inch thick and made a good sturdy place for me to stay. I didn't have to worry about the rain because I was under an overpass. I stayed there until just before Christmas of 1989, during which time I worked very little—except for panhandling, and if you think that's not work, try it sometime. I did work occasionally, but mostly I panhandled and sold blood. It was a bad time for me.

When I first moved in under the overpass, there weren't many other people there, but the closer it got to Christmas, the more people came. The reason for this being it was a favorite drop-off place for the people of Houston, who at that time of year, Christmas, began thinking about the homeless, and trying to help them. The rest of the year we were invisible. People meant well, but I believe if you're going to help someone, you make a habit of it, not just at Christmas when you're feeling guilty about not doing anything.

It was while I was staying there that I met Pops, another homeless person of the older generation, whom you just called Pops more or less out of respect and for the lack of anything else to call him. Pops had only been in the streets for two years, and had been trying to get on Social Security all that time. Pops was fifty-five and had a bad heart—what they called congenital heart disease—along with a bad case of arthritis in both his arms and legs.

Two years earlier he had failed a physical at work, and they had to let him go because he could no longer do what was required on his job. He had worked at the same place all his adult life, and had been a supervisor of a large warehouse complex. He had always lived from paycheck to paycheck, and didn't have much saved for such a contingency. Before long, he found himself in the streets, with no other place to go. He had been married a couple of times and had two children, but they were grown and living elsewhere. He didn't want to leave Houston. He was a divorcee, and had no parents. They had died a few years back, so he had nowhere to turn.

He applied for Social Security Disability as soon as he couldn't work anymore, but it taking as long as it does to get the paperwork through, he found himself in the streets with no money coming in and no way to get any. He couldn't work, so he collected cans, and after a while started panhandling. He had to swallow a lot of pride to do this—he had been self-sufficient all his life, but he didn't know what else to do. He was lost. The endless paperwork and time involved in obtaining Social Security left him with no other option. I'm not blaming the people who work in Social Security. It's not their fault. They have rules to follow, but I think the government could work a little faster for these people who have no other options.

Pops spent a lot of time at the doctor's office and in the emergency room for his condition. He had nine medications that he was supposed to take regularly, but couldn't afford the cost of the prescriptions so most of the time he went without. Social Security had already turned him down once, and he had to reapply, but it was taking forever and he was rapidly getting worse. He couldn't get help until the Social Security Department determined him disabled. We could improve on this process, at least give a person the medical help they need until they can make a determination.

Pops was a gentle creature. He was deeply saddened by the way he had to live and what he had to do to survive, but he had no other choice, and this hurt him deeply. He didn't really even want Social Security and would have preferred to keep working, but his health wouldn't allow it, so there he was, between a rock and a hard place.

In June, Pops had a massive heart attack in his sleep and died alone under an overpass, with no one around to comfort him, another of the Walking Wounded who shouldn't have been there in the first place. Maybe he was your neighbor at one time or even a friend, who knows. So how can we judge such people? My grandfather use to say, don't ever judge another man until you have walked a mile in his shoes, and who of us, including myself, have ever honestly done that?

Just before Christmas, the people of Houston started showing up in droves, with blankets, coats, food, anything a homeless person could use. With them came the media, with the cameras and everything, talking to the people who came to help, as well as with some of the homeless. I was one of those they interviewed, and did I give them a piece of my mind! I was a bit tipsy at the time, a bad mistake for them. On camera, I asked them where they had been the rest of the year. That I had been there since March, and no one paid me any mind. Why do we only need help at Christmas?

I didn't mince any words, and from what I heard they televised that segment, though with a lot of bleeps. My language was highly descriptive as I remember it. They showed the cardboard box where I lived. I had cut holes in the side that had the appearance of windows and they got a big kick out of that. To me, those holes served a purpose: no one could sneak up on me at night, and they provided ventilation so my home would not become musty. I guess they thought I was crazy, and who knows, maybe I was. I only know how pissed I was that they only thought about us once a year. Where were their consciences the rest of the time?

Shortly after this time, just before Christmas, I checked into the Salvation Army for yet another try at getting better. This was in December of 1989. I remember it was cold that day, especially for Houston, and I was sick and tired once again of living the kind of life I was living, and sick of drinking. I didn't even want to drink anymore, but had reached the point that I had to, just to be able to function in the streets. I knew that somehow I had to get out and try again to straighten out my life.

It was during this stay at the Salvation Army that I met Lenny. Lenny was at one time a well known sports personality. His fame was short-lived, but if I told you his real name, or for that matter what line of sports he was in, you would probably be able to put two and two together, and figure out who he is. For now, I'll just say he was a well-known sports figure. Lenny made the mistake of trusting others to handle his finances. At one time he had a seven-figure payday, and could have been set for life, had his money been managed intelligently.

Lenny himself was not a well-educated man. He had a heart of gold, and would do anything for anybody if he thought they needed it. When his name became synonymous with his sport, the vultures closed in, and people he hadn't seen in years showed up. Lenny being the kind of person he was, made room for as many as he could, and they bled him dry. Lenny was a young man still, in his late twenties, but had already been through a fortune. Lenny himself didn't have any vices. His only vice that I knew of was his complete trust of others, and while this could be considered a good trait, for him it was his Waterloo.

Another thing about Lenny that set him apart from the others was his attitude. He didn't blame anyone but himself for the position he was in, and he never complained about where his decisions led him either. For a few years after he went broke, he lived in the streets, just like me and many others. He worked out of the labor pools for minimum wage, so sometimes he could afford a bed at one of the local flophouses. Other times he stayed down at the Pierce Elevated like the rest of us. Another thing about Lenny is that he never changed, even when he didn't have much money at all, I seen him help others out when they needed it, ignoring his own needs over theirs. I just couldn't believe this man. Here was a young black man who had once had it all, and was taken to the bank by his so-called friends and associates, yet still his attitude hadn't changed. He still believed that there was good in everyone; talk about the power of belief!

His mom deserves the credit for this. Lenny often said that was how she raised him. His father left the family when Lenny was still young, and so his only role model growing up was his mother. She should have been named Mother of the Century, because while overcoming her own difficulties, she still took the time to instill in her children a belief system that made them all, in my opinion, exceptional people, and beyond reproach. I really liked Lenny. He taught me that no matter what the circumstances you face in life, good can come of it if you learn, don't give up and accept at least some responsibility for your situation. Because no matter how much others may have been involved in any given situation, they were in your life because of who you were, and because you allowed them to be. But as long as you didn't give up, and kept putting one foot in front of the other, everything—no matter how bad it may seem at the time—will get better if your beliefs don't falter.

What a man! I could never be like him completely, but it was something to strive for. He never allowed anything to get him down. He tried to do better with each passing day. Lenny did eventually get off the streets, and last I heard, was on the lecture circuit, talking to young people and signing autographs. He had some new agents that believed in him and didn't use him for their own ends, but rather to benefit him. So you see, some of us do make it. Lenny was such a person, though he should have never been in the street in the first place. Wherever you are Lenny, I love you. I learned much from your experiences, and I often think about you when things are not going well for me.

As usual, it didn't take me long to land a payroll job at the Salvation Army. You see, most of the jobs in the center were non-payroll, but there were some critical positions in the center that were needed for its operation that were deemed payroll jobs so the center would function more smoothly. I was one of those people who had been around the Salvation Army for so long, I had held virtually every job in the center at one time or another. Because of this, it never took me long to secure a payroll position.

I'm not very proud of it, but many times I took advantage of my positions to benefit myself and my own needs. One day it is my dream to repay the Salvation Army, in part, for all they have given me over the years. I could not have survived the streets as long as I did had it not been for them. The Salvation Army is one of a kind, and if you ever contemplated giving to any charity, it is one of the best. In my opinion, they've helped more people in more ways than any organization known to man, and do more good than any of them. The Salvation Army will always hold a special place in my heart.

At any rate, I didn't stay long. I saved every penny I earned—and even some I didn't—and soon had enough to buy another car. With that, I was on the move again, headed east, and once again not sure of my destination. It was in late March of 1990, and the one thing I did right when I left Houston was not drink. I drove straight through to New Orleans, arriving late on a Friday night. I had a few dollars in my pocket, so I done something else that was out of character for me, I rented a room. My mistake was the room was above a bar, and it wasn't long before I was broke again and without my car, sold to drink on. Broke and in the streets, I stopped in my tracks and then and there quit drinking. I spent a week looking for a place to get help, and finally found it at Bridge House.

This was a place that helped those who couldn't get help any other way by taking them off the streets, and into a program to overcome their problems, whatever they might be. Bridge House is another place I owe my life to. You see, things at this time were beginning to fall into place, and even though it would take me a couple of more years to finally get it right, Bridge House provided one of the main ingredients, they loved me when I couldn't love myself. This is where I first began this book, and was when I was written up by the *Times Picayune*, the local paper. I even managed to get a couple of editorials published about the homeless.

I was beginning to feel good about myself, and that there still might be hope for me, and this was one more of the ingredients needed to live a life without alcohol. The others would follow ever so slowly in the next couple of years, but I now had HOPE, something that had been missing in the past. Bridge House gave me that hope, and made me believe in myself. I stayed at Bridge House for five months, and when things were getting better, I left to work offshore again. I done all right for the first couple of months, but then for whatever reason, I can't even remember now, the demon returned. Again I lost everything I had gained, and was on the move to Florida.

It was late September of 1990, and I ended up in Orlando, where I achieved more sobriety than I had ever known. I even managed to go to school for a year, while living in a homeless shelter and not drinking, a very difficult task for an alcoholic like me. With help from the Coalition for the Homeless in Orlando, I was able to hold things together for over a year. It wasn't easy, and there were many times when I just wanted to give it up, but I hung in there hoping this would be the time I made it. And because of some very caring people I became involved with at the shelter, I was able to put together a substantial stretch of sobriety. During this time I met quite a few people who were and had been homeless like me for quite some time. The first one I'd like to tell you about is Janet.

Janet was the only female Vietnam veteran that I ever met living in the streets. I'm not saying she was the only one, just the only one I knew. She was a pretty lady, not really beautiful in the physical sense of the word, but her inner beauty was unlike any I had ever seen before. Never had I known anyone who lived in the streets that had so much concern about others, ignoring her own circumstances. It was almost as if she was put there to help others, and her own plight was just an afterthought. That's the best I can explain it.

She was a small lady, only about five-foot-two, and she was a Registered Nurse. She had brown hair and green eyes, and dressed as if she were still in the Sixties. When she came home from Vietnam, she got involved in the peace movement and the hippie generation. We often ignore the fact that there were many women who served their country in the Vietnam conflict, and that many of them returned with some of the same problems that combat soldiers had. Nurses seen more death day in and day out than a front-line infantry man. It was a constant in their lives that they faced every time they went into the operating theater or a hospital ward.

Until I met Janet, even I had no idea how much this war affected the women who served; it's just something I had never thought about. Our government is still, to a great degree, ignoring the plight of the female veteran, and that needs to change. Janet was in one of the most active areas of the conflict, the northern provinces. She had been in Vietnam about the same time I had, and had gone through the Tet Offensive of 1968, the same as me. I never knew her while I was there, as I was in the southern provinces around Saigon and she was up north around Da Nang. Most of the soldiers she dealt with were Marines and I was in the Army. I can only imagine the pain that Janet felt having to deal with the amount of death she dealt with every day and trying to remain detached from it in order to do her job.

Janet went to Vietnam for the same reason many of us did, to serve our country, and to try to make a difference. I imagine how Janet was before she went to 'Nam, but I knew enough about her to know that she wasn't the same person that returned. She had the same desire to help others, but it was directed more to prevention, rather than intervention. Her ideals had changed and her belief that she could make a difference if only she done the right thing had been shook to the core. Like many of us, she didn't like to talk about what had happened, and never, but never, expressed her feelings. It was as if the war had made her detached from reality. She still lived in the culture of the Sixties and just wanted to forget what had happened to her. At times it seemed like a dream.

When she returned from 'Nam, she tried, like most of us, to adjust to the world the way it was, but couldn't accept it in the context of what had happened over there. Janet never had a drug problem that I knew of, other than alcohol. We all needed something to relieve the pain, if only temporarily. It was the coping mechanism that allowed us a temporary peace in the war we still carried around inside. When I met Janet, she was staying at the shelter where I was, run by the Coalition for the Homeless. But she had no desire yet to do anything about her plight. She refused when help was offered, and lived in a world she created that was free from the terror of her mind. I use to talk to her for hours on end. We were close to the same age.

At times she was completely coherent. Other times she made no sense at all and was living in her fantasy world, a perfect world with no war, and especially no death. Janet's problems ran much deeper than one could imagine, her mental state had suffered greatly over the years. She was gradually retreating further and further into her imaginary world, and was almost beyond reach at times. I wish I had the answers as to how she could have been helped, but I believe she had already crossed that invisible line where help was beyond her reach, a sad tale, but true.

202

I had known many a man who had reached that state in their lives, but this was the first time I'd ever seen it in a woman. The best thing I could have done for Janet was to let her know she wasn't alone and that she had a friend, and that's just what I done. Janet never stayed in the shelter for long periods of time; she came and went. One day you would see her around, and then she would disappear for a while. She was from Buffalo, New York, but she never talked about her family, whether she had ever been married, or had children. I never heard that anyone came around looking for her. In that sense, it was almost as if she didn't exist.

Another of the Walking Wounded, I think. She deserved more, but had lost her sense of reality—in order to protect herself and not "lose it"—if that makes any sense to anyone. It does to me. When I left Orlando over a year later, she was still living in the streets. I doubt she ever got the help she needed, mostly because she wasn't receptive to it. She had accepted her fate.

At the shelter I met another woman named Angel. She was thirty-nine and originally from Memphis, Tennessee. She had been married and had three children, but was divorced. Her ex-husband had custody of the children. Angel had had a normal childhood and as far as I could tell, it played no part in her homelessness. What was a major factor was she was disabled. Seven years before, at age thirty-two, she had had a stroke, and it left her partially paralyzed on the left side. She could still get around by herself, but walked with a limp, and her left arm and hand were not fully functional. I'm sure many of you have seen people just like her at one time or another. It was a common affliction of stroke victims. People don't usually associate pride as a problem of the female gender, but believe me when I tell you it is just as much a factor for them as it is in males, just not as pronounced. This was one of the reasons she was in the streets—she didn't want to be a burden on her family. She received a check every month from the government, but that went fast because she liked to drink, and drank to forget, as a lot of us done.

After her stroke, her husband couldn't accept her imperfections, and couldn't deal with a wife that was so visibly disabled. A year after she had the stroke, he divorced her and obtained custody of the children on the premise of her disability—that she couldn't take care of them herself. She never recovered from that rejection, and even in a way accepted it as true. She blamed herself and her disability for her circumstances in life. Her husband convinced her that she was less of a woman the way she was, and she believed him.

Yes, Angel drank too much, and yes the things she believed to be true were in fact, not true, but you couldn't convince her of that. She had been in and out of mental institutions since her stroke, mostly for depression and the suicidal tendencies she had. She talked about death often, and had even tried to kill herself a couple of times. This always ended her up on a mental ward for a couple of weeks, then right back into the streets. People treated Angel badly, even some of the street people; to them she was a freak.

Angel was not a beautiful woman, in fact I guess you could call her a plain Jane. But she was just the opposite inside. She really cared about others, and it hurt her deeply that people looked at her as a freak. She wasn't a violent person, and was a harm to no one except herself. She had become a loner, mostly sticking to herself, although she did have one female friend.

Other than myself, I only seen her with one other man. He had befriended her in the beginning for all the wrong reasons: he wanted to share in her monthly windfall when she got her check. He used her for this purpose only, but she would always let him back into her life after they broke up, which was usually once a month after her money had run out. But I guess she needed the physical contact to make her still feel like a woman, and even though she knew he was only there for her money, she accepted that fact in order to have that personal touch in her life that helped her feel normal.

You couldn't badmouth him, because she always stuck up for him, saying that at least to him she wasn't a freak, and he made her feel like a woman again. I can almost understand how she must have felt; we all need that contact from time to time to make us feel alive, and with her, she felt she wasn't good enough for anyone else. In a way I believed she really loved him, even him being the asshole he was. It was a match necessary in both of their lives—she felt no one else would have her, and he was the kind no one else would have ever put up with. A match made in heaven—

think about it—it may have been the only thing that was keeping her alive, that contact in one's life that gives it purpose. She was living like that when I left Orlando, and as far as I know, if she isn't dead, she still is.

Another person I came to know well while I was at the Orlando Coalition for the Homeless was Junior. Junior was a black man in his mid-fifties who was kind of a mentor for the homeless. He was the one who knew everyone and everyone knew him. Originally from somewhere in Mississippi, he had lived in or around Orlando for most of his adult life. He couldn't work anymore; he had one of the worst cases of asthma I had ever seen. He was never without his aerosol pump, and sometimes when he had an attack you'd swear he was going to die. He was a very thin man. His hair was black mixed with just a little bit of gray. He always dressed in jeans and a long-sleeve shirt, even in the summer, and always wore tennis shoes.

He had a bicycle to get around with, although at times he couldn't ride it because of his asthma. He was always loaning it to someone. I don't know how he ever kept track of it. Junior was one of those people who were on and off the streets from time to time depending on his circumstances. But even when he was off the streets, he still hung around the street people. He had a girlfriend who was younger than him by at least twenty years. She was heavy into drugs, and when she wasn't in rehab or in the streets herself, Junior stayed with her. You could always find him during the day and into the early evening hours around the shelter.

They all knew Junior well, and when he was around he helped the people who ran the shelter, handing out meal tickets and bed assignments. Bed assignments consisted of a spot on a bare cement floor. You had to provide your own blankets—what few they had went to the women and children first, and were usually gone by the time it got to you. Many just slept on the cold cement. I liked Junior. He was good people, and would do anything for you if he could. Had it not been for him those first weeks that I started school and couldn't work, I wouldn't have had any cigarettes. He use to buy me a pack of Bugler (loose, roll-your-own tobacco) everyday.

Junior's one vice was he liked his wine, and usually had a drink for anyone who needed one to get over the night before.

He did drink vodka from time to time when he could afford it, but for the most part it was his wine, Wild Irish Rose. The shelter itself slept over two hundred people and as far as shelters go it was new and crude, but better than the streets. At least you had a roof over your head to protect you from the weather. They were always hoping to build a better shelter with beds and everything, but for as long as I stayed there it was just a spot on a cold cement floor.

You almost had to fight to get anything to eat. It was like feeding cattle at meal times, with people cutting into line and going through the line three or four times. I usually waited in the background for things to quiet down, then went up to get whatever was left over, which usually wasn't much. I lost a lot of weight while I lived there. I quit drinking after about a month in the shelter because I was trying to get into school. I thought if I could learn a good trade, I wouldn't want to drink anymore. I did get into school, Mid-Florida Tech, and I stayed there almost a year. During this time Junior was a big help to me, encouraging me to continue when I wanted to quit, and making sure I got something to eat every day and had smokes.

When he was living off the streets with his girlfriend, he would invite me over on the weekends to watch TV so I wouldn't be so bored. This was good, especially during football season, because I really loved football. Other times it was just nice not to have to hang around the shelter watching your things all the time so they wouldn't get stolen. There was no honor among thieves, and if it wasn't watched or tied down, they would steal it. The shelter was divided into two parts by a flimsy tennis net. The women and children stayed on one side of the net, and the men on the other. I never cared for the set up they had there, and had it not been for Junior I probably would not have stayed.

Junior was the one you went to if you needed advice, or to know how to get over on whatever; he knew all the ins and outs of the system and how best to approach any given problem because he had already been there. He was also the one you went to if you just needed a friend, because if there was one thing Junior knew how to be, it was a friend. He asked for nothing in return and was one of the most unselfish persons I ever knew. I use to hang around him a lot, and came to depend on him often. When I left the shelter, Junior and his girl were separated, for whatever reason, and he was living in the shelter, the same as the rest of us. If Junior is alive and still there, he may be running the place.

I didn't stay at the center the whole year I was in Orlando. I met a guy I went to school with who needed a cook and a baby-sitter on the weekends to take care of his two boys while he was at work. So we reached a mutual agreement, and it worked well for both of us as long as the arrangement lasted. I was really doing well—I hadn't drank for almost a year, and my studies were coming along. I was entered in a course where you could work as fast as you wanted to as long as you could pass. In a year's time, I was already into the course six months ahead of everyone else.

Then I made a fatal mistake—I met a woman. We ended up moving in with one another, and before long I was drinking again, and the relationship was down the tubes. As quick as it had started, it ended. We were on summer break, so I never made it back to school. I had gotten a check for the time I did attend school the year before, and with that check I left town. Surprise! Sound familiar to you? It should, it's been my pattern throughout.

It was in the early spring, somewhere around April of 1991, and I was back in New Orleans, working offshore and back to my old tricks. But the end was near, and I hadn't even seen it coming—one day it was just there and all the key ingredients were right. But first I had to endure another year and a half before I put it all together, during which time I met a few more people I must tell you about.

The first is a young man I had met earlier when he was in the streets. He had since come to Bridge House, where I got to know more about him. His name was Jerry, and he was one of the success stories that you don't hear enough about. Jerry was twenty-six years old, and one of the kindest and gentlest people you'd ever want to meet. He was from somewhere around St. Louis, Missouri, and had left home by choice, looking for something better. He didn't have much book learning, but made up for it in street knowledge. He had more common sense than most of us ever hoped to have. Jerry and I were good friends at a time when I needed friends.

One of Jerry's main problems was that he was such a trusting person, and there were those in the streets who often took advantage of this fact. He would do anything for anyone, no matter what the circumstances, even if that meant he would have to go without himself. Jerry related to me some horrendous stories about his childhood; the physical abuse he endured from his father was unbearable, and out of respect for Jerry I'll not go into that. He was trying to forgive and reestablishing a relationship with his mother. Did I mention how forgiving he was?

Jerry was slow in a lot of ways, and he had a speech impediment that took time to get use to, but his character made up for his shortcomings. Besides it wasn't his fault, but rather a result of what he had been through as a child. Jerry in some ways was still a child but he wanted more than anything to be independent and to provide for himself. His whole time at Bridge House he concentrated on this end, as well as addressing his alcoholism. With help from counselors at Bridge House and other agencies in town, he learned a trade: how to cook.

Jerry had fought insurmountable odds growing up and in the streets, but had his sights on becoming a better person, and wouldn't let anything or anyone turn him from that purpose once he made the conscious decision to do something about his problems. He went to speech therapy and was getting much better than he had been when I first met him. Jerry fought all the demons of his afflictions, and was winning. He taught me a lot, and I'll always be grateful to him for allowing me to be one of his friends.

He left Bridge House before I did, and got a steady job at a local restaurant washing dishes. It wasn't the cooking job he wanted but was a step in the right direction. He felt you had to start at the bottom in order to reach the top of your goal, but as long as a person worked towards those ends, they were making progress, and for now he was content with his job. He use to say how good it felt to have a steady job and be a productive member of society, and not have to depend on anyone else. Jerry was a treasure, and a testament to those who work so tirelessly to reach their goals. I still think about Jerry when I start to question my own methods and become dissatisfied with my own progress.

If Jerry can do it, anyone can; they just need the right ingredients to succeed.

By now I hope you understand that I had returned to Bridge House in New Orleans after leaving Houston, and was trying to get my life in order. But it didn't seem the same as before. Almost all my old friends had moved on, either to better things or back to their old habits somewhere else. I used this as a reason not to stay too long. When I left, I moved in with Jerry for a brief time, until I could get on my feet. While I was with Jerry he helped me keep my goals in mind and my life on track.

Then came the time I chose to leave and at once my life began to fall apart again. I was relying on myself for salvation and you'd think I'd have learned by now that that doesn't work. Armed with the best knowledge and the best intentions, you cannot make it in this life if you choose to be an island. I was still fooling myself after all this time that I could do it on my own. I returned to the streets and back to working offshore, hoping for the quick fix. It was at this time that I met Tony.

I had been living in a weed patch just off Annunciation, and during one of my binges Tony came wandering into my campsite. At the time I didn't know it, but Tony was a mirror image of myself, only more advanced. He was Italian American, black hair and brown eyes, and physically trim—in that respect, he could not have been farther from where I was. But mentally, and what he had been through, he was my exact copy: a Vietnam veteran who ran into the same problems as I did when he got home. He was in the streets for all the same reasons, and had been battling his alcoholism for a long time. He had wanted to change and had been trying to change for quite a few years now, but as yet, like me, had not found the right combination. Tony was rapidly approaching the point of giving up and accepting his fate. I, on the other hand, had not reached that point yet. It is because of Tony that I started looking at my own situation with more respect. Tony was one of the catalysts that was instrumental in putting me on the right track.

Physically Tony was further down the ladder than I had gone so far; he already had cirrhosis of the liver. He was rapidly approaching the end and didn't know it yet; at least that's what he made you believe. I watched over the next couple of months as Tony got worse and worse. The pain he endured, the emotional state he went through during this time was indescribable. He was drinking only wine at that time, about two gallons a day. He supported this habit as much as he could through his friends and panhandling.

Unable to work, his sole purpose in life was to find his next drink. Three months after walking into my camp, Tony was found dead in an alley in downtown New Orleans, a victim of his disease. I didn't know much about Tony's family, and don't even know if they knew that he had died. He died alone, having found no answers to his questions and having accepted his fate. He had given up. I saw myself down the line just like Tony, alone and dead in an alley somewhere, my loved ones not knowing what happened to me.

For the first time in my life of drinking, I was scared. One of my biggest fears was that I would give up before I found the answers, or that others would give up on me before I gave up on myself. It was through Tony that I began to see where I was headed, and it didn't look good. It's true that there are those who have to die in order that some of us might live. Tony was this for me: he gave his life in order that mine might be saved. His contribution, and those of all the others I had encountered along the way who had nurtured me, were beginning to come together. I was slowly getting the message, finally! This wasn't an immediate change, but it was taking shape, ever so slowly, but would I find the rest of the puzzle before it was too late?

It was late April of 1992 and I was going through a lot of changes. Trying everything I was ever taught to get out of my situation, I run the whole gambit: missions, the Salvation Army, back to Bridge House, and the streets again, with lots of AA meetings in between. Still nothing seemed to work, until I met Betty Gail over a year later. Then the missing part of the puzzle came together and I knew things were going to change. In late June of 1993, I was working offshore and living out of hotels and flophouses, drinking like there was no tomorrow, when all of a sudden Betty came into my life.

God's Wisdom

When the heart is lying heavy
And the world seems crushing down
When the mind can see no reason
And your pain, it knows no bounds

When your life is often measured
By the hours and minutes of your day
That life's meaning loses its aura
And your feet don't know the way

When things often look their darkest
And human reason no longer seems
To answer questions, yet unspoken
And real life plays like a dream

It's only then you find the answer
From deep within your soul
That lasting makes the difference
And by preserving, can reach our goals

'Cause the walk is often hardest
When no answers lie in sight
And the actions lose their meaning
If the walk has lost its might

Only then, and only when
We choose to step aside
Does God allow his greatness
To abide with us inside

When we choose no longer to be the problem
And seek solution, by our faith
To look to the heavens for the answer
That God's wisdom sets us straight

Because when we're no longer the problem
And allow God to do his THING
We release the bonds of slavery
And the bells of freedom ring

Freedom from the days of drudgery
Of trying to go it alone
We realize God has taught us to be stronger
And his true WISDOM has he shown.

— April 10, 1997

212

~ 8 CHAPTER 8 ~

Free at Last OR *God's Wisdom*

In the past twenty-five years, I had been through a lot, and met a lot of people just like me, who for whatever reason found themselves homeless. I've tried as best I could to relate these stories to you as I encountered them, and for the most part have remained true to what really happened. During this time, I learned a lot. As I traveled this country, I picked up bits and pieces of what one day I would put together to finally finish the puzzle, and find what I was looking for all along. Many of those lessons were learned from the people I met. As to why it took me so long to get the complete message is anybody's guess. Who knows why it takes some longer than it does others to find his or her dream? It just does.

At any rate, what I learned in the end is that it takes several factors, and one by itself does not constitute a solution. You must learn them all and then put together a package that will work for you. Some people find it, and some don't. Some have the solution, but never put the different parts together. Maybe some of the parts never appear, who knows? All I know is it took me twenty-five years to have all the ingredients in one spot, at one time. The final ingredient for me was a woman, and her name was Betty Gail.

In the past, I had known many women, and why it didn't work with them I guess was because some of the other parts were missing. I do know that when Betty arrived in my life, all the elements were there. I was living on the East Bank of New Orleans in a flophouse, working offshore off and on, and things weren't going very well for me. I decided to move, but not far. I moved to the West Bank, to a town known as Westwego. I still worked offshore, but I had a better place to stay—a one-room efficiency that I kept even when I was offshore and working. I was tired of bouncing around the country like a nomad, going from job to job and working for minimum wage. I was also getting real tired of drinking. It no longer gave me the relief it once had. Now if you've followed along, you just seen four of the final ingredients it took to make me finally see the light. But the end had not come yet.

I continued to drink, searching for the escape that had long since disappeared. I was becoming more and more despondent, and was rapidly reaching the point in my life where I didn't know what I was going to do anymore, even drinking didn't help. In four words, "I was really tired." One of my times off work I went to a place called

214

the Canal Bank Inn, a bar in Westwego. As I sat there drinking, I happened to look down the long bar and there standing at the end of it was Betty. The first thing I noticed about Betty was how beautiful she looked to me, and I wondered if she was alone. I was brave when I was drinking, and asked the barmaid, who seemed to know her, if she was alone, and the reply came that she was. I told her to give the lady a drink, whatever she was drinking, and to not allow her to buy a drink herself as long as she or I was still there.

Much to my surprise she was drinking Diet Coke; she didn't drink alcohol. She had came to the bar at the urging of a friend, and had almost decided not to come, but at the last minute did. I could see she liked to dance, and seemed to be popular with some of the locals as a partner. I figured what the hell, what have I got to lose? So on the very next dance I asked her to join me. Much to my surprise she did. In the past I had often asked others, but they seldom accepted. The rest of the night was like a dream—we talked and danced the night away.

Even on the West Bank, most of the bars were open twenty-four hours, and by midnight I was getting very drunk, and asked her if she would take me home and she did. She stayed with me a couple of hours at my efficiency, and we talked, among other things. She gave me her phone number, and told me to call her some time, and after a couple of hours she left. At the time, I remember thinking, well that's the end of that.

The next evening I went out drinking again, and on a whim, gave her a call. I couldn't get her off my mind. Much to my surprise she came, and we stayed at the bar for a while, then went out to get something to eat, much earlier than the night before. We talked on incessantly that evening, and I learned a lot about Betty. She was a single mother, divorced, who still had three of her six children living with her. She had been separated from her ex-husband now for almost eight years, and was having a tough go of it. She was physically unable to work herself, and was living in subsidized housing not far from the bar where I met her. Besides having three teenage daughters at home, she was taking care of her ailing mother who was slowly dying of cancer. It was July of 1993, and one thing led to another, and on the third date I moved in with her. Exactly how that finally came about I'm not sure, it just happened.

She only had one rule: she didn't say right away that I couldn't drink, she just told me that she wouldn't allow alcohol in her home. I respected that, not suspecting that my drinking days were rapidly coming to an end, at least the drinking days like I had known in the past. I immediately fell in love with Betty and her family. I felt they needed me, and that word "need" became another very important ingredient in my final decision to try and quit drinking for good and without reservation.

Our first Christmas together was very special to me. I spent over four thousand dollars on her and the rest of her family. I wasn't trying to impress anyone; it's just that now that I had cut way back on my drinking, hardly drinking at all, I had all this money left over. I was making over eight hundred dollars in a two-week pay period working offshore. Makes you kind of realize just how much I was drinking before. Yea! Anyway, according to Betty, her family had never before known a Christmas like that one of 1993, and it made me feel so good to do it. Someone finally needed me as much as I needed them—YES, the final piece of the puzzle that had always been missing.

I now had a purpose in life: this family depended on me and me alone to provide for them. It felt so damn good I could hardly stand it, and I was falling in love with Betty and her family more and more every day. I felt as though I belonged. Now it's as I said, Betty had three girls at home. Betty Gail, the youngest, Shannon, the next in line, and Kelly, the oldest. She also had two other daughters who were married, Rhonda and Liz, and a son named Dudley who was living on his own. I truly loved them all, and in my book they could do no wrong. I would have died for any of them.

Now I'd like to say that everyone lived happily ever after, but let's get real, even the best of relationships have their ups and downs, and mine and Betty's was no different. Betty had a certain way she thought her children should be raised, and would have no interference from anyone concerning this matter, and this is as it should have been. They had been through a lot together, and who better to know how to treat one's children if not the mother. Betty's kids were no angels, but they were all good kids. Yet I found it very hard sometimes to bite my tongue when they did something wrong. I tried real hard, but sometimes it was impossible. This was the main cause of disagreement between Betty and me. And I must interject at this time that Betty was right. What right had I, a stranger up until just a few months before, to correct her children? I didn't even have any experience in this area. But sometimes they use to talk to Betty really bad, and this upset me very much. When I said anything, though, Betty got mad at me, as she should have.

I was completely unprepared for this type of relationship—I had no experience how to act, and on top of that, I was just learning what real love was all about. I tried my damnedest but often fell far short, and in the first two years we were together I'd gotten mad four or five times, and left and went out drinking. But these excursions didn't last long, and as quick as they started, they were over. It wasn't the same anymore, and I couldn't live without Betty and the girls, I loved them so much. I only wish I had known better how to show them this, and to prove it to them. I failed miserably in this area. No matter how hard I tried, it always seemed to come out wrong and Betty deserved so much more. It's just that I was so ignorant about love and what a relationship based on love was about, or how to act, and many times I made a real ass out of myself.

Betty and I were together for almost three years and they were three of the happiest years of my life. I really wanted it to work, but unbeknownst to me, I was ever so slowly driving Betty and the kids away with the way I acted sometimes. Now don't get me wrong, we had a lot of good times, but the bad times became too much for Betty to bear, and in the end it drove her away and I was the one who did the driving. One day just two weeks before Christmas of 1996 Betty left me, and I knew that nothing I could say would bring her back. Once she had made up her mind that was it. I had lost the one thing in my whole life that I had been looking for all along, because until I met Betty I didn't know what love was, and I didn't know how to act.

I was devastated, and right away I could think of only one thing, and that was to go back to drinking, which is just what I did. But after two weeks, for the first time in my life I was scared to return to the streets, and I knew if I stayed there I would be dead in no time. Then I remembered one thing, the thing I needed most in life was to feel needed. So one evening, two weeks after Betty left, I called my mother and she told me to come home. I had always said when my mother got old that I would take care of her, and I intended to do just that, and this is where I have been ever since. Now to say I don't miss Betty and the girls would be a gross understatement. I can never replace the love Betty and her family gave so freely to me, and I'll always love them, and do for them whenever I can. But at least now I know I don't need to drink anymore. I just need to stay around those I love and who love me, to contribute, and feel needed.

Today that is the one most important item in my life, along with not drinking anymore, and except for the sadness I feel from having lost Betty and the girls, they at least taught me that there is more to love than just saying, "I love you." Today I am trying to apply this lesson in life, and am learning more and more everyday. Thank you Betty, you gave me much more than I ever gave you, and even though we are not together today, you are still a big part of my life. I owe my life to you and your family, for loving me for who I was and showing me that there is a way in life that doesn't have to include drinking, and that I could be loved and in a small way return some of that love. You and your family will always be in my thoughts and prayers, and some day I hope to make it all up to you for the pain I may have caused trying to have the kind of love that I knew nothing about at the time. God bless you all always, I miss you all very much.

The end is often a new beginning . . .

Life's Design

Life is often like a piece of art
A mosaic we do not clearly see
Events that just don't make no sense
Like the backside of a tapestry

We try to understand the chaos
In a world filled with disarray
But we do not see the whole picture
And allow things to stay as they lay

Because it's easier to ignore the problem
Than to figure the pattern of life
We tally the consequences
And neglect the power of its might

But the true strength of the entire vision
Is God's alone to understand
We're not asked to perceive the whole picture
Only to do the best that we can

So we must learn to walk through life
And not ignore every right or wrong
But it's better to do what's right in the first place
'Cause in God's world we must all get along

—May 9, 1997

~ C H A P T E R 9 ~

In Summary - Life's Design

Even though every book has an ending, this book is one that could go on and on. I've covered many stories here, and there are many others that I could relate to you of those I met during years of being homeless myself. But after a while they start repeating themselves, over and over again. Combine that with the fact that my memory is not as good as it once was, and I'm sure there are a couple of stories I should have told you that for some reason or another have escaped me.

The thing to remember here is the scenario remains the same: many who are homeless are not there out of a conscious choice or because they thought it might be a good idea. They are there because of the circumstances they found themselves in that they knew no other way out of, through no fault of their own. I'm not going to insult your intelligence by saying they are all there because of circumstances beyond their control, but most of them are.

A large percentage of the homeless population is made up of families, women and children. This is based not only on figures from various government and social agencies but also on my own observations, having been there.

There is and always will be a small number out there completely by choice; for whatever reason it suits them. Some of these can even be reached, if approached in the right manner, although many others—perhaps most—you couldn't reach no matter what you tried, because they are happy where they are and do not want to be anywhere else. This is a very small percentage, yet I believe this is what the general public's vision of the homeless is based on.

I would like you to see that this is not the case. As I've said throughout, many of the people out there were once your neighbors, friends and perhaps even family members. Like everything else in life, we have to be careful not to label a group of people by the most obvious aspects of their situation. We have to look deeper, to what led them to be there and whether in fact they had other choices.

And as I've said before, I'm not here to blame anyone or any agency, including the government, only to say that more has to be done to address this matter. I also don't want to leave the impression that no one out there cares, and that nothing is being done at all to address the problem. There are a lot of well-intentioned persons and agencies out there set up to help the homeless that try to

222

address the problem, but they are too few to help so many. Their resources are inadequate, and there is no space available to handle the growing numbers of homeless and the different situations they face. Because of this there are many who slip through the cracks. We as a society—and I include myself—must do more to address these problems. While we have been improving, we still have a long way to go. One of the first things we must face is how we look at the homeless, and how we perceive them.

Another thing you may be asking yourself is: Why do some people faced with similar situations make out all right and others don't? The answers lie a lot deeper under the surface of the problem. It starts with the way a person is raised, what they're circumstances are at the time, as well as the lack of strong family ties, or no family at all to fall back on in tough situations. We have to look at all the circumstances of a person's life, from the beginning, not just concentrate on the dilemma that put them in a situation where the streets were the only alternative. I hope, in a small way, I have answered some of these questions and that you will come away with a different outlook on the plight of the homeless.

It is my hope that in some small way, by telling these stories, I will be able to draw attention to the problem, and help others to see what I saw through my eyes. If everyone was to do just a little, so much more could be done to help the homeless out there. This has been a long-time dream of mine. I started writing this book in 1991 while in a jail cell, and it has taken me this long to complete the project.

We are one of the best societies on earth, and individually, do more to help others than any other society I know of, but so much more has to be done. Everybody in a society like ours, no matter what the circumstances, should have the guarantee of a home. No one in this world should have to live like an animal. We are better than that, and I believe in my heart that between us, we can all make a difference.

Thank you for reading my story.

My Dearest Sister Jeanine,

Well needless to say it's been a long, long
time girl. I'm afraid I haven't been much
of a brother. I've spent most of my adult
life running from myself and those I hold
so dear. I could blame it on alot of things,
I just haven't been the same since Viet Nam,
I've tried very hard to forget it but it
just hasn't gone away. But that to, I have
to shoulder the blame, I've used it as an
excuse for so many years. I'm trying to
learn today to live with that and to except
the responsibility for myself and my actions.
It hasn't been easy, it was always so much
easier to blame someone or something else
for my own inadequacy's, didn't want to
look at myself, the pain was to great, then
I tried to drown that pain in alcohol which
only compounded the problem. Oh the nights
I've ~~laid~~ layed awake crying for the love
of my family, the lonliness I've felt and the
emptyness I've carried all these years has
really seasoned me. In a way that makes
it difficult to fight my way back. But by
the grace of God he is doing for me what
I could not do for myself, I just have to

224

The Times-Picayune

Re the Jan. 7th editorial, "Homeless and the public," and *The Times-Picayune's* continuing effort to make the public aware of the homeless in New Orleans, a commendable and admirable task:

I am speaking from experience as one who was once homeless and fought the difficulties of trying to get help. Believe me when I say it's not easy.

And anyone who believes the homeless do not want help is sadly mistaken. While it's true there is a small percentage (very small) who choose to be where they are, even they would not pass up a chance for a better life.

The real problem lies in the situation; once you find yourself there, it's hard to work out of it.

People don't realize what it's like to walk around with just the clothes on your back, not knowing for sure where your next meal is coming from or even if you'll have a place to stay the night, to experience the prejudice one meets when he or she doesn't meet society's standards.

Many, like myself, turn to alcohol or drugs to escape the pain and reality, only to quickly get caught up in addiction.

In New Orleans there is little or no help for the numbers of those who truly want and need it. The space is just not available to handle so many.

I personally know of people who have died in the streets, waiting to get help. I wanted help long before I got it, and but for the grace of God and Bridge House, I would have been one of those people.

I am now recovering and trying to put my life back together. It's a long, hard road, but better than the one I came from. And if there were more places like Bridge House, the chance would be greater and much easier.

I can only hope and pray that you will continue your battle to make the public more aware of the plight of the homeless— so many lives depend on it. You are truly to be congratulated, and God's direction is with you.

Wayne Compton

226

left to right: the author's son, Winfred III; the author's father, Norman Delos Compton; and the author, Winfred II, who is named after one of his other ancestors

POETRY FROM
THE STREETS

1982 - 1998

The Power of Prayer

When the heart is down, and spirits low
And the pain just lingers on
When nothing seems to work for you
And all your friends are gone

When the world comes crushing in on you
And you think you've lost your way
When the days turn into weeks and months
The only answer is to pray

Because there's nothing like a heart in pain
That brings out the truth in you
And a heart in pain is a line to God
He knows when you're feeling blue

So never underestimate a heart in pain
That's lifted up in prayer
'Cause that's the truest form of exigency
And that's what makes God care

'Cause it's not important what we want
It's a question of what we need
And need is what our Savior gives
And it matters not the deed

The Lord sees what is in our heart
It's the picture of our despair
So never underestimate a broken heart
That's lifted up in prayer

— December 1972

At the Crossroads

I dreamed one night I passed away
And left this world behind
I started down a long wide road
Some friends of mine to find

I came to a signboard in the road
With directions it did tell
Keep right to go to Heaven, it said
Turn left to go to Hell

I hadn't been too good on earth
A hopeless, wandering fake
So I knew there at the crossroads
The path I'd have to take

I started down that rocky road
That leads to Satan's place
With tear-filled eyes and broken heart
Not knowing what I faced

Old Satan met me at the gate
Said, what's your name my friend?
I said, it's just ole homeless Wayne
Who's met an unkind end

He glanced through some files and said
You've made a mistake, I fear
You're listed here as homeless
And we don't want you here

I said, I'm looking for some friends
And a smile stole on his face
He said, if your friends were homeless too
They're in the other place

So I went back the way I came
Till the crossroads I did see
I then turned right to Heaven
As happy as I could be

St. Peter met me at the gate, a smile upon his face
Come in my friend, he said to me, for you I have
        a berth
'Cause you've been homeless most your life
And you lived your Hell on Earth

There I saw my ole friend Pete
And friend, ole bag girl Sal
And all the rest, my homeless friends
I thought had gone to Hell

So listen friend, to what I say
If you were homeless here on earth
Your place in Heaven has been reserved
Since before your very birth

So if someone should judge you here on earth
When you're not feeling well
Just tell them you're on your way to Heaven now
And they can go to Hell

— October 1976

To Survive Is to Forgive

When on and on you go through life
Just doing the best that you can
When all seems lost, and days seem long
When you wonder of your fellow man

You try to survive 'cause you know it's right
To give up, would admit that you're wrong
So you walk through this world with head held high
Because you know, in your heart you belong

But on and on you search through this land
Seeking the answers that lie
Just around the next turn in the road
As the seasons go passing by

One step at a time, you travel the distance
To survive is a way to forgive
For all that is wrong, and all that is gone
It's a way you have learned to live

In a land that hasn't always been fair
When things have not always gone right
When memories linger, and dreams do fade
When the sun doesn't always shine bright

But somewhere you know, is the place you seek
When once again you can dream your dreams
Where the sun shines bright, and the rain renews
And God once again rules supreme

— November 1979

Memories Gone

Years gone by and memories past
Reflections of yesterday gone
Like the morning dew on petals bright
And the beauty of a warbler's song

Ever so fleeting, like a passing wind
Searching for the canyon's end
Moonbeams glistening on a midnight stream
Where does it all begin

When do recollections cease to be
Part of one's daily meal
When do reflections no longer echo
That which the heart doth feel

How do the ages fleeting by
No longer a probability
Cease to be a familiar face
And are now just a memory

When do we open that forbidden door
And walk away from reality
Only to become a voice in the wind
Lost in our own productivity

When do the eyes no longer see
The measure of one's own soul
When do our feelings sour and die
When the heart loses sight of its goal

It's a measure of time passing by
Like the setting sun in an evening sky
It's the aging of one's own memories
And allowing those memories to die

It's a wake-up call for all to hear
So remember and remember well
Your memories are a part of you
And never bid them farewell

'Cause when your memories no longer live
You too will cease to be
You'll walk alone in a crowded world
And you too, will be a memory

— May 1981

- -

In Just One Moment

In just one instant a life may change
No one knows what lies in the cards
One moment your life seems whole
The next, just living is hard

One moment you may have all that you need
The next what you need is gone
And all that is left are your memories
You no longer feel you belong

What once was a life filled with hope
Is now filled with uncertainty
What once was the norm is now the exception
Yesterday is just a memory

When once you believed what tomorrow would bring
Now tomorrow you fear to tread
Because just to make it through today
Has become what you fear, instead

For nothing in this world is a guarantee
That all will remain the same
What you take to bed with you tonight
May tomorrow just be a game

So remember when you see a man with no shoes
Or a woman pushing a grocery cart
Or a child living in a cardboard box
Remember they were once a part

A part of a family that once was whole
Someone who someone still loves
An aunt, an uncle, sister or brother
Some once well thought of

For we're all no different than anyone else
We're all just a paycheck away
From being that person in the cardboard box
And having our dreams go astray

— February 1983

· ·

Badge of Shame

For years I've carried a lot of pain
A stigma that I cannot bear
Inside me lies an empty hole
A badge that I must wear

'Cause long ago, in a faraway land
I faced the devil's rage
Doing what I believed in
While inside the battle raged

I crossed the sea, a younger man
And returned an empty soul
To a country that didn't understand
The man no longer whole

The body stood tall, but the mind was weak
All I wanted was to relieve the pain
Of the things I'd done, and the things I saw
Horrors that I couldn't explain

So I turned to alcohol to ease
The nightmares of my dreams
I choose to bury it deep inside
Along with my self-esteem

And along the way, I made mistakes
Not knowing what the cost
A man who fought for what he believed in
Now in a country that he lost

Lost to a piece of paper
That demeaned his very being
That said we no longer want you
After he gave his everything

To God and Country he gave his all
When asked, he didn't hesitate
He held the banner high and proud
For a country that couldn't tolerate

Someone who couldn't face pain
Who had made a few mistakes
Because he didn't understand
A world so full of hate

— November 1984

Wall of Tears

There is a place where grown men go
Women and children too
To remember a war once fought
A place known by more than a few

It's a place of redemption, but filled with tears
Memories of those who were lost
As well as a place you can finally let go
And to finally count the cost

Of the many lives that mark the wall
And to the ones who had made it back
Finally recognition for all they gave
And for all that our country has lacked

It's well known as the Wall of Tears
Where finally a man can let go
Of all the pain and suffering he knew
And the tears can finally flow

The tears held in for so many years
'Cause the country didn't understand
A place you went as a boy
And came back a full-grown man

Unable to speak of untold things
Because no one wanted to hear
And no one wanted to right the wrong
Or to wipe away the tears

Of those who were there and didn't come back
And those who did, but not whole
It was those who still suffered the cost
Whose names you didn't see on the scroll

But now at the Wall they could release the pain
And finally get on with their lives
Lives that would still never be the same
But where deliverance had finally arrived

— *July 1985*

The Ultimate Sin

We ask ourselves, how could this be
How could the world be so cruel
How can we sit by so idly
Have we forgotten the Golden Rule

When everywhere we look is wrong
Wars against our fellow man
Children starving by the horde
Are we doing all that we can

Or do we simply sit back and say
It's God's will and it's in His plan
Or do we just choose to ignore it
Because we really don't understand

But I tell you this simple fact of life
God doesn't intend for the world to be
They way man has made it in his quest
It's the responsibility of you and me

God gave this world to man to transform
And rarely does He interfere
It's not God not doing His job
It's within our scope and range

Instead we sit back and blame someone else
It makes it easier to face the day
We bury our heads in the sand and say to ourselves
This is just God's way

But I tell you it's man who has dropped the ball
God is holding up His end
We've forgotten the Golden Rule my friend
And that's the ultimate sin

— February 1986

The Master's Plan

There are many seasons in one's own life
And they vary as the shifting winds blow
Each change has its own place in wisdom
It's a process where we learn to grow

From the Spring of our lives it all begins
A time of spontaneity and free
From all the decisions that mark our years to come
Now are made for you and me

The time to follow is the Summer of being
From here we must learn to decide
From the temptations and trials we face each day
That come at us like an endless tide

Here we begin to shape our senses
And prepare for the times to come
It's here we fashion who we are
And it's trying times for some

From here we move to the Fall of our lives
Ever changing like the autumn leaves
Choices made from options bestowed
And what we've come to believe

It's here, too, we shape mankind to come
When our influence on others is strong
When what we say and do ourselves
May choose where another belongs

Here we enter the Winter of our souls
When we sit back and view our works
Our job's not done, it just moves on
A responsibility we cannot shirk

But it's also a time of quaint reflection
When the harsh winds of Winter touch deep
When what you are and have become
Matters what we choose to keep

It's also here where our faith grows strong
As we know we've done the best we can
When it matters not what tomorrow will bring
'Cause we now know the Master's Plan

— February 1988

The Memories of '68

My memories go back to a time in my life
When times went against the wind
The sun didn't shine and the rain didn't fall
It wasn't as it should have been

I'd given my all and suffered the watch
And the tour was over for me
But the pain lingered on, and the memory didn't fade
It just wasn't as it was meant to be

The silence was loud, and the warrior fought on
To quiet the voices in my mind
They haunted my dreams, and taunted my soul
And gave me a look at mankind

The way it really was at the time
When things were not right with this realm
You were right to be back, but the feeling not right
I was completely bewildered and overwhelmed

It was a time in my life when things weren't clear
The memories of sixty-eight
A time in my life that shadowed the sun
And made me a part of my fate

The fate that led me to where I came
From the pain of the memories
The years I fought the demons alone
'Til once again, my heart I could appease

— Summer 1988

Real Happiness

Happiness comes in many forms
In many shapes and sizes
For some it means more than most
And it lies in many disguises

Sometimes it's as fleeting as the wind
And others it's a constant thing
But true happiness lies in one's own heart
It matters how the pendulum swings

It's as individual as a snowflake
And for each it's not the same
But through it all, one thing is constant
It still makes a sad heart sing

The amount really doesn't matter
It's the quality it makes one feel
It lies not in the tangible
But rather what is real

What's real in one's life to know
That what is done is what is right
It causes no one else to pain
And it ignites another's light

'Cause true happiness comes in making others
Feel the happiness that you know
By putting another ahead of yourself
And letting the free wind blow

By allowing others just to be
The way they are at any given moment
You put their happiness first
And draw yours from the other

— April 1993

Haunted Memories

Where once were hopes of things to come
And things that once were there
Are now filled with Haunted Memories
And times that seem unfair

But who's to say what is right
In times so hard at best
Who's to say, why me ole Lord
When all have stood the test

For the rain, it falls on everyone
At some time or the other
We have to take the good with bad
They come with one another

But through the veil of Haunted Dreams
Still lie magnitudes of uncertainty
Of times that were and times that are
Of how you wished it could be

Once again the way they were
When your heart was young
When your dreams, not yet your memories
And your songs were yet unsung

When Hope still sprung eternal
And the world lay at your feet
When times were much more simple
And the world seemed more complete

— May 1995

Yearning to Belong

In the process, we all call life
Comes a process we call learning
That makes a person who they are
And satisfies a yearning

A yearning to belong somewhere
When where you're at is alien to you
When what you've learned thus far in life
No longer applies to what you say and do

A search that begins in No-Man's Land
A place you've never been before
In hopes that there you'll find yourself
Or at least, you'll learn the score

Because where you're at, just don't make sense
And inside, you're not the same
As who you once perceived to be
Life has changed the game

Because what is life, if not a game
A game we play to win
And when does life choose not to be
The place we all begin

So search we must, to find the place
That once again we will fit in
To belong in a world we somehow lost
We must find a new place again

So you hit the road, in hopes there'll be
Somewhere on down the line
A place where others like you have gone
To find a place called yours and mine

— May 5, 1997

The Shadows

The City grows dark and weary
As the sun sets in the evening sky
Shadows of pain and man's sorrow
Memories of dreams that won't die

A man who walks along in the shadows
Because he no longer can stand the light
The sadness of all those around him
Will occupy his thoughts tonight

His home always lies in the shadows
In the feeling of his own despair
His address is an open number
In yesterday that cannot compare

Compare with the sanctity of manhood
A long time gone and now lost
In the shadows of his memories
Lie the recollections of what they cost

Cost to his very existence
When existence is a fact of life
Just to survive till tomorrow
Is a fact that cuts like a knife

'Cause the shadows can only bear witness
To the sorrow he bares in his soul
In the light the others can see him
And know he's no longer whole

In the shadows there's comfort and convenience
'Cause he knows its contents so well
He knows he is going to Heaven
'Cause he's already been to Hell

— June 1997

Empty Arms

There is a loneliness in this world
That some don't associate with
The empty arms of a mother's love
And it's more than just a myth

The passing of a loved one
Or a loved one no longer near
Is measured by a mother's tear
And imagined through her worst fears

It's an emptiness that cannot be explained
A hole in the pit of your soul
Of someone once very near
No longer in the fold

A person who once occupied
The empty arms that you now feel
Once a part of your intricate day
Now a memory that's so unreal

'Cause it seems like only yesterday
That your arms were always full
Now the laughter has turned to sorrow
And the sorrow is so painful

But what you once had is never lost
If the memory remains in your heart
Of the good times once shared by everyone
And the happiness they impart

And it's OK to feel the emptiness
If the emptiness is still a part
Of the love once shared by everyone
And it still remains within the heart

— June 1997

Quiet Place of Rest

There comes a time in everyone's life
When you have to stop and smell the roses
When life becomes too much to bear
And you don't like what it proposes

When all around you, all seems lost
And your world is tumbling down
When laughter no longer occupies
Your lonely part of town

When the sadness that lies within your heart
Grows more with each passing day
And each day becomes a memory
And you no longer have a say

It's then that you must realize
Even soldiers need a quiet place to rest
Even the best of us cannot hold up
When our heart is put to the test

Of the strength of God's great wisdom
We must learn to accept the good with the bad
At the same time we must know when to rest
And count the blessings we always had

Cause in the worst there lies a lesson
And the lesson cannot be learned
Until we take our quiet time
And count what we have earned

And in that quiet place of rest
We'll count our every hour
And realize God's great wisdom
And feel His amazing power

— June 1997

The Hard Way

As I saunter through this realm called earth
In a macrocosm of all living things
Assimilating all around me
And the lessons that they bring

I have a tendency to overlook
The obvious right in front of me
And store the information deep within
That will one day set me free

But first I suffer many times
Before the warning finally takes hold
And return again to see the mirror
Regardless of what I've been told

Because a lesson learned is best remembered
By the repetition of living again
Over and over we repeat the trip
And ignore the obvious pain

If learning once is too easy
Twice cannot be too hard
Three times seems a little excessive
Four times, the ego is charred

It's the hard way that we're taught most things
Just why nature acts this way
Is best answered by the messenger
And just what he has to say

We put up blocks and pretend to be
Knowledgeable in the ways of man
When in reality, we're truly lost
And actually don't understand

Through repetition nature learns to evolve
As the evil begins to decay
Man learns his lesson, and learns it well
By learning it, done the Hard Way

— June 1997

250

For All the World to See

There's nothing in this world so great
That fills an empty soul
As true love and commitment is
That fills the heart and grows

With each new day, a new beginning
And each new beginning starts anew
The process of learning from one another
And to know what's really true

That I love you is not an answer
We give just to hear our voice
It's a commitment that is to be cherished
And a song to be rejoiced

'Cause when you've really found each other
Nothing else can take the place
Of two hearts that come together
And commitment, face to face

And in the hard times that may follow
That nothing truly means much more
Than what we offer to one another
Not what the other may restore

Because it's not in what we have to gain
But rather what we both can give
Love only grows when it is nurtured
And only true love can forgive

The little things of happenstance
To the largest of them all
True love and commitment can only happen
In a marriage "GOD" installs

As His blessings, truly meant by Him
For all times to achieve
The joy of growing old together
And for all the world to see

Dedicated to my beautiful niece, Christy, and her
betrothed, Lee, this 29th day of June, 1997

The Choices We Make

We all make certain choices in life
In the paths that we choose to take
And the choices all have circumstances
Depending on the choices we make

Good, bad, or even indifferent
They're there for all the world to see
And often they're lessons, painfully learned
Not just by you, but by me

Because sometimes the choices affect others
Depending on the direction you go
And as adults, we have to learn to live with others
But from them we can also grow

For there are never what we call failures in life
If we learn from the lessons we face
But sometimes the lessons hurt others
Yes, in the choices we make

And even though it may seem cruel to you
From them, the choices I choose
It doesn't diminish my love for you
But it's in those choices I lose

Because in them it sometimes drives you away
And in that, it truly breaks my heart
Because my life is empty when you're gone
And our hearts grow further apart

But I really have no other way to go
I am truly at my wit's end
I've done all I can in my life for you
And I no longer know where to begin

Because my choices were made from what you gave
And were the lessons that I had to learn
Sometimes you have to allow things to take their course
To avoid yourself being burned

And even though it hurts my heart so say no
And not pull you into my loving arms
If I do, you will not learn your lesson in life
And in that, I will do you more harm

So for now I will keep you in my prayers
And hope someday you'll come back to me
Sometimes in order to have something you love
You must first learn to set it free

— June 1997

Forever

In all the world to cherish
There's none that means so well
As the love we share together
And the commitment it compels

For in the time we've been together
We've learned what true love really is
And it's sharing with one another
Not what the other can give

To place our hearts above our minds
And allow each other to grow
We allow the space it takes a heart
For our true love to know

And I know from deep within my heart
When I know what true love can be
I will always know it means so much
Because you gave so much to me

And in the gift you've given me my love
I give myself to you
To love and cherish always
In all I say and do

And because I know the feeling is mutual
And the love you offer runs so deep
I offer my love to you forever
And my heart for you to keep.

— June 1997

Free at Last

For many years I have carried the guilt
Of the pain that was wrought against me
I always thought it was the way it was
'Cause that was the way I made it to be

I thought it was my fault, the way things were
That I was paying for the things that I'd done
I never realized it was a reflection of
What I was really running from

Things that happen in a person's life
That cannot be predicted or known
Things that change a person's being
And cause the heart to groan

An empty hole in the pit of your soul
A part of your life taken away
That cannot replace the loneliness felt
That grew with each passing day

Demons faced that could not be beat
Because they came one after the other
Memories of a child's mind
That were only met by another

A process that shaped a young man's life
That confused his very thoughts
Never knowing what true love really was
Or the feelings that true love brought

Having to go it alone in the world
That I had no understanding of
Forced to draw from what I'd learned
It's best not to face push with shove

But ever so slowly, I began to see
That by living it wasn't the plan
It was how I perceived things to be
Not what the mind could understand

I had to let yesterday die
And to forgive the pain of the past
It was only then and only when
I could then feel free at last

— July 1997

. . . .

When the Going Gets Rough

There is nothing in this world so important
Than a tie that is bound by blood
The adhesive that holds a family together
Is sanctioned by the Lord above

It is always as it was meant to be
Its imperative to man's survival
Man cannot lie as an island
It's wisdom straight from the Bible

Without the coherence of the family unit
Man has to go it alone
In a world already set to trials
Man has to have a home

Somewhere to go when his heart is low
A love who can understand
That the tears he cries are a call for help
And make him no less of a man

Where an embrace is a means of relieving pain
Wrought by the trials of the day
Scratching out an existence as best he can
Trying to find his way

It's a family unit that makes him whole
Alone he is only a part
Of a world already set to hard times
Man needs an independent and understanding heart

To make his journey an easier walk
The family unit is set up to be
One of the parts that make the whole
That helps the man to see

The direction that he has chosen in life
Is the mandate that is best for all
That what he has culled is best for everyone
To prevent him from taking a fall

The family is set up to cushion the trials
And to be there when the going gets rough
To make the walk worth the trip
And be there when life gets tough

— July 1997

. . . .

Beauty Is in the Eye of the Beholder

Seldom do you have a chance in life
To meet someone perfect in every way
Who can light up a room when they enter
And brighten the world each day

Someone who is aware there is more to life
Than the beauty that the eyes can perceive
Who knows that there is more to a heart
And you can't always believe what you see

Because it's not till you see the whole package
That you can begin to understand
It takes more than the physical aspect
To make up a woman or a man

It takes how they feel on the inside
In nature life begins with a seed
The flower won't bloom, till the process is finished
And it doesn't rely on greed

It takes what the good Lord has given it
And then does the very best that it can
It takes the good along with the bad
Thus is the making of a woman or a man

'Cause when they say beauty is in the eye of the beholder
They mean it's through the eyes of the heart we see
And we cannot begin to see the distinction
Until we can set our emotions free

And allow the heart to make the choices
That the eyes have no perception of
Because the heart can see the whole picture
It's a gift God gave us from above

Because we limit our choices greatly
When we allow the eyes to choose
We let the best of life pass by us
And in doing so, we lose

Because the one you may have been searching for
Is often hidden in the perception we understand
Because the outside was an ugly duckling
While on the inside was the real woman or man

— July 1997

One in a Million

I have traveled this world and then some
And there are few surprises left for me
But it's been a long time since I saw a vision
As the one yesterday that I did see

Because no sooner had you walked into the room
Than your smile lit up the whole place
Your presence was a matter of loveliness
And an excellent example of taste

You carried yourself with pride and distinction
Your beliefs and convictions rang so true
You not only believed in others
But believed in what you could do

Your confidence was very refreshing
And it showed in the way that you walked
You were more than what showed on the outside
And I could tell by the way that you talked

That there was more to this woman in front of me
Than the obvious that my eyes could see
Your beauty ran deeper than attraction
Because you were confident in what you believed

And still your personality was infectious
You made one comfortable to be around
To be in the same room with you
Made the whole experience sound

As one would expect the voice of loveliness
To sound if it had an expression
You left me in awe of your beauty
And left one Hell of an impression

On a man who doesn't take lightly
And chooses his words very well
You came across as a woman I'd choose as a friend
And a gift that I would not sell

So always stay just as lovely as you are
Because you're one of the very few
You're one in a million, and then some
'Cause God really broke the mold when he made you

— July 1997

. . . .

My Fall of Tears

There is a sadness that's crept over me
In the twilight of my years
My frailties have made me feel less a man
And brought back my fall of tears

I look on the mirror in sadness now
Not liking what I see
My physical person has not become
The person I want to be

My heart beats much slower now
And sleep is but a passing thing
It comes in measures of the night
And I don't like what daylight brings

Another day trapped in this shell
That no longer moves with stealth
A prisoner locked within himself
A captive bound by his own health

Not wanting to be a prisoner no more
Yearning for the days of yore
When I was young and sleek at heart
I long to be like once before

Before the twilight of my years
Took away the distinction of my vitality
And locked me in this shell so frail
That cries out for reality

And I fear how others see me now
When they look at this unsightly shell
That has made me a prisoner of mind
And provided its own private Hell

I fear I'll not be loved no more
Nor experience a woman's loving arms
The warmth of having another near
To protect you from all harm

Never again to feel that tender touch
That only a good woman can provide
Because they fail to see my child within
And the tenderness my unsightliness hides

— July 1997

. . . .

God's Gift to Man

There is nothing more that makes a man
Feel as splendid as he can feel
That the loving arms of a woman he loves
That makes his life so real

For a woman has that tender touch
That can wipe your tears away
And remove the pain of a broken heart
And turn your darkness into day

Her soft voice warms the winds that blow
The winters of your heart
When all around is drab and gray
And you know not where to start

She gives that special tenderness
Through the sunshine of her eyes
A smile that lights the darkest day
And tells you, you're her guy

She's the freshness of a morning breeze
That stirs the spring time flowers
The beauty of the setting sun
That inspires the heart for hours

She's everything and much much more
Than words can ever voice
She's all that's been or ever will
She's yours by God's own choice

And if you're lucky enough to be
The one God's chosen for her
You better treat her right my friend
And make her own heart stir

Tell her what she means to you
And never let her down
Don't ever cause her heart to pain
Or her face to wear a frown

And never let a day go by
That you don't express your undying love
To her and all she's done for you
'Cause she was sent from God above

—July 1997

According to How You Act

I look back on all the yesterdays
That God has given to me
And think in sadness of what I've done
Of what it's turned out to be

A lifetime strewn with broken hearts
Of lives I've left behind
In the wake of my own selfishness
And the many times I've crossed the line

When God has given all He can
And I've given nothing in return
I took for granted all His gifts
And left the lies to burn

In the hearts of those I've touched
I've left emptiness and pain
I didn't know a time would come
When no longer they'd remain

I thought the times would always be there
And the cup would always be full
I treated God's gift with pure disdain
And filled my life with bull

And now I'm paying the price I wrought
The good times long since gone
I've taken my full measure of what God gave
And now must play along

With a life that's filled with emptiness
And the long hard lonely nights
There's no one left for God to give
I've fought and lost the fight

So let this be a warning to you
When God is good to you
Respect his gifts and treat them well
And watch what you may do

Because the time will come, when you
Wish you could have them back
But you can't turn back the hands of time
God gives you according to how you act

— July 1997

. . . .

Woman

A woman is the most precious thing
That man could ever hope for
She's all that makes a man feel whole
And holds what life has in store

She's the foundation of the family
That holds the body together
When all else seems like fortuity
She's the bind that ties forever

All that there is meant to be
In a world where frailty appears
To be the judgment of the day
She erases all the fears

Of life's great trials and tribulations
She stands and faces them all
And in the face of danger
No one stands as tall

As a woman protecting her family's whole
Nothing can threaten her domain
To cross the line and challenge her
You reap her deepest disdain

She's always there when all else is gone
And her fight seems almost lost
She'll stand the watch to fight again
It matters not the cost

Because her family is her life
And when nothing else remains
She knows she still has all there is
And has everything to gain

As long as she can hold them all together
She knows they'll never be alone
Her family is all that is important to her
And holds more love than she's ever known

So you see there is nothing stronger than a woman's love
For her family that she holds so dear
And there is nothing she wouldn't do for them
And nothing this woman fears

—July 1997

Her Name Is Chastity

You're seventeen, a new day's dawn
And the sun is shining bright
You're on the threshold of womanhood
Your future is in your sight

You've walked the path so many trod
It's been a long time coming
It's been a long, hard road to hold
But we love what you're becoming

A woman bright, and caring too
Whose beauty knows no bounds
Who sees herself for who she is
Who deserves to wear a crown

You've made us proud of who you are
And who you want to be
You've taken up the slack and more
Your name is Chasity

And though we'd like to take the credit
For the way you've turned out today
We only gave the direction
It's you who found the way

So as we gather on this day
To celebrate your womanhood
We wish you all the best in life
And all that's pure and good

— July 1997

Bridge to the Future

The future holds the message
That so few can comprehend
That people hold the answer
Of the place where time began

And the message that they carry
Is the answer to it all
That God has put man on this earth
To hear man's fateful call

That the future is our garden
Only if we can improve
The yesterdays we let pass by
And the tomorrows we can renew

To reach our hands across the sky
And make a difference when
All the world's against you
Is the place we must begin

To make a difference in this world
You first must take a stand
And reach out to your fellow man
And lend a helping hand

The future lies within your grasp
But first you must withstand
Heart and hand to God in trust
Is the bridge you have to span

— February 1998

North Mississippi Medical Center

It's been said that time enough's not spent
In the healing of the soul of man
But here at North Mississippi we try
At least to believe and understand

That the soul begins with the physical being
First we heal the pains and then go on
To treat the person as a whole
But from there, we go beyond

Because healing doesn't stop with therapy
Until the regiment has made it through
Dealing with the needs of the inner man
Is the only way we can renew

The commitment that we've made to ourselves
At North Mississippi Medical Center we care
We reach out to touch the spirit of man
And the needs we learn to share

It's a commitment we made to God and man
To treat the entirety of the need
To reach out beyond the physical being
Is the motto of our creed

Because if we only treat the half of the man
The rest will soon fade and die
A complete healing means treating all of him
We're not perfect, but we always try

— February 1998

The Millennium

We fast approach a milepost
In the substance of our lives
When issues must be answered
And the soul must be revived

We must ask ourselves where we're going
And must look from deep within
To find the answers yet not answered
In an inquisition we first began

What is the meaning of life itself
And where does man belong
In our fateful search for significance
How can we be so strong

When everyone lies within themselves
And are blind to what they see
How can a man rise above it all
To practice what he believes

We must first look deep within our climate
And ask ourselves how come
We let it go so long thus far
How could we be so dumb

The answer's been there all along
God made the point so clear
He gave us life to make it better
But we must learn to volunteer

— February 1998

The Call

Hands that reach to heaven
Hearts that search for man
Caring that knows no limit
In a world that understands

That nothing is more giving
Than a mind that gives its all
When all else seems so futile
It's the heart that hears the call

— February 1998

. . . .

The Season of Change

Hearts to God and hands to man
The bridge that spans the ages
The future's held within our grasp
But we must turn the pages

A journey begins with just a step
But the direction that it takes
Is mindful of the effort we make
And the interest that we awake

— February 1998

Hands Across Tomorrow

Our hands reach out tomorrow
In the hope we'll understand
That somehow we'll make a difference
In a world we can't command

And yet we seek the season
That the heart can comprehend
That man can live in harmony
With the season he began

Began in love and wonder
Is the body of the mind
And yet it needs the mending
Of a hand that's not confined

To measures not restricting
When help is held so dear
We'll be there with the helping hand
To wipe away the tears

And in the morrow that follows
In the future we'll be there
Hands across tomorrow
Of the hearts we can repair

In the minds that carry the message
We'll be the hands that carry the load
When no one else knows the passage
We'll be the ones who hold the road

— February 1998

Trust in Him

Nothing can cause more distress in the present
Than to worry about all of the yesterdays
And to wonder what will happen tomorrow
When all that we have is today

For you cannot bring back all the yesterdays
Nor predict what the future will bring
To do so, you lose all the energy
And your step will lose all its spring

For things are never as bad as they seem to be
Or as we can project in our minds
For yesterday's gone, and we can't see the morrow
All we have is this moment in time

If we project, we must do it positively
Never plan the outcome of it all
Allow God to have all the freedom
Don't put your back up against a wall

For only God knows what tomorrow will bring
And He's already forgiven you for yesterday
If we trust Him to make all the decisions
Then we can take care of today

For today is all He really gives us
To live in tomorrow, life grows ever dim
It's all right to plan for the future
If we leave the outcome up to Him

— April 1998

The Love of a Family

There are many lessons to be learned in life
But none more important can be
The value of health, home and family
Lesson's that sometimes take awhile to see

Man more often than not loses sight of his goal
And his being is consumed by his domain
Blinded by a drive to succeed in this world
With the promise of riches and fame

In the process he loses a part of his soul
And believes that he's doing the right thing
That his reasons are other than personal aims
It only matters what the outcome will bring

And he doesn't learn 'til much later in life
When more often than not, it's too late
His health, home and family have long since been lost
And pain and despair has been left in its wake

So when all around you humanity is driving to be
Number one, and the best at the game
Keep in mind what's important is waiting at home
And they're more important than riches or fame

So take it from someone who's learned the hard way
The best things in life are all free
Riches of fame will never replace
The love of your family

— May 1998